Hiking
Grand Canyon
National Park

by

Ron Adkison

FALCON™
GUILFORD, CONNECTICUT
AN IMPRINT OF THE GLOBE PEQUOT PRESS

ΛFALCONGUIDE®

All black-and-white photos by author unless stated otherwise.
Front cover photo by Cheyenne Rouse.

Library of Congress Cataloging-in-Publication Data

Adkison, Ron.
    Hiking Grand Canyon National Park / by Ron Adkison.
        p. cm.
    "A Falcon guide"—CIP t.p. verso.
    ISBN 1-56044-566-1 (pbk.)
        1. Hiking—Arizona—Grand Canyon National Park—Guidebooks.
    2. Backpacking—Arizona—Grand Canyon National Park—Guidebooks.
    3. Grand Canyon National Park (Ariz.)—Guidebooks. I. Title.
    GV199.42.A72G732   1997
    917.91'320453—dc21   97-19745
                                                              CIP

Manufactured in the United States of America
First Edition/Eighth Printing

CAUTION

Outdoor recreational activities are by their very nature potentially hazardous. All participants in such activities must assume the responsibility for their own actions and safety. The information contained in this guidebook cannot replace sound judgment and good decision-making skills, which help reduce risk exposure, nor does the scope of this book allow for disclosure of all the potential hazards and risks involved in such activities.

Learn as much as possible about the outdoor recreational activities in which you participate, prepare for the unexpected, and be cautious. The reward will be a safer and more enjoyable experience.

♻ Text pages printed on recycled paper.

CONTENTS

CONTENTS

ACKNOWLEDGMENTS

The Grand Canyon is a monumental landscape, and writing a guidebook to the Canyon's trails evolved into a monumental task. Yet the task has inspired in me a profound affection for that landscape, and I yearn to return there.

The staff at Grand Canyon National Park have many responsibilities, yet these dedicated professionals graciously took time out to answer an endless barrage of questions. They offered a great deal of generous support throughout the project, helping to make this book useful and informative.

Foremost among them, my old friend John Rihs deserves great credit. John took time out from his busy schedule to join me in the backcountry from time to time. He shuttled me to trailheads and generously offered his home during my lengthy stays at the Canyon. Throughout endless brain-picking sessions and through stacks of documents he shared, the landscape, trails, and role of the Park Service at the Grand Canyon began to make sense. John also shared some of his excellent photographs for this book.

Long hours were also spent with Andy Thorstenson, who shared his great knowledge of Grand Canyon vegetation. Andy also helped me to gain a deeper appreciation of how it *feels* to hike in the Grand Canyon.

Few people know the Grand Canyon's trails as intimately as Backcountry Ranger Bil Vandergraff. For a time, Bil and I developed a habit of bumping into each other at trailheads and in the backcountry. During those impromptu question-and-answer sessions, Bil shared with me his vast knowledge of the Grand Canyon backcountry, and I am most grateful we met.

Bryan Wisher, Corridor ranger, kindly volunteered the information contained in the chapter "Why Suffer?" To date this is the most useful information available to Grand Canyon hikers. Bryan did an excellent job compiling the material, and he deserves much credit.

Many thanks to Steve Sullivan at the Backcountry Reservations Office for his enduring patience. Steve helped me to make sense of the intricacies of BRO operations, and he also shared a wealth of backcountry information.

Helen Sairley, staff archaeologist, generously offered me guidance regarding the Park's archaeological and historical resources.

There were also countless people I met in the backcountry, some of whom unselfishly offered assistance when I needed it most, and they all offered great insights into Grand Canyon hiking and contributed enormously to this book.

Finally, without the unflagging support and understanding of my wife, Lynette, and children, Ben and Abbey, this book would never have materialized.

> *Ron Adkison*
> *January 1997*

MAP LEGEND

Interstate		Picnic Area	
U.S. Highway		Campground	
State or County Road		Bridge	
Interstate Highway		Mine Site	
Paved Road		Cave	
Unpaved Road, Graded		Cabins/Buildings	
Unpaved Road, Poor		Ruins	
Trailhead		Ranger Station	
Main Trail		Elevation	X 9,782 ft.
Secondary Trail		Butte	
Trailless Route		Cliffs	Top edge
Colorado River		Falls, Pouroff	
River/Creek, Perennial		Pass/Saddle	)(
Rapids		Gate	
Drainage, Intermittent Creek		Sand Dunes	
Spring			
Forest/Wilderness/ Park Boundary		Map Orientation	N
State Boundary	ARIZONA UTAH	Scale	0 30 60 Miles

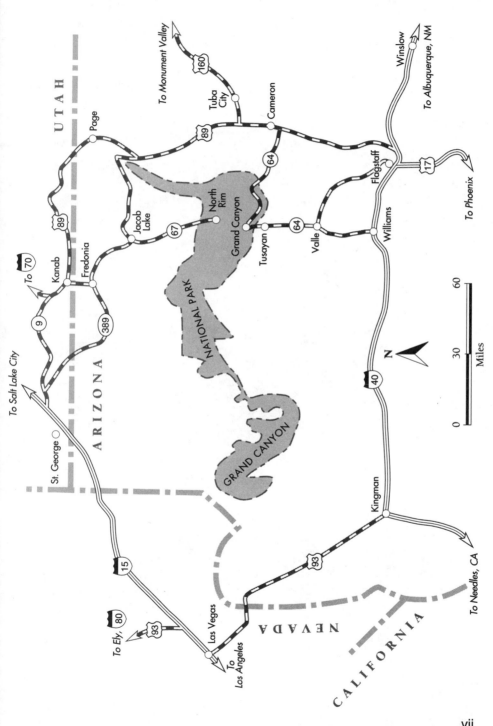

HIKE LOCATOR MAP

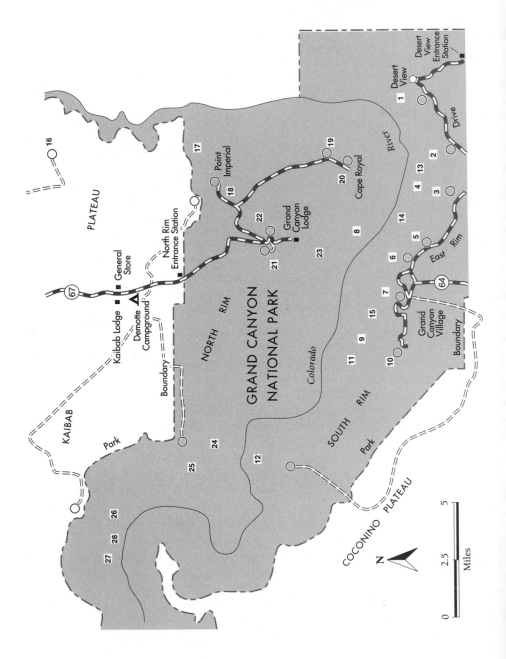

USGS TOPOGRAPHIC MAPS INDEX

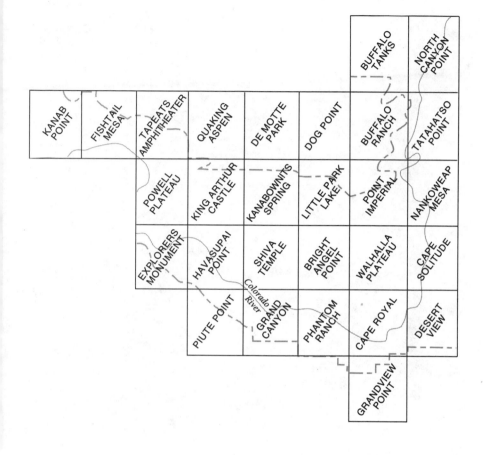

Looking north along the Colorado River from Beamer Trail. Photo by John Rihs.

INTRODUCTION

The Grand Canyon of the Colorado River, one of the world's great natural wonders, offers much more than just incomparable scenery. Camping, scenic driving, challenging whitewater, fishing, and, of course, hiking are among the major attractions of the magnificent landscape of Grand Canyon National Park. Above all, Grand Canyon is a hiking park. Facing hundreds of miles of trails, and many more miles of possible off-trail routes, hikers can meet the challenges of one of the world's greatest desert canyons.

Much of the Grand Canyon's 277-mile length is protected within the boundaries of the 1,215,735-acre Grand Canyon National Park. Within the Park, about 1,179,700 acres are considered backcountry, and much of that backcountry is proposed for federal wilderness designation. Due to its rugged landscape and inaccessibility, the Park's backcountry retains much of its primeval character.

Most rim overlooks and inner Canyon trails are located in the eastern part of the Grand Canyon where, in its great depths, bold towers, cliffs, and terraces of ancient rock typify the landscape. As you gaze into the Grand Canyon from the rim, it soon becomes clear that it is not simply one canyon, but rather a canyon system. The veins of countless tributary canyons—many of them major gorges in their own right—feed the artery of the river, which courses through its inner gorge, the canyon within the greater canyon the river has carved. Each side canyon displays its own unique characteristics, and many of these canyons funnel trails into the inner gorge; thus each trail provides a different wilderness experience.

It is difficult to appreciate the immense breadth and depth of the Grand Canyon without abandoning roadside viewpoints and hiking into the abyss of "the Big Ditch." People's impressions of foot travel in the inner Canyon vary widely. To some viewers on the rim, hiking in the Canyon appears nearly impossible. To others, the Canyon's depths seem to be deceptively close and easy to reach. Grand Canyon hiking is, in reality, somewhere in between these two extremes. Hiking in this grand, natural museum offers the promise of quiet and solitude, of the discovery of nature's improbable secrets, and of self-discovery. Yet to explore the depths of the Grand Canyon, hikers must pay the fee of sweat and toil to be rewarded at the end with vivid memories and an unparalleled sense of accomplishment.

HOW TO USE THIS BOOK

Grand Canyon National Park has a wide variety of hiking opportunities, ranging from brief day hikes to extended rim-to-river and long-distance, point-to-point trips. This guidebook covers more than 200 miles of trails in Grand Canyon National Park.

Perhaps more so than any other hiking area in the country, hiking in the Grand Canyon requires more pre-trip planning. The hike descriptions in this book give you all the information you need to be well prepared for your backcountry outing. Most of the information in each hike description is self-explanatory. Yet there are a few points that require further discussion to help you get the most out of this book.

The **general description** notes if the hike is suitable as a day hike, a backpack, or both. For extended backpack trips, the average number of days required to complete the trip is listed.

The **difficulty** rating is based on the average hiker's ability and may vary depending on a number of factors, including your physical condition, state of mind, and weather conditions.

Average hiking times are based on the average hiker. Most hiking times listed are conservative estimates; many hikers will make a trip in less time. It makes more sense to plan your hiking days based on how long the hike will take, rather than simply how far. Mileage is difficult to determine on the Grand Canyon's up-and-down trails. The average hiker will walk downhill with a full backpack at 1.5 to 2.5 miles per hour. Hiking out of the Canyon when you are tired, and perhaps sore, may take twice as long as the hike in. Most hikers can walk uphill on Grand Canyon trails at 1 to 2 miles per hour.

The **type of trail** lists whether or not a trail is maintained and gives its general condition. An "excellent" trail is maintained and fairly smooth with few obstacles. A "good" trail is easy to follow, generally smooth but unmaintained, with occasional obstacles. A "fair" trail is typically narrow, may be obscure in places, and presents numerous obstacles, such as boulders and rockslides. A "poor" trail is most often hard to follow; the tread is narrow and may occasionally be nonexistent. Obstacles are common. A "route" is where there is no obvious trail and is usually shown by cairns.

Elevation loss gives the total elevation difference between the trailhead and the low point, which is usually the Colorado River. Remember, you must regain all that lost elevation on the hike out of the Canyon, so plan your hike based on how much of that elevation you think you are willing, and able, to regain in one day.

Knowing **water availability** is critical to a safe and enjoyable trip in the Grand Canyon. I scouted the trails in the book during the dry seasons of a dry year, so many accounts of running water are conservative. Always check with the Backcountry Reservations Office for up-to-date information on water availability before heading into the backcountry.

Suggested cache points offer general recommendations for convenient locations to cache water. Particularly on trails where the only water source is the river, hikers are strongly advised to cache adequate water en route for the hike out.

The **optimum season** listing indicates the seasons with the greatest probability of avoiding extreme summer heat and winter snow and cold. Since the North Rim has a limited season, the summer is included in the season listing for trails that begin there. Hikers must be aware of the dangers of hiking in extreme heat and adjust their hiking schedule accordingly. Of course you can hike in the Grand Canyon year-round, but summer and winter hiking present challenges that cannot be taken lightly.

At first glance, **Use area codes** may seem confusing. Yet hikers need to know which Use Area they will camp in to apply for a Backcountry Use Permit. Obtain a copy of the "Backcountry Trip Planner" from the Backcountry Reservations Office (listed in Appendix B), and perhaps a copy of the Trails Illustrated Grand Canyon topo map, both of which show Use Areas, their boundaries, and codes.

Management zones give an indication of camping and trail conditions and the likelihood of contact with other hikers on each trail. (See "Trails of the Grand Canyon.")

Key points shows cumulative mileage between prominent features and junctions.

Best day hike destinations are included for longer trails, where part of that trail is suitable for an enjoyable day hike. Many of these destinations are splendid inner Canyon viewpoints that also offer camping areas for backpackers budgeting their time and energy.

Unnamed features mentioned in the hike descriptions are referred to as "Point," "Hill," or "Butte," followed by a number.

AUTHOR'S RECOMMENDATIONS

Easy day hikes suitable for novice hikers and families with small children

Hike 5 (Shoshone Point), Hike 19 (Cape Final), Hike 20 (Cliff Spring), and Hike 26 (Monument Point)

Moderate day hikes

Hike 7 (Mile-and-a-Half Resthouse and Three-Mile Resthouse), Hike 9 (Santa Maria Spring Resthouse), Hike 17 (Saddle Mountain Saddle), Hike 18 (Ken Patrick Trail), Hike 21 (Widforss Trail), Hike 22 (Uncle Jim Trail), Hike 23 (Supai Tunnel), and Hike 25 (Muav Saddle Cabin and Powell Plateau).

Strenuous day hikes

Hike 3 (Horseshoe Mesa), Hike 6 (Cedar Ridge), Hike 7 (Indian Garden), Hikes 7 and 15 (Plateau Point), Hike 10 (Dripping Spring), Hike 17 (Marion Point Ridge), and Hike 23 (Roaring Springs).

Backpacks for first-time hikers to the Grand Canyon in good physical condition

Hikes 6 and 7 (Bright Angel Trail to Indian Garden Campground or South Kaibab Trail to Bright Angel Campground), Hike 19 (Cape Final), Hike 21 (Widforss Trail), Hike 22 (Uncle Jim Trail), and Hike 23 (North Kaibab Trail to Cottonwood Campground).

Backpacks for first-time hikers to the Grand Canyon in good physical condition, with ample backcountry experience and good judgement

Hike 3 (Horseshoe Mesa), Hike 4 (Grandview Trail Loop), Hike 9 (Hermit Trail to Hermit Creek Camp), Hike 23 (North Kaibab Trail to Bright Angel Campground), and Hike 25 (Powell Plateau).

Backpacks slightly more challenging than Corridor area trails

Hike 3 (Horseshoe Mesa), Hike 4 (Grandview Trail Loop), Hikes 7 and 23 (North Rim to the South Rim via the North Kaibab and Bright Angel trails), Hike 9 (Hermit Trail), and Hike 25 (Powell Plateau).

Extended trips for those who have explored several Grand Canyon trails and want more of a challenge

Hike 1 (Tanner Trail), Hike 12 (South Bass Trail), Hike 26 (Bill Hall/ Thunder River trails), and Hike 27 (Deer Creek Trail).

For backpackers who think they have seen it all, demanding routes that stretch the meaning of the word "trail"

Hike 2 (New Hance Trail), Hike 11 (Boucher Trail), Hike 16 (South Canyon), Hike 17 (Nankoweap Trail), Hike 24 (North Bass Trail).

Long-distance backpacks for hikers who don't mind intense heat and lugging gallons of water

Hike 8 (Clear Creek Trail), Hike 13 (Tonto Trail, New Hance Trail to Grandview Point), Hike 14 (Tonto Trail, Grandview Point to Yaki Point), Hike 15 (Tonto Trail, Hermits Rest to Bright Angel Trailhead), and Hike 28 (Tapeats Creek to Deer Creek loop).

Short backpacks that offer good campsites on the top of the Redwall, about halfway between the rim and the river

Hike 1 (Tanner Trail; camp from Seventy-Five-Mile Saddle to Cardenas

Butte), Hike 2 (New Hance Trail), Hike 3 (Horseshoe Mesa), Hike 11 (Boucher Trail; camp below Yuma Point), Hike 12 (South Bass Trail; camp on the Esplanade), Hike 17 (Nankoweap Trail; camp on Marion Point and Tilted Mesa ridges), and Hikes 26 and 27 (Bill Hall/Thunder River trails; camp on the Esplanade).

HIKING IN THE GRAND CANYON

Grand Canyon National Park offers a greater variety of extended trail trips than any other place on the Colorado Plateau. The Park's vast network of trails, both on the rims and in the inner Canyon, offer something for every hiker. While there are many rim-to-river trails and connecting trails (such as the Tonto Trail), which can be arranged into a variety of long-distance trips, you need not be a seasoned backpacker and commit to many days of strenuous hiking to enjoy the Grand Canyon's trails.

Short, nearly level trails that visit panoramic viewpoints on the rims offer destinations for novice hikers and people budgeting their time and energy. More experienced day hikers have many fine destinations to choose from, both on the rims and on inner Canyon trails partway between the rims and the river.

Backpackers wishing to experience the Grand Canyon need not hike the long distances down to the Colorado River. Numerous fine campsites, though lacking water, lie on the Supai rock layer less than halfway from the rim to the river on trails including Tanner (1), New Hance (2), Grandview (3), Boucher (11), South Bass (12), Nankoweap (17), North Bass (24), and Thunder River (26). These sites offer the opportunity to enjoy the Canyon from the inside out with a minimal investment of time and effort, not to mention the memorable panoramas these sites afford. These sites also offer good destinations for experienced day hikers. First-time Grand Canyon backpackers should consider the advantages of an overnight trip partway into the Canyon before undertaking a strenuous rim-to-river trip.

From the plateau rims to serpentine side canyons, broad desert terraces, and the inner gorge of the Colorado River, the Grand Canyon's trails survey the spectrum of Park landscapes. Most inner Canyon trails follow side canyons en route to the Tonto Platform or the Colorado River. Each one of these canyons is unique in the nature of its landscape and the drama of its natural beauty, thus each trail is also different.

The Grand Canyon is at once an exciting and an overwhelming spectacle. Unlike many other hiking areas in the Colorado Plateau canyon country, when you enter the Grand Canyon, you leave the context of the plateau; there are no distant landmarks to help you locate yourself. You are entering a separate realm, the unique realm of the Grand Canyon. It envelops you; it seems the whole world becomes the Canyon. Some people find the feeling unnerving, while others revel in it.

Views from Huxley Terrace reach into Shinumo Creek canyon and up to Powell Plateau.

The Grand Canyon's trails begin on the rims at elevations between 6,600 and 8,800 feet, and drop 4,000 to 6,000 feet to the Colorado River, a phenomenal elevation change that must be regained on the hike out. Going down is the easiest part of Grand Canyon hiking, and these trails tend to lure unprepared hikers deeper into the Canyon. These inner Canyon trails are long, rugged, and strenuous. Many trails can be viewed from the rims, but don't be lured onto them without ample information and planning. Distances here are telescoped by the clear desert air; what appears to be a half-day hike from the rims may actually be a one- to two-day trek.

Rim-to-river hiking in the Grand Canyon is likely to be the hardest hiking you will ever do. Yet the hike itself is just as rewarding, sometimes more so, than the destination. Since each trail begins by descending, hiking here is contrary to most people's experience. Even seasoned hikers in excellent condition find that Grand Canyon hiking is far more demanding than they expected. That is not to say that you cannot have an enjoyable backpack trip; most people do. Yet an extended trip requires careful planning and adequate physical and mental conditioning, more so perhaps than any other hiking area outside of Alaska.

Some first-time hikers in the Grand Canyon make mistakes in judgment and preparation. And, once here, hikers who allow the immense landscape and great elevation changes on the trails to overwhelm and sometimes defeat them. Their trip, then, becomes an ordeal to forget rather than an experience to remember. Those who come armed with a positive attitude, an awareness of their limitations, and adequate physical conditioning are also overwhelmed, but in a different way. Once they set foot on the trail, the magic of the Grand Canyon begins to cast its spell.

The intrinsic rewards of simply being in the Grand Canyon, combined with the sense of accomplishment gained from hiking from the rim to the river—and back—add up to a truly unforgettable backcountry experience that draws hikers back to the Canyon time and again.

TRAILS OF THE GRAND CANYON

Grand Canyon trails range from wide, well-maintained thoroughfares trod by thousands each year, to lonely routes that see few hikers. All inner Canyon trails—those that descend into the Canyon from the rims—are, regardless of their condition, very strenuous and demand a serious commitment of time and energy. These trails are exceedingly steep, and most are very rocky and rough. They all descend severely from the rims to the river. The only "easy" trails in the Park are those that follow the rims. (See Hikes 5 and 18 to 22).

The backcountry of Grand Canyon National Park is divided into four management zones, and trail conditions vary in each zone. The Corridor Zone includes the North and South Kaibab trails and the Bright Angel Trail. These trails are wide with a generally smooth tread, and are regularly maintained and patrolled by rangers. These are the only trails available for stock

A thunderstorm rumbles behind Vishnu Temple in this view from the South Kaibab Trail.

traffic in the inner Canyon (except for the Whitmore Trail in the western Grand Canyon), and mule trains use them daily. On Corridor trails you will find ranger stations, designated campgrounds, emergency telephones, toilets, and piped drinking water. In this zone, there is the probability of continuous contact with other hikers.

Backcountry rangers strongly recommend that backpackers use Corridor trails for their first hikes into the Canyon. These trails are not easy, but they are less demanding than other inner Canyon trails. And should an emergency arise, help is usually not far away.

In all other management zones, the trails are generally old prospectors' trails that pre-date the establishment of the Park. Some were rebuilt around the turn of the last century to accommodate tourist traffic. Park Service trail crews occasionally work to stabilize portions of these trails, but they are not maintained or regularly patrolled and are considered wilderness trails. They are narrow, rocky, very steep, and often brushy. Help is generally far away, and good judgment and self-reliance are essential for a safe and enjoyable trip.

Threshold Zone trails are unmaintained, rough, and rocky, but are in generally good condition and easy to follow. Junctions are marked and designated campsites and toilets are provided, but water sources are few and may be separated by considerable distances. Threshold trails include the Hermit, Grandview, and Clear Creek trails; the Tonto Trail between Hermit

The well-groomed North Kaibab Trail is the North Rim's only maintained trail.

Creek and Indian Garden, and the Cape Final, Widforss, and Uncle Jim trails. Backpackers are advised to have previous Grand Canyon hiking experience before attempting inner Canyon trails in this zone. On Threshold Zone trails, you are likely to have frequent contact with other hikers.

All other inner Canyon trails covered in this book fall within the Primitive Zone. Considerable Grand Canyon hiking experience is a prerequisite to a safe and successful trip on these trails. Route-finding skills are often necessary since trails are faint, narrow, and sometimes nonexistent. Junctions are unmarked and only occasionally indicated by cairns. Trail segments may be only "routes" where the way is defined only by the boot tracks of previous hikers or by sporadic cairns. Hikers can camp at-large, or wherever they wish, in this zone. Toilets are not provided, and water sources are scarce, separated by many miles. Self-reliance, ample planning, and good judgment are essential on Primitive Zone trails. Here, you will likely have infrequent or no contact with other hikers.

This book does not cover the Wild Zone, a mostly trailless area accessible only to Grand Canyon hikers with the advanced skills necessary to navigate it.

TRAILHEADS

Grand Canyon trailheads range from paved parking lots alongside major Park roads to remote turnarounds at the end of poor, rough, seldom-used dirt roads. A few offer drinking water, toilets, and pay telephones, such as Hermits Rest and the South Kaibab, but at most trailheads, you are far removed from assistance should you need it.

The last thing you want after an arduous trek out of the Grand Canyon is a vehicle problem. The best insurance for a trouble-free trip to and from Grand Canyon's remote trailheads is pre-trip planning and prevention. Be sure your vehicle is in good condition. Fill your gas tank and bring along a tool kit, tow rope or chain, jumper cables, and perhaps a roll of duct tape. Squirrels, particularly on the Kaibab Plateau, have a nasty habit of investigating the engine compartment of vehicles, and sometimes they chew through hoses.

Carry several gallons of water and extra food and clothing. An axe or a bow saw may help you get through blowdowns that can block forest roads.

Some dirt roads, such as the roads to South Bass and Swamp Point trailheads, can become difficult, if not impossible, to travel when heavy rains or snowmelt turn the roadbeds into corridors of bottomless mud. Even four-wheel-drive vehicles have difficulty negotiating these "gumbo" roads. A winch could get you out of a mudhole, provided you can find an anchor point. If your vehicle becomes stuck in the mud, you may have to wait a day or two for the road to dry out. It is best to avoid attempting to drive wet, muddy roads; not only could you get stuck, but the deep ruts you leave behind cause long-term damage to the roadbeds.

The North Rim is open seasonally from mid-May through mid-October. Depending on snowpack, roads leading to trailheads on the Kaibab National Forest may become passable earlier. In the early season, expect the possibility of blowdowns blocking North Rim trailhead approaches. Snowstorms can occur unexpectedly into May and at any time by October. Forest roads and Arizona Highway 67 can then become snowpacked and icy.

AZ 67 remains open until the first major snowstorm in autumn, after which the gate is locked at Jacob Lake and the highway is closed for the winter. Following the first major snowstorm, the highway is usually plowed only once, allowing visitors and Park Service vehicles to leave the area before it becomes snowed in. However, the highway to the North Rim can remain open until December, but no services are available. Travelers should expect winter driving conditions and be prepared to leave the area on short notice. Hikers' vehicles have been stranded in the snow at the North Rim for the duration of winter.

The South Rim remains open all year, but snowstorms in winter can create hazardous driving conditions and temporary road closures. Trailheads on the South Rim are accessible during winter, though snow and mud can render Forest Road 328 to the South Bass Trailhead impassable at times from December through March.

Cellular phone users should note that service is spotty on both rims. The range of cellular service includes high points on the South Rim, particularly West Rim Drive, points on the North Rim with a clear path to the South Rim, and the Monument Point and Swamp Point trailheads on the North Rim.

MAPS

A good map is an essential piece of equipment for any Grand Canyon hiker, and there are several excellent maps available. The maps in this book show the correct configuration of trails based on my field work, but they are designed to give a general overview of the trails and are not intended for serious navigation in the backcountry.

Maps that are useful for navigation include two Kaibab National Forest maps, one for the North Kaibab District (covering the Kaibab Plateau and North Rim) and the other covering the Tusayan, Williams, and Chalender districts (and showing the South Rim). These maps, particularly the North Kaibab map, are very helpful for navigating the maze of forest roads en route to remote trailheads.

Another map, the most popular with Grand Canyon hikers, is the Trails Illustrated Grand Canyon National Park topographic map. This useful map covers the Park from Lees Ferry at River Mile 1 to River Mile 173 near Tuckup Canyon. This map is printed on waterproof, tearproof material and shows roads, the general configuration and location of trails, and Use Area codes and boundaries, making it most useful for trip planning and backcountry permit application.

The map is on a scale of 1:73,530 (7/8 inch = 1 mile), with a contour interval of 80 feet. Study this map carefully when planning your trip; a lot of area is squeezed into a small space. What appears to be a one-day hike may actually take much longer.

Trails Illustrated maps are available at many stores and gas stations in communities adjacent to the Park, the visitor center, Babbitt's General Store on the South Rim, the general store on the North Rim, and the North Rim Country Store on the Kaibab Plateau. To order Trails Illustrated maps from the visitor center call 1-800-858-2808.

Earthwalk Press produces two topographic maps that cover part of the Grand Canyon backcountry. The Bright Angel Trail map, on a scale of 1:24,000 (2 5/8 inch = 1 mile) covers the North Rim and South Rim in the Corridor Zone. This is one of the best maps for hikers on the North and South Kaibab trails, and the Bright Angel Trail. Earthwalk also produces a Grand Canyon National Park map, showing the North Kaibab Trail and South Rim trails from Horseshoe Mesa in the east to the Hermit and Boucher trails in the west. Since this map is on a scale of 1:48,000 (1 inch = 1.25 miles), it gives a better representation of the terrain than the Trails Illustrated map. These maps are available at Babbitt's General Store on the South Rim.

The Grand Canyon is now covered by USGS 7.5-minute topographic quadrangles. These maps, on a scale of 1:24,000, with contour intervals of 40 feet, offer the most detailed representation of the Grand Canyon landscape. USGS topo maps show the most accurate configuration of trails, and veteran backcountry travelers prefer them. For most trails covered in this book, you need only carry two or (seldom) three USGS quads. USGS quads are available at Babbitt's General Store on the South Rim, but popular maps, such as the Grand Canyon and Phantom Ranch quads, sell out quickly. Outdoor shops in Flagstaff, Arizona, also carry USGS maps of the Grand Canyon.

Topographic quadrangles (all maps listed in this book are Arizona quads) are available by mail from the USGS. The cost is four dollars each, with a handling charge of one dollar on orders under ten dollars. Order well in advance of your trip since orders often take two months or more to process. You'll find the address in Appendix B.

You can get Kaibab National Forest maps at the Tusayan Ranger Station, a short distance north of the town of Tusayan, near the south entrance to the Park; at the North Kaibab Ranger Station in Fredonia, Arizona; and at the Kaibab Plateau visitor center at Jacob Lake, Arizona. Or you can request a map by mail (at a cost of three dollars each) from the Kaibab National Forest. The address can be found in Appendix B.

Another useful addition to your Grand Canyon map collection is the geologic map of the eastern part of the Park. This map covers the area from Tatahatso Wash in Marble Canyon to Havasu Canyon. The contour interval is 80 feet, and the scale is 1:62,500. This colorful map shows the thirty different rock formations present in the Canyon, as well as slumps, slides, faults, and folds. This large map can be cut into sections and carried with you in the backcountry to aid identification of geologic features. The map is available at the visitor center on the South Rim.

SEASONS

Hikers come to the Grand Canyon year-round, but by far the majority come during summer. Since the inner Canyon is a desert environment, with daytime high temperatures exceeding 100 degrees Fahrenheit almost daily from June through August, summer is the most unfavorable time of the year to hike in the Grand Canyon.

The extreme heat of summer and the unrelenting sun pose serious hazards to hikers. Rangers must attend to more than a thousand hikers each summer, with most incidents due to heat-related illness and dehydration. Despite ample warnings in Park literature, at trailhead bulletin boards, and from rangers, too many hikers get in over their heads in summer, either because the heat overwhelms them or they didn't bring enough water.

Any seasoned desert hiker knows you cannot fight the desert heat, but you can adapt to it. In summer, hike from the pre-dawn hours until early morning, then rest in the shade during the hottest part of the day. Resume your travels after 5 p.m., when shadows begin to fill the canyons.

During extreme heat, use of all inner Canyon trails (except the North Kaibab Trail to Supai Tunnel) may be periodically restricted between 7 a.m. and 5 p.m. Violating this restriction carries the prospect of a significant fine, and you also will be putting yourself into a hostile, sun-baked environment where the consequences could be fatal.

Temperatures increase as you descend into the Canyon, and precipitation decreases. Keep in mind that while you descend into the Canyon, you are going from environments that mimic those of northern coniferous forests (on the rims) to the Sonoran Desert of Mexico (at the Colorado River). In general, daytime temperatures at the Colorado River average 20 degrees warmer than the South Rim, and 25 degrees warmer than the North Rim. Temperatures are slightly cooler at the river's edge.

This is why spring and autumn are the preferred seasons for backcountry trips. Canyon weather is always unpredictable and weather patterns vary from year to year. Spring weather (March through May) can be highly variable. Occasional cold fronts from the west and northwest can bring cold, windy conditions, rain showers in the inner Canyon, and perhaps snow on the rims, particularly in March and April. Generally, warm, dry weather prevails between storm systems.

As spring progresses, temperatures warm and storm systems are pushed farther north, but often-dry cold fronts may still brush the region. The most noticeable effect of these fronts are slightly cooler temperatures for a day or so and strong winds. From a water standpoint, early spring is one of the best times of year to hike in the Grand Canyon. Springs and seasonal streams are likely to be flowing, and slickrock waterpockets will hold rainwater longer at this time of year, providing more flexibility and a margin of safety in the backcountry.

Usually by late May, there is the onset of searing summer heat, which can persist into mid-September. From late June or early July through early Sep-

The Hermit Ranger Station.

tember, the summer monsoon occurs. Moist tropical air masses over Mexico circulate an almost daily parade of thunderstorms over the region. Often torrential, but usually localized, rainfall accompanied by strong, gusty winds and lightning characterize midsummer weather in the Grand Canyon.

As cold fronts once again begin to brush the region in early autumn, the thunderstorm pattern is shunted southward. Autumn provides some of the most stable weather of the year. Often clear, warm, and sunny days and cool nights make this one of the most delightful seasons to visit the inner Canyon. Although summer thunderstorms have little, if any, affect on spring and stream flows, deeper waterpockets filled by those downpours often persist into early fall due to cooler temperatures and reduced evaporation. Stronger cold fronts can sweep through the region as autumn progresses, and by mid- to late October, these fronts can drop temperatures significantly for several days or longer. Snowfall on the rims is not uncommon.

Winter in the Grand Canyon is cold on the rims and cool in the inner Canyon. Extreme cold temperatures of –16 degree F on the South Rim and –25 degrees F on the North Rim attest to the severity of winters at high elevations. Winter storms, though generally infrequent, can dump considerable snow on the rims. On the South Rim, 65 inches of snow fall in an average year, but most snow often melts between storms. The North Rim, in contrast, averages 125 inches of snow, and a deep snowpack often develops there, lasting until spring.

On the sheltered, generally north-facing cliffs and slopes below the South Rim, snow and ice can persist through much of the winter, roughly down to about the level of the Hermit shale. Daily freeze-and-thaw cycles make the upper portions of South Rim trails dangerously icy. Winter hikers must be prepared for conditions of cold weather, sudden storms, deep snow, and ice. Gaiters, instep crampons, and a pair of hiking or ski poles are essential items for winter hiking in the Grand Canyon. For a list of average monthly temperatures and precipitation, see Appendix C.

BACKCOUNTRY REGULATIONS

The Grand Canyon may at first glance appear to be a durable landscape, but Park resources exist in a delicate balance and can be easily disrupted. The long list of backcountry regulations below may seem burdensome, but for the most part they embody common sense practices to help preserve not only resources, but also the qualities of wilderness that visitors seek. Study the regulations below *before* you venture into Grand Canyon backcountry.

1) A Backcountry Use Permit is *required* for all overnight backcountry use and *must* be in your possession while in the backcountry.
2) No wood or charcoal fires are allowed. However sterno or backpack stoves are permitted.
3) Carry out all trash. Burning or burying trash or toilet paper is prohibited.

4) Firearms and bows and arrows are prohibited.
5) Pets are prohibited below the Rim.
6) Leaving a trail or walkway to cut between portions of the same trail or walkway, or taking a shortcut to an adjacent trail or walkway, is prohibited.
7) Throwing or rolling rocks or other items inside caves or caverns, into valleys or canyons, and down hillsides or mountainsides is prohibited.
8) Feeding, touching, teasing, frightening, or intentionally disturbing wildlife is prohibited.
9) Possessing, destroying, injuring, defacing, removing, digging, or disturbing from its natural state any plant, rock, animal, mineral, cultural, or archaeological resource is prohibited. Walking on, entering, traversing, or climbing on an archeological resource is prohibited.
10) Motorized vehicles and all wheeled vehicles, such as motorcycles, baby buggies, and bicycles, are prohibited on trails below the rim.
11) Fishing requires a valid fishing license or nonresident permit.
12) Writing on, scratching, or otherwise defacing signs, buildings, or other property is prohibited.
13) Overnight private stock use requires a Backcountry Use Permit. Use is restricted to trails and campsites designated for stock.
14) More than one party/group from the same organization may not camp in the same designated campground or non-Corridor Use Area per night. Violating a closure, designation, use, activity restriction or condition, schedule of visiting hours, or use limit is prohibited.
15) Use of soap in creeks or camping within 100 feet of any water source is prohibited.
16) The Backcountry Use Permit is valid only for the campsites and dates specified on the permit. *You must follow your itinerary.*
17) Commercial use of the backcountry must be authorized by concession permit or commercial use license.

FISHING

The Grand Canyon may seem like an unlikely place to go fishing, but many people do fish here. Perennial streams, such as Bright Angel, Tapeats, and Shinumo creeks, harbor populations of small trout. But anglers out to land a lunker need look no further than the Colorado River. The river offers excellent fishing for rainbow trout, adding a unique dimension to a hike in the Grand Canyon desert.

Prior to the construction of Glen Canyon Dam in 1963, the ebb and flow of the river—low in winter, high during spring from snowmelt—created a wide fluctuation in water temperature. In winter, the waters would approach the freezing mark, while in the heat of summer the river would rise to 75 to 85 degrees F. Native fish adapted to the pre-dam river included humpback chub, bonytail, roundtail, flannelmouth, bluehead, and razorback sucker. Most of these fish no longer exist in the Colorado River in the Grand

16

Canyon. Their original habitat has been erased by the cold waters released from Glen Canyon Dam.

The often clear, cold waters of the river in Grand Canyon now support one of the most productive trout fisheries in the Southwest. Anglers frequently land large rainbow trout on the river in the depths of this desert canyon. Attesting to the productivity of this fishery, bald eagles now gather in the Canyon, feeding in winter on spawning trout at the mouth of Nankoweap Creek

If you intend to fish in the Grand Canyon, an Arizona fishing license is required for anyone over the age of fifteen. The daily limit is four fish. Licenses are available at outdoor shops throughout the state and at Babbitt's General Store on the South Rim.

HIKING WITH CHILDREN

Hiking with your children in the Grand Canyon has its limitations. Steep descents and ascents quickly take their toll on children, and sheer dropoffs present a constant danger. Needless to say, parents must closely supervise their children near the rims and on inner Canyon trails where sheer cliffs plunging hundreds of feet are common.

Children need physical conditioning to prepare for the rigors of Grand Canyon hiking just as adults do. Start slow with hikes on the rims. If your children are not afraid of heights and want to explore the inner Canyon, begin with easy day hikes below the rim on good trails, such as the South and North Kaibab or Bright Angel trails. Progress to more demanding destinations, such as the top of the Redwall limestone, a good turnaround point on most inner Canyon trails, for well-conditioned children and adults alike.

For that first backpack trip in the Grand Canyon, begin with Corridor area trails. An overnighter to Indian Garden, for example, is a good way to introduce your children to Grand Canyon hiking. Progress to longer backpacks as your children gain confidence, to Bright Angel Campground from the South Rim or Cottonwood Campground from the North Rim.

Following is a list of suitable day hikes or overnight trips for families, with suggestions for destinations and whether the trip is a day hike, overnighter, or both. Because each family's abilities are different, carefully read each hike description in this guide and study the maps to determine a hike's suitability for your family.

Hike 3   Horseshoe Mesa, day hike or overnighter
Hike 5   Shoshone Point, day hike
Hike 6   Cedar Ridge, day hike
Hike 7   Mile-and-a-Half Resthouse, day hike, Three Mile Resthouse, day hike, Indian Garden, overnighter
Hike 9   Santa Maria Spring, day hike
Hike 10 Dripping Spring, day hike
Hike 12 The Esplanade, day hike or overnighter
Hike 17 Saddle Mountain saddle, day hike or overnighter

RIVER RUNNERS, AIRCRAFT, AND YOUR WILDERNESS EXPERIENCE

During your travels in the Grand Canyon backcountry, you will, at times, experience various intrusions on the natural quiet and solitude the Canyon provides.

Oar-powered rafts, commercial motorized boats, and dories float the Colorado River through the Grand Canyon from May through September. Depending on your viewpoint, the presence of river runners can range from an intrusion to welcome yet unexpected company. During the day at many beach campsites on the Colorado River, you may feel that you have the Canyon all to yourself. Perhaps you have been watching rafts float by. Usually by midafternoon, those raft parties begin searching for a campsite. If

This beautiful beach at the end of the North Bass Trail is popular with river runners.

you are camped at a beach frequented by river trips, such as South Canyon, Nankoweap, Tanner, and North and South Bass, you may be invaded by river parties. In theory, we are all supposed to share the beach, river runners and backpackers alike. After all, we are all here for the same reason—to experience one of the world's most majestic canyons from the inside out. Keep in mind that though you may have been waiting for several months to take your backcountry trip, private raft parties are on a twelve-year waiting list to float the river.

Backpackers sometimes find the surprise company too much to bear, often yielding to river parties and moving to a more secluded spot. If you wish to avoid an invasion of river runners, choose a site well away from the beach, a site next to rapids, or a rocky or brushy stretch of beach where rafts are not likely to land. On the positive side, river parties will often share their food and beer with you, and their assistance could save a life in the event of a medical emergency.

Tour aircraft, on the other hand, are a significant intrusion, not only in the backcountry but on the rims as well. From sunrise until sunset, an endless procession of helicopters and twin-engine Cessnas crowd the flight corridors over the Park. Hikers on the remote and rugged Boucher and Nankoweap trails may feel as if they have spent all day hiking to the outskirts of a busy airport rather than into the remote reaches of the Grand Canyon.

The air tour industry touts scenic overflights as "eco-tourism" that "does not disrupt the natural setting of the Canyon." It is difficult to imagine that an average of eighty thousand air tour overflights per year does not disrupt visitors' experiences, both visually and aurally. In addition, a steady stream of commercial jets en route to Las Vegas and southern California fly directly over the Grand Canyon twenty-four hours a day.

As of 1996, only 45 percent of the Grand Canyon was flight-free, and only 31 percent of the Park experienced natural quiet 75 to 100 percent of the time. The Park Service is working with the Federal Aviation Administration to restore natural quiet to much of the Park. New guidelines adopted by the FAA in 1997 may increase flight-free zones and are a good first step toward the restoration of natural quiet that visitors expect. Overflights of the Park will likely never be banned entirely, but one can hope that things will quiet down in the future.

LEAVE NO TRACE

Backpacking use of the Grand Canyon represents slightly more than 1 percent of total Park visitation. Since backpackers are in the Canyon hiking and camping, they have the potential of creating the greatest impacts on the overall integrity of the ecosystem.

These impacts are readily apparent in the backcountry. Multiple trails,

Cryptobiotic soil crust is common along many Grand Canyon trails, especially on the Esplanade. Photo by John Rihs.

the evolution of new trails, the spread of impacted campsites, trampling of delicate vegetation, and contamination of water sources are some of the legacies of past hikers.

The desert landscape of the Grand Canyon appears deceptively durable, but actually is very fragile. Once damaged, the desert recovers slowly and may not heal completely in your lifetime, if at all. Soils in the Grand Canyon are thin to nonexistent. Plants and desert creatures have evolved a delicate balance of survival. The simple acts of walking off the trail, even for short distances (crushing plants or moving rocks), can disrupt the balance that desert plants and animals have achieved. Shortcuts and excavation at campsites hasten erosion of the thin soil cover, reducing and, in some instances, eliminating habitat for plants and animals. Shortcutting trails can lead to the eventual destruction of a good, but perhaps unmaintained, trail.

Most Grand Canyon hikers have long since learned to employ no-trace practices. Along most of the Canyon's trails and at its campsites, you will seldom find trash, food scraps, discarded items, soap suds in precious water sources, evidence of illegal campfires, or unnecessary excavations or alterations. Consider the following ideas for no-trace travel as guidelines for preserving the wilderness resource, not only for the Canyon's native inhabitants, but also for those who follow in your footsteps.

CAMPSITES

When observed from the rim, it appears as though you could camp almost anywhere in the inner Canyon. In reality, campsites are more scarce than you would imagine, due to rocky terrain or a mantle of coarse, rigid desert growth. Corridor and Threshold Use Areas have designated campgrounds and campsites that concentrate use. But in the Primitive Use Areas, where you camp at-large (wherever you wish), campsite selection is important.

Choose a previously used site, thus concentrating your impact rather than spreading impact to new locations. Unfortunately, many previously used sites are located in riparian areas or too close to water. *Avoid these sites.* Select a site on bare mineral soil, sand, or even slickrock, where minimal evidence of your passing will remain. A free-standing tent allows greater flexibility in campsite selection where soils are thin or where slickrock dominates.

Backpackers are drawn to desert oases—either springs, streams, or the Colorado River. Although Park regulations specify that campsites must be located at least 100 feet from water sources, backpackers should make an extra effort to camp at least 200 feet from springs, streams, and waterpockets to prevent water pollution and allow undisturbed access for wildlife. Better still, tank up with water at springs or streams and move on to a dry camp at least 0.25 mile away.

Avoid making unnecessary improvements at your campsite, such as construction of rock walls or trenching around your tent. The bottom line is to leave no lasting sign of your passing.

PROTECT WATER QUALITY

Scarce water sources in the Grand Canyon are the lifeblood of wildlife and hikers alike. Springs, waterpockets, and sluggish streams are highly susceptible to contamination. Stirring up silt, using soap, or depleting a waterhole can have an adverse affect on water quality.

Avoid digging in a waterhole with a soil bottom to enlarge it. You may break the seal formed by fine silt and algae, and the water may drain away into the ground. Using too much water from a limited source may deprive wildlife or other hikers of a much-needed drink.

For bathing and dishwashing, take water only from larger streams and the Colorado River. Wash up and discard your soapy water at least 200 feet from water sources and drainages. *Never use soap in any water source.*

When at the Colorado River, urinate directly into the river or in wet sand. This may sound contradictory to what most of us have learned, but the large volume of the river will rapidly dilute urine. Urinating on sterile beach sand leads to a buildup of uric acid and the accompanying odor. Dishwashing water may be strained through a fine screen or handkerchief directly into the river, but the garbage that collects in the screen must be packed out.

WASTE

Garbage and food scraps attract animals, ants, and flies. Pack out your garbage and leftover food scraps with the rest of your trash.

Human waste must be deposited at least 200 feet from campsites, trails, water sources, and drainages. Choose a spot with organic soil and dig a cat hole 6 to 8 inches deep, covering the waste with soil.

Do not bury or burn your toilet paper. Fires from burning toilet paper have devastated parts of the Canyon; Deer Creek and Hance Creek are examples. *You must pack out all used toilet paper in the Grand Canyon.* Ziplock bags are useful for this.

TRAVELING OFF TRAIL

The passage of too many feet creates a lasting trail in the Grand Canyon desert, whether it be from campsite to water source or an off-trail route that can evolve into a trail. Use established trails where they are available. Your boot tracks in trailless areas will encourage others to follow. Although the majority of backcountry trails in the Grand Canyon are unmaintained, hikers maintain them simply by using them.

When traveling off-trail, spread out to avoid concentrating the impacts of too many feet. Choose routes through washes, across slickrock, or over unvegetated areas as much as possible. Desert plants are stiff and spiny, yet fragile. Crushed plants may take many years to recover from damage, if they recover at all.

Restrain the urge to build cairns (small piles of rocks). Some trails may be ill-defined, but there are almost always cairns to show the way. Unfortunately, there is a profusion of unnecessary cairns, constructed by misguided hikers, and you could be led astray. On faint trails, consult your topo map and look for the next cairn before proceeding, but please don't build any more cairns. Let the next person enjoy the challenge of route-finding as you did. If you need the guidance of cairns and other "handrails," stick to well-defined trails instead.

CRYPTOBIOTIC SOIL CRUST

In some areas of the Grand Canyon, particularly on the Esplanade, you will find large areas of soil covered by a black or gray lumpy crust. This cryptobiotic soil crust is a delicate assemblage of mosses, lichens, blue-green algae, and fungi that forms a protective layer against wind and water erosion and aids in the absorption and retention of moisture, allowing larger plants to gain a foothold. The passage of a single hiker can destroy this fragile crust, and it may take twenty-five years or longer to redevelop. In areas covered by cryptobiotic soil crust, choose your route carefully to avoid it. Follow routes through sandy areas, washes, or slickrock instead.

BE A GOOD NEIGHBOR

Many hikers seek out places like the Grand Canyon for quiet and solitude. Hikers in Use Areas that allow at-large camping should make the extra effort to allow ample distances from other parties and keep loud noises to a minimum.

ARCHAEOLOGICAL AND HISTORICAL SITES

Evidence of ancient cultures and prospectors-turned-tour-guides abounds on Grand Canyon trails. Indeed, all trails except the South Kaibab Trail have evolved from routes used by ancient inhabitants that were later improved upon by nineteenth-century prospectors. Along such trails (Nankoweap, Beamer, Thunder River, Deer Creek, North and South Bass, Hermit, Boucher, and the Bright Angel), you may encounter archaeological and historical ruins and artifacts.

The majority of archaeological sites date back to between A.D. 1050 and A.D. 1200, a time when the Anasazi widely occupied the Grand Canyon region. Granaries, rock art, ruins of dwellings, pot sherds, the gray ash and charcoal of mescal roasting pits, prospectors' cabins, and mining and camp relics are among the cultural resources hikers may find in the Grand Canyon backcountry.

Keep in mind that these nonrenewable resources offer archaeologists insights into past ways of life in the Grand Canyon and can be easily disturbed and damaged by curious hikers. Although federal and state laws protect cultural resources, ultimately it depends on each of us to walk softly and treat these resources with the respect they deserve. Excavation and stabilization of many sites has yet to take place. Although hikers are likely to encounter many sites on Grand Canyon trails, this book will not lead you to them, preserving for hikers the sense of discovery.

Ancient granaries and ruins are very fragile. Restrain the urge to enter them and climb on their stone walls. Walk carefully around the slopes that support these structures. Ruins are an interesting highlight of a hike, but are inappropriate places to make camp.

After observing an archaeological site, move on before having meals. Food crumbs and garbage may attract rodents that could then nest in the site.

Pigments of ancient pictographs are easily destroyed by skin oils. Restrain the urge to touch them, particularly hand-print pictographs. Never add your own graffiti to irreplaceable rock art panels.

If you happen upon an archaeological site where artifacts remain, you may photograph them, but if you pick up or rearrange objects you may be destroying an important link to the past. Once an artifact is removed or disturbed, it becomes merely an object with little meaning to archaeologists.

There are cultural sites within the Grand Canyon that are off-limits to visitation. Only one trail covered in this book passes by such a place. Because the site has great religious significance to the Hopi people, I won't give its location but I will reiterate the importance of respecting these sites.

PLANNING YOUR TRIP

A Grand Canyon backpack trip is a physically and mentally demanding experience. Yet anyone in good physical condition can have an enjoyable trip in the Canyon. The more you prepare for the rigors of 4,000- to 5,000-foot descents and ascents, the fewer problems you are likely to have.

The best preparation for Grand Canyon hiking *is* Grand Canyon hiking. Begin with preliminary day hikes into the inner Canyon, progress to short backpacks on Corridor trails, and, finally, as your conditioning and confidence grow, strike out on the Park's unmaintained wilderness trails. Unfortunately, few of us live close enough to the Grand Canyon to use its trails as a training ground. Thus, we must seek out local hiking areas to prepare for the rigors of hiking in the park.

Physical conditioning is important for a safe and enjoyable trip, and with adequate conditioning you have won half the battle. Beyond proper conditioning, the second most important thing to bring with you is a positive attitude, an adaptable attitude for the changing conditions you meet on the trail. You can't fight the heat, the steep and rocky trails, or the interminable ascents. On the hike out, don't stare up at the rim and convince yourself it's too far. Put your mind at ease, take one step at a time, and rest as often as you feel necessary. Take each step as a victory and focus your attention on looking down at what you have gained rather than up at the elusive rim.

Rarely are you able to set a steady pace on Grand Canyon trails, to let your mind wander and crank out the miles. Rugged trails and steep ascents and descents require you to constantly adjust your pace, and the incredible views that unfold at every step distract you from your labors. Your pace, and your schedule, will be based on your condition and that of the members of your party. It will also depend on what the Canyon serves up, whether it be extreme heat, heavy rains, strong winds, cold, or snow. Be prepared to modify your plans. Don't exceed your limits by trying to rush on a self-imposed, unrealistic schedule that may jeopardize the well-being of you and your party.

Everyone wants to get the most out of their hiking experience in the Grand Canyon. Unfortunately, for some hikers, that means trying to squeeze a two-day hike into one long, exhausting day. *Do not attempt to hike from the rim to the river and back in one day!* Many of those foolhardy enough to try this don't make it and require assistance from rangers. The less-fortunate have been evacuated by helicopter in a body bag.

Before you leave home for a backcountry trip to the Grand Canyon, leave a detailed itinerary with a family member, friend, or employer. Include the name of the permit holder or trip leader, the trailhead where you will be hiking out, your vehicle make, model, and license number, and the date your trip ends. Make arrangements for a friend to initiate a search if you do not return home or contact that person by a specified date. Be sure to notify that person upon your return to avoid an unnecessary search. To report a lost or overdue hiker, phone (520) 638-7888, then press 2.

Even with good conditioning and a positive attitude, problems may still develop. Summer heat, generally lasting from May through September, can be debilitating. Heat-related illness is the number one problem suffered by Grand Canyon hikers. Like Canyon wildlife, hikers must avoid the sun and the heat. Yet you can adapt, though it takes from four to seven days to acclimate to the heat and dryness of the Canyon. Steep descents, at the least, often cause intense soreness in calf muscles, usually unnoticeable until the next day when muscles tighten up. Cold weather may intensify soreness since your muscles are already tight to begin with. This soreness often persists for a few days and may slow you down on the hike out.

More serious are ligament strains; the knees are most susceptible. A strained knee can make your hike a painful ordeal and, in the worst case, require a dangerous and expensive helicopter evacuation. To help take the strain off knees and legs, many hikers use a staff. Better still is the use of a pair of lightweight hiking or ski poles. These will help you on the way down and give you an extra push on the hike out.

Be prepared with items in your first-aid kit to prevent and treat blisters. If you tend to develop knee and ankle problems, discuss your hiking plans with your doctor. Over-the-counter or prescription pain and anti-inflammatory medications, and sturdy elastic or neoprene knee and ankle wraps will help you cope in the backcountry.

Camping below Cardenas Butte, Tanner Trail.

BACKCOUNTRY PERMITS

All overnight backcountry use—backpacking, overnight cross-country skiing, and camping at rim sites outside of developed campgrounds—*requires* a backcountry use permit. Permits are not required for overnight stays at Phantom Ranch or for day hiking in the Park.

Permits are issued only by the Backcountry Reservations Office (BRO), in person or by mail. Permits are not issued over the telephone. On the South Rim, the BRO is located at the former Maswik Transportation Center, adjacent to Maswik Lodge (to the east of the lodge, next to the railroad tracks), 0.25 mile south of the West Rim Interchange near Bright Angel Lodge. The North Rim BRO (open mid-May through mid-October) is located in the Ranger Station, 1.4 miles north of Grand Canyon Lodge.

BRO offices issue backcountry permits only. They *do not* make reservations for lodging, campgrounds, river trips, mule trips, or Phantom Ranch lodging.

To maintain the qualities of wilderness that visitors seek, and to minimize the degradation of the fragile desert environment, strict limits on the number of overnight users are in effect in the Grand Canyon backcountry. An average of sixty thousand people stay overnight in the Grand Canyon backcountry each year, yet you are likely to encounter few other hikers on your overnight trip. The exceptions are Corridor area trails, heavily used by day hikers and backpackers alike. Corridor area campgrounds have a large capacity and are filled most nights from spring through autumn. Each Use Area, campground, and designated campsite has a limit on the number of groups (seven to eleven people) and parties (one to six people) that can use the area each night.

The high demand for permits far exceeds their availability. A reservation system allows you to apply for a permit up to four months in advance of your trip. Before you apply for a permit, however, you should consider your plans carefully. First, get a copy of the "Backcountry Trip Planner" from the BRO, either in person, by mailing a request, or over the telephone. It contains a permit application, a map showing backcountry Use Areas and their letter/number codes, and ample information on permit application procedures.

Plan your trip using topo maps and the trail information in this book. Remain flexible in your dates and itinerary, but don't choose an unreasonable alternative trail or destination where you may get in over your head. You are required to follow your itinerary. For example, if this is your first backcountry trip in the Grand Canyon, you will probably be hiking Corridor trails (Bright Angel, North and South Kaibab), and staying in one of the three campgrounds (Indian Garden, Bright Angel, Cottonwood). If those areas are unavailable, apply again for different dates rather than choosing a more difficult trail that is available. First time hikers who choose, for instance, the Tanner, Boucher, or New Hance trails may end up getting into trouble.

Permits are issued on a first-come, first-served basis. So if you arrive at the BRO expecting to obtain a permit for that day, week, or even month, you will very likely be disappointed. The reservation system allows you to apply for a permit, by mail, in advance. Requests will be accepted for any date during the month your request is received and for the following four months. For example, you can apply on or after March 1 for any dates from March 1 through the end of July. The postmark on the envelope will determine the validity of mail-in requests. Letters postmarked earlier than the requested date (i.e. the first of the month) will not be accepted.

If an opening is available for the dates and itinerary you requested, your permit will be mailed to you, usually within about two weeks. You are advised, however, to include alternate dates and itineraries in the spaces provided on the request form. The permit is valid only for the trip leader, number of persons, and itinerary specified on the permit.

A twenty dollar fee is required for the permit and the correct amount must be submitted with your mail-in request. You must add another four dollars per night, per person "impact fee." For example, if there are five people in your party and you stay four nights in the backcountry, the total fee for your trip will be a hundred dollars. If you take more than three backcountry trips per year in the Park, you can save money by buying a one-year "frequent hiker" membership for fifty dollars. The frequent hiker program allows a trip leader and members of his/her party or group to take as many backcountry trips in one year as they wish, based on the availability of permits. You must still pay the nightly impact fee.

If you cancel your trip after paying for a permit, the fee is not refundable. A fee-recovery system allows 80 percent of the monies collected from permit fees to fund backcountry operations in Grand Canyon National Park.

The permit system and user fees may seem complicated and burdensome, but the process is fairly straightforward. More planning is necessary in the Grand Canyon than for most other hiking areas, yet there is only one Grand Canyon, and the rewards of a backcountry trip here far outweigh any inconvenience.

Cancellations occasionally make permits available, and you may be able to get a permit in person at either BRO at your time of your arrival. A few Corridor area campsites are held from the reservation system and are available daily on a first-come, first-served basis at the BRO beginning at 8 a.m. A waiting list is maintained for these few permits when demand exceeds availability. You may place your name on the waiting list, but you must be present at the BRO at 8 a.m. each day to maintain your place on the list for as many days as necessary to get a permit. A wait of two to three days is often required.

Hikers en route to remote trailheads in the Park, such as South Bass and Swamp Point, can apply for a backcountry permit and camp at or near those trailheads. These permits are often easier to get for your date of choice than permits for backcountry trail trips.

Be warned: Rangers check for backcountry use permits on Canyon trails. If you backpack in the Canyon without a permit, be prepared to hike back out to the rim and/or pay a substantial fine.

The Backcountry Reservations Office is open seven days a week (except federal holidays) from 8 a.m. to noon, and 1 p.m. to 5 p.m. (Arizona is on Mountain Standard Time year-round; Arizona does not observe Daylight Saving Time.) Backcountry information is available over the telephone from the BRO, Monday through Friday, between 1 p.m. and 5 p.m., by phoning (520) 638-7875. This is an extremely busy line and you will likely have to try repeatedly to get through.

To request a permit, include the following information:

1) name, address, and telephone number of the trip leader
2) organization name if applicable
3) number of people
4) campground or campsite name, or Use Area code for each night of the proposed trip
5) preferred trip dates
6) vehicle state and license numbers, if applicable
7) indicate if you will accept variations in trip dates and/or trip campsites
8) list two alternative proposed trips and dates
9) include appropriate fees (personal check or credit card number and expiration date).

Refer to Appendix B for the BRO address.

Don't Overpack

Grand Canyon trails are demanding enough to test the endurance of the most well-conditioned hiker. An overburdened pack puts unnecessary stress and strain on a hiker and can dramatically increase food and water requirements. Carry only what you will need, taking into consideration the time of year. Plan your equipment, food, and water requirements carefully.

Some hikers lighten their load by eating cold meals, leaving the stove and fuel at home. In the heat of summer, some foods will spoil quickly. Use any perishable foods early in the trip to avoid the risk of a debilitating intestinal illness.

A tent may seem unnecessary in the hot, dry environment, and many hikers leave their tents at home and sleep under the stars instead. But a lightweight tent gives you a place to retreat on those summer nights when rain comes suddenly, and during cooler times of the year a tent offers a warm haven. A tent is also not a bad idea for people who prefer not to be startled out of their slumber by mice, tarantulas, scorpions, frogs, or those large black and red ants that seem to come out only at night.

From June through August, inner Canyon high temperatures average above 100 degrees F and nighttime lows seldom dip below 70 degrees F. During very hot spells, overnight lows may only dip into the mid- to upper 80s. To save weight and space, consider leaving your sleeping bag behind during summer, instead packing a sheet, lightweight blanket, or sleeping bag liner.

Protect Your Food Supply

Animal raids, both day and night, are a problem at many campsites in the Grand Canyon backcountry. Mice, squirrels, skunks, ringtails, and even deer have grown accustomed to human food, particularly at popular campsites and Corridor area campgrounds. Any established campsites are susceptible to the silent raids of these hungry animals. These critters associate the smell of plastic with food, and they will chew through backpacks, and even tents, to reach it.

Pack poles are provided for hanging packs in Corridor campgrounds, but ringtails have learned to climb them and search packs for food. (Use the ammo cans provided in these campgrounds for food storage.) Many hikers suspend packs and stuffsacks from trees and shrubs with nylon cord, but mice and ringtails can easily walk the tightrope to your food supply.

Instead of nylon cord, hang your food using fishing line; 20- to 30-pound test works best. Fishing line is slippery and thin enough to thwart the climbing efforts of the most determined mouse or ringtail. Put all of your food, plastics, toothpaste—anything you want to protect from damage—into a stuffsack and hang it at least four feet off the ground, high enough that a ringtail can't reach it. Hang your empty pack or leave it on the ground with zippers open

---

WATER SOURCES IN THE GRAND CANYON

Although water is responsible for carving the Grand Canyon and its many tributaries, surface water (except for the Colorado River) is scarce. Water is the single most limiting factor to travel on Grand Canyon's trails—you must reach a water source each day or carry all the water you will need until you reach that source. Some creeks and springs flow year-round (see "Perennial Water Sources" below), while others flow unpredictably following prolonged rainfall or snowmelt. From late autumn to early spring, when evaporation is reduced, some springs and streams resurface.

The Backcountry Reservations Office (BRO) maintains a list of seasonal water sources, updating the list based on the reports of rangers and hikers. You should always check their reports before any inner Canyon hike. These reports will help you maintain a margin of safety. Several times I have been told by the BRO that certain springs or streams were dry, and instead I was pleasantly surprised to find flowing water. However, I have yet to receive a report of flowing water and then find it dry.

Hikers must always carry water on any Grand Canyon trail, even on the Bright Angel and North Kaibab trails, where drinking water is provided at intervals. Breaks in the trans-canyon pipeline that supplies that drinking water can occur at any time. Water requirements are based on heat, exertion, time of day, and the time of year you hike. (For a complete discussion on water requirements, see "Why Suffer?" below.) As a rule, and for a measure of safety, hikers should always carry at least 1 gallon of water on extended trips away from known water sources. To paraphrase Park Service

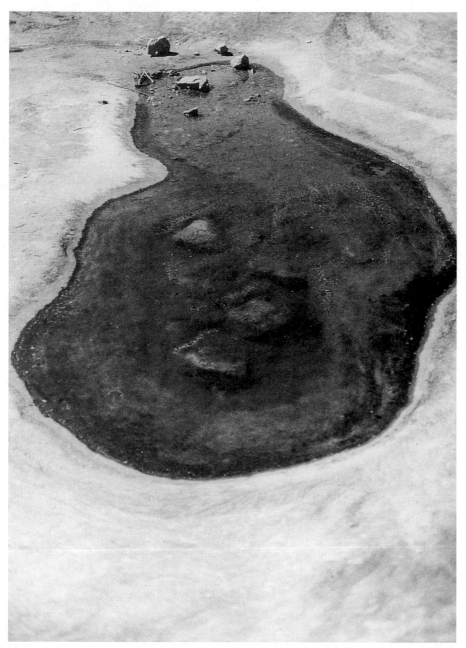

Rare waterpockets in the slickrock are important to both hikers and Grand Canyon wildlife.

recommendations, your water supply should be the heaviest item in your pack. Running out of water on Grand Canyon trails is the single largest mistake you can make, and occasionally people die for lack of water here.

You will drink at least 1 gallon of water per day while hiking in the Grand Canyon. If you are bound from the rim to a dry camp, you will need to pack at least 1.5 gallons, provided you reach a reliable water source early on the following day. If you are hiking to a known water source, but the trip takes all day, you are still advised to pack a full gallon of water for the trip in the event unforeseen situations develop that prevent you from reaching water.

Always prehydrate prior to your trip, and during your trip before your most strenuous hiking days, such as prior to your hike out to the rim from the river. Drink large amounts of water over a period of several hours in the evening at camp and in the morning before leaving camp. It is essential, however, that you balance your water intake with electrolytes.

Since adequate water intake is so critical to a safe and enjoyable trip in the Grand Canyon, it is surprising that so many hikers carry their precious water supply in fragile containers, particularly thin plastic milk jugs. These jugs burst easily if dropped, and in summer, when rocks are too hot to touch, the bottom will quickly melt if you set your jug down. Instead of large, flimsy jugs, transport your water in several smaller, more durable containers. Nalgene 1- and 2-quart bottles are best, and they take up little more room in your pack than larger jugs.

Caching water on your route of travel is a popular means of lightening your load and ensuring a water supply when you need it on the hike out. Most hikers cache water roughly halfway between the rim and the river, usually on top of the Redwall cliff. Two quarts per person comprises the typical cache, but hikers intending to camp on the way out should cache 1 to 1.5 gallons.

When caching water, mark your containers with your name or initials and the date you expect to retrieve it. Conceal it well, preferably in the shade. Too many hikers leave their cache in full view, sometimes at the trailside. There are, unfortunately, inconsiderate hikers, usually those with little Grand Canyon hiking experience, who jeopardize other hikers by consuming their water cache. Always remove your cache; pour out the water if you don't need it and pack out the container.

Water sources in the Grand Canyon range from green, scummy pools brimming with tadpoles to seeps, dripping springs, spring pools, cold and vigorous creeks, and the refreshing waters (when running clear) of the Colorado River, which maintains a year-round temperature of 48 to 50 degrees F. Wherever you obtain your water, it must be purified before drinking or even brushing your teeth. Life is concentrated around precious desert water sources, including life forms you cannot see. Microscopic bacteria and protozoans may inhabit any surface water in the Grand Canyon, including *Giardia*, *E. coli*, *campylobacter*, or the virus that causes Hepatitis A. Boiling water for at least 5 minutes is the old standby for rendering water potable, but the extra weight in fuel required, and the time to boil an adequate supply and allow it to cool, are reasons enough to use a pump-type water filter instead.

Filters such as Katadyn, Pur, First Need, Sweetwater, and MSR have been proven to eliminate most waterborne organisms. For added insurance, choose a filter or attachment that removes viruses as well. These filters are widely available at outdoor supply stores, or you can get them at the last minute at Babbitt's General Store on the South Rim.

Filters can clog with silt easily, so choose a filter that you can clean in the field. When the Colorado River is silt-laden, you will need to set water aside (a collapsible bucket is useful for this) and allow the sediment to settle before filtering.

During winter, some water sources may be frozen. Then you will need some means of chopping the ice and a stove to melt it.

PERENNIAL WATER SOURCES IN THE GRAND CANYON

(An * indicates sources accessed by trails covered in this book.)

Boucher Creek*
Bright Angel Creek*
Buck Farm Creek
Clear Creek*
Colorado River*
Crystal Creek
Deer Creek*
Dripping Spring*
Garden Creek*
Grapevine Creek*
Hance Creek*
Haunted Creek
Havasu Creek
Hermit Creek*
Little Colorado River*
Kanab Creek
Miners Spring*
Monument Creek*
Nankoweap Creek*
Olo Creek
Pipe Creek*
Phantom Creek*
Royal Arch Creek
Santa Maria Spring*
Shinumo Creek*
Tapeats Creek*
Thunder River*
Vasey's Paradise

The foaming waves of Hermit Rapids lie at the end of the Hermit Trail.

LODGING

See Appendix B for reservations information at lodges.

Demand for lodging accommodations in and around Grand Canyon National Park far exceeds availability. During spring through fall, the busiest seasons, you must make advance reservations for lodging or you cannot expect to find a room available.

There are six lodges in Grand Canyon Village on the South Rim. Accommodations range from hotel suites to rustic cabins, and you pay a premium for the privilege of staying the night on the rim of the Grand Canyon. Advance reservations (several months in advance) are strongly recommended.

Phantom Ranch has cabins and dormitories adjacent to Bright Angel Campground in the inner Canyon. Breakfast, lunch, and dinner are available by reservation. Some people hike in to Phantom Ranch, but most take the round-trip mule ride. Again, make reservations several months in advance of your trip.

Grand Canyon Lodge, located at Bright Angel Point, at the road's end on the North Rim, offers motel rooms and cabins.

The town of Tusayan, located on Arizona Highway 64, 1.5 miles south of the Park's south entrance, features several large motels, a private campground with RV hookups, groceries, restaurants, and fuel.

A wide variety of lodging and services are available outside of the Park, in the towns of Flagstaff, Williams, Page, and Fredonia, Arizona, and Kanab,

Utah. For more information contact the chambers of commerce listed in Appendix B.

CAMPGROUNDS

See Appendix B for reservations information at campgrounds.

There are three campgrounds and one RV park in Grand Canyon National Park, all but one of which are on the South Rim. The 320-site Mather Campground is located south of Babbitt's General Store on the South Rim. This campground lies in a forest of ponderosa pine, pinyon, and juniper, but offers no Canyon views. The campground access road is paved, and campsite spurs can accommodate RVs (no hookups available). Mather provides water, toilets, tables, fire pits and grills, and six handicap-accessible sites. A fee is charged. The campground is available on a first-come, first-served basis from December 1 through March 1. At other times, you must book sites well in advance.

The 84-site Trailer Village adjacent to Mather Campground has RV hookups. Desert View Campground is a fifty-site campground on the South Rim at Desert View, 26 miles east of Grand Canyon Village on East Rim Drive. Set in an open woodland of pinyon and juniper, the campground offers views into both the Grand Canyon and the Painted Desert. Facilities include water, tables, toilets, fire pits, and grills. A fee is charged. The campground is usually open from mid-May through mid-October and is available on a first-

The picnic area at Shoshone Point, South Rim.

come, first-served basis only. Visitors are advised to arrive early in the day to secure a site.

On the North Rim, there is the eighty-two-site North Rim Campground, open from May 15 through October 15. This pleasant campground lies on the rim above The Transept in a forest of pine, fir, and aspen. The Transept Trail follows the rim of that cavernous defile for 1.5 miles from the campground to Grand Canyon Lodge. Facilities include water, tables, toilets, fire pits and grills, and campsite spurs that can accommodate RVs. A fee is charged. Some sites may be available at your time of arrival, but to insure a site, you should make reservations.

When conditions permit, you may build a campfire in Grand Canyon campgrounds, but you must bring your own firewood. Wood gathering is not permitted in the Park.

The Kaibab National Forest also offers campgrounds, one near the South Rim, and two near the North Rim. The seventy-site Ten X Campground lies 3 miles south of Tusayan off AZ 64. This fee campground is usually open from May 1 through October 31. The Jacob Lake Campground, with fifty-four sites, is located just north of Jacob Lake and the junction of Arizona Highway 67 and U.S. Highway 89A. A fee is charged here, and the campground is usually open from May 15 through November 1. The twenty-three-site DeMotte Park Campground is located high on the Kaibab Plateau off AZ 67, 25.7 miles south of Jacob Lake. The campground is usually open from June 1 through November 1. A fee is charged. All national forest campgrounds are available on a first-come, first-served basis and feature tables, water, toilets, fire pits, and grills.

The private Kaibab Lodge Camper Village is located 0.25 mile south of Jacob Lake off AZ 67. This fee campground offers fifty tent sites and sixty RV sites with hookups.

The Kaibab National Forest is open to at-large camping, and many hikers who are here for solitude prefer that type of camping to developed campgrounds. Many excellent, secluded sites can be found along any forest road en route to either rim. Campers must be aware of fire restrictions (if applicable), off-road travel restrictions, and camp at least 0.25 mile from paved roads and water sources.

Forest roads leading to Nankoweap, South Canyon, North Bass, and Bill Hall trailheads all offer many possible campsites. Forest Road 328, which leads to the South Bass trailhead, offers a wide selection of car camping areas. Another excellent, but often overlooked, area in which to camp is Forest Road 310. This road, marked for Arizona Trail, branches off from East Rim Drive 2 miles east of the Grandview Point turnoff. This dirt road leads 0.6 mile to the Kaibab National Forest boundary, beyond which are many miles of open ponderosa pine forest offering ample room for car camping. Camping along this road is useful for hikers wishing to get an early start from East Rim Drive trailheads.

ACCESS AND SERVICES

Despite its remoteness, Grand Canyon National Park attracts 5 million visitors a year. The North Rim, even more remote than the South Rim, receives one-tenth that number of visitors. Visitors must come prepared and realize that the services available in an near the Park are limited. And you must often pay a premium for those services.

Grand Canyon Village at the South Rim can be reached from Interstate Highway 40 in the south. From Williams, Arizona, drive north on AZ 64 for 59 miles to reach the village. Or from Flagstaff, follow U.S. Highway 180 and AZ 64 for 78 miles. From the east, find the junction of AZ 64 and U.S. Highway 89 at Cameron, on the Navajo Indian Reservation. Cameron is located 82 miles south of Page, Arizona, 58.3 miles south of the US 89/89A junction, and 16 miles south of the US 89/160 junction. Grand Canyon Village can be reached from Cameron by following AZ 64 west for 57 miles. Cameron offers your last chance for fuel until you reach Desert View, 30.7 miles ahead.

At the South Rim at Desert View, there is a general store and gift shop. The Grand Canyon Association bookstore and gas station at Desert View are open spring through autumn only.

The majority of South Rim services are located in or adjacent to Grand Canyon Village (see the map of the South Rim). Grand Canyon Village is much more than a typical national park development, it is a self-contained town. Hundreds of Park Service and concessioner employees live here, and a variety of services are available to meet not only their needs but the needs of the millions of visitors who come each year.

Gas, diesel, and propane are available at the gas station opposite the visitor center. Babbitt's General Store offers a wide selection of groceries and an outdoor department, where a full range of backpacking supplies, topo maps, and equipment rentals are available. Adjacent to Babbitt's you will find a post office and bank. A medical clinic, offering 24-hour emergency services (dial 911), a pharmacy, and dental service, is located on Center Road, south of the village area; ample signs point the way to the clinic.

Other village services include vehicle repair at the garage located next to Grand Canyon National Park Lodges General Offices, and a Western Union telegraph office located in the General Offices building at the Y junction just east of the train depot and the lodge complex. Laundry and showers are located south of the visitor center on the Mather Campground access road. Pet kennels are located off Rowe Well Road south of Maswik Lodge.

For more information about the South Rim, request a copy of Park information and a trip planner, see Appendix B.

To reach the North Rim from the east, follow US 89, either south from Page for 25.8 miles, or 58.3 miles north from Cameron, to the junction with US 89A. Follow US 89A north, then west, for 57.25 miles to Jacob Lake, on the Kaibab Plateau, at the junction with southbound Arizona Highway 67 (the Kaibab Plateau-North Rim Parkway). Jacob Lake can also be reached from the north via US 89A, 29.8 miles south of the US 89A/Arizona Highway 389 junction in Fredonia, Arizona, and 34 miles south from US 89 in Kanab, Utah. The North Rim entrance station is located 31 miles south of Jacob Lake via AZ 67. The road ends at Grand Canyon Lodge, 11.7 miles south of the entrance station.

Services at the North Rim are limited and available only between May 15 and October 15. At Grand Canyon Lodge there is a restaurant, snack shop, bar, and post office. A general store is located adjacent to North Rim Campground. Limited camping and backpacking supplies are available at the store. A gas station is located just west of the main Park road on the campground access road. You will find a laundry and showers adjacent to the campground. Medical services are available at the clinic adjacent to the lodge.

Kaibab Lodge, located off AZ 67, 25.5 miles south of Jacob Lake, offers lodging and a restaurant. Opposite Kaibab Lodge is the North Rim Country Store, offering gas and diesel, and limited groceries.

In Jacob Lake, you will find a service station offering gas, diesel, and propane, and minor vehicle repair. Adjacent to the service station is Jacob Lake Lodge, offering a restaurant and rooms.

On US 89A east of Jacob Lake, additional services are available. Marble Canyon Lodge, a short distance southwest of Navajo Bridge and the turnoff to Lees Ferry, is located 14.25 miles northwest of the US 89/89A junction and 43 miles east of Jacob Lake. The lodge provides a motel, restaurant, gift shop, telephones, and fuel. Vermilion Cliffs Lodge, 17.7 miles from the US 89/89A junction and 39.6 miles from Jacob Lake, offers a bar and grill, fly shop, motel, restaurant, telephones, and fuel. Cliff Dwellers Lodge, 23 miles from the US 89/89A junction and 34.25 miles from Jacob Lake, offers rooms, groceries, a restaurant, and fuel.

SHUTTLE SERVICES

A variety of shuttle services are available at both the North and South rims, allowing hikers greater flexibility for point-to-point trips. Many hikers leave their vehicles at the trailhead where they plan to emerge and ride a shuttle back to their starting point.

West Rim Shuttle

West Rim Drive is closed to private vehicles to relieve congestion from late May through September. During that time, the West Rim Shuttle operates daily, running every 15 minutes from 7:30 a.m. to sunset. There is no fee. You can board the brown and tan bus at the West Rim Interchange bus stop adjacent to Bright Angel Lodge and the Bright Angel trailhead.

Kaibab Shuttle

The Kaibab hiker's shuttle connects the Grand Canyon Village area with the South Kaibab trailhead for a small fee. The bus departs from the front porch of Bright Angel Lodge at 6:30, 8:30, and 11:30 a.m., and from Maswik

Lodge at 6:50, 8:50, and 11:50 a.m. daily. The bus leaves the South Kaibab trailhead at 7:10 a.m., 9:10 a.m., and 12:10 p.m.

Park plans eventually call for the closure of the South Kaibab trailhead to private vehicles, at least during the peak season. At that time, a free shuttle will offer access from Grand Canyon Village to the trailhead. Check with the BRO for current information and schedules.

Private Shuttles

To reach more distant South Rim trailheads along East Rim Drive, hikers have two choices for transportation. The Fred Harvey Company conducts daily bus tours to Canyon overlooks (some of which are trailheads) along East Rim Drive. You can join the tourists on one of these tour buses (for a fee) and disembark at your trailhead en route.

Fred Harvey also operates a 24-hour taxi service for a higher fee. Despite the fee, the taxi service offers much greater flexibility for hikers, and the taxi also serves the remote South Bass trailhead.

Contact the transportation desk at Bright Angel Lodge for information regarding bus tour transportation, or phone (520) 638-2822 or (520) 638-2631. To hire a taxi, phone (520) 638-2631, extension 6563.

A rim-to-rim shuttle is available to trans-Canyon hikers for a substantial fee. For information or reservations, contact any lodge transportation desk, or phone Trans-Canyon Shuttle at (520) 638-2820. This shuttle leaves the North Rim at 7 a.m. and arrives at the South Rim at 11:30 a.m. Later, it leaves the South Rim at 1:30 p.m. and reaches the North Rim at 6:30 p.m.

On the North Rim, a hikers' shuttle, available for a small fee, departs from Grand Canyon Lodge and takes hikers to the often full North Kaibab trailhead parking lot. The shuttle is available from 6 a.m. to 8 p.m. daily when the North Rim is in full swing, mid-May through mid-October.

PLAYING IT SAFE

The rocky depths of the Grand Canyon are neither barren wastes nor a hostile landscape where poisonous creatures and spiny cacti lie in wait to inflict painful injury on passersby. However, the Canyon does contain its share of cacti, thorny shrubs, and creatures that can injure you if you are careless.

Flies are common in the Canyon, but biting flies and mosquitoes are largely absent. Only during the cooler months of the year will you encounter mosquitoes, and then only in limited numbers, primarily near seeps, springs, and sluggish streams.

Various spiders, including black widows and tarantulas, and scorpions and centipedes inhabit the Canyon. Of them all, the scorpion is the most

The Grand Canyon pink rattlesnake is found only in the Canyon's depths.
Photo by John Rihs.

common. Most can inflict a painful sting, but their venom is rarely life-threatening. The exception is the bark scorpion, *Centruroides sculpturatus*. This scorpion, less than 2 inches long, spends daylight hours beneath the bark of cottonwood trees. Its venom is more toxic than that of a rattlesnake.

A scorpion's sting is a defensive reaction; it doesn't seek out humans and attack them. Most stings are incurred after someone steps on one or touches it. Scorpions are nocturnal hunters, spending the day in the shade under rocks or in dark crevices of logs and bark. Hikers should be careful where they put their hands and feet and avoid picking up rocks. At night always wear shoes—not sandals—around camp and look before you sit. Shake out your boots, shoes, and clothing before putting them on, and either shake out your sleeping bag before retiring or wait until bedtime before preparing your bed.

Perhaps the most frightening insect in the inner Canyon, particularly along the Colorado River, is the tarantula hawk wasp. These large black wasps, with orange wings, can reach lengths of 2 inches. There are no reports of tarantula hawks stinging people, but they do have the nasty habit of flying into your face.

Ants are ubiquitous throughout the Canyon; you can't avoid them, but you can keep them at bay. Red harvester ants can inflict a memorable sting, and there are tiny red ants that march in columns toward your pack and food. Camp away from anthills and avoid discarding food scraps that will attract ants.

Great Basin, Hopi, and Grand Canyon rattlesnakes inhabit the Canyon. The endemic Grand Canyon rattlesnake, unmistakable with its pinkish hue, is most common in the inner Canyon, generally in the lower reaches of side canyons and along the Colorado River below about 3,000 feet. Although rattlesnakes often are seen by hikers, they are generally not aggressive, and few hikers have been bitten in the Canyon. Snakes rest in the shade to avoid midday heat, so hikers should use caution when stepping over logs and boulders and watch where they put their hands and feet.

Beware of the spines of cacti, yucca, and agave. Although cactus spines are painful, they can usually be removed with tweezers. The glochids— those tiny hairlike spines—are more difficult to remove and cause painful irritation. Probing with fingernails or tweezers often imbeds glochids deeper into your skin. Try removing them with adhesive tape instead.

Yucca and agave have large, stiff spines on the tips of their leaves that can inflict a painful puncture wound. If one of these spines breaks off in your hand, leg, or arm, it can be very difficult to remove and you may have to endure the remainder of your trip until a doctor can remove it.

Mice are ubiquitous throughout the Grand Canyon, and though they represent no direct threat to hikers, save for their annoying campsite foraging habits, they are potential carriers of the dangerous *hantavirus*. The virus is spread by inhaling airborne particles of the droppings, blood, urine, and saliva of mice. Symptoms of the respiratory illness caused by the virus resemble the flu, but worsen as the lungs fill with fluid. If the illness is not detected and treated in its early stages, it can progress to coma, respiratory failure, and death. For this reason, extra precautions are warranted when camping in a mouse-infested campsite. Sleep in a tent rather than on the ground. Protect your food supply from mice and never keep food in your tent. If mice do chew into some of your food, don't eat it; pack it out to the rim and discard it.

Solar radiation is intense in the Grand Canyon's dry desert air and there is often little shade. Protect yourself from sunburn by using a sunscreen with a Sun Protection Factor (SPF) of at least 15. Wear a light-colored long-sleeved shirt, a hat, and sunglasses with ultraviolet protection. Most Grand Canyon hikers wear shorts, but long pants protect your legs not only from sunburn and afford some protection from rocks, stiff brush, and cactus.

Keeping your feet happy can be a challenge in the Grand Canyon. Sweaty feet combined with the Canyon's steep trails are precursors to rubs and blisters. Wear well-broken-in boots and bring at least one change of socks, moleskin, and tape. If you feel a rub or blister developing, stop at once, air dry your feet, and change into dry socks (allow your sweaty socks to dry on the outside of your pack). Apply moleskin or tape as needed.

During the summer monsoon season in July and August, sudden torrents of rain are unleashed from towering thunderheads in hit-or-miss fashion throughout the Canyon. This heavy, localized rain pours off the slickrock and thin soils and gathers in rivulets, which in turn flow into larger and larger side canyons. The result can be a flash flood. Flash floods are always a danger to be reckoned with, and they are even more powerful and dangerous in the steep, precipitous side canyons. Although many canyon-bottom campsites are inviting, they can become death traps in the event of a flash flood. Avoid camping in canyon bottoms and washes during stormy weather, particularly during the monsoon season. Some canyons can flash with a 10-foot or higher slurry of water, mud, rocks, branches, and logs. When scouting for a campsite in a canyon, you will likely see debris left behind by past floods lodged on ledges above a wash. Choose your campsite above that debris line. If you anticipate a flash flood while hiking or camping, look for escape routes to higher ground immediately.

Lightning goes hand in hand with summer thunderstorms. Keep your eye on the sky; dark cumulonimbus clouds herald the approach of a thunderstorm. If one is approaching, stay away from ridges, the base of cliffs, solitary trees, shallow overhangs and alcoves, and open areas. Seek shelter in thickets of brush or in pinyon-juniper woodlands where trees are plentiful, small, and of uniform size. Barring that kind of shelter, retreat to a boulder field or low-lying area.

Flows in the Colorado River in Grand Canyon are regulated in response to storage and hydroelectric energy demands at Glen Canyon Dam. Water is drawn from Lake Powell 200 feet below the surface, so the river in the Grand Canyon, which often resembles the crystalline waters of its source in the Rocky Mountains, maintains a near-constant temperature of 48 to 50 degrees F. The river is deep, cold, and much more powerful than it appears. Restrain the urge to swim in the river; people have been swept away to their deaths by the strong currents. Also be wary when you draw water from the river; be sure of your footing.

WHY SUFFER?

The following unofficial information on avoiding dehydration and other safety hazards was compiled by Corridor area rangers, who generously allowed it to be reprinted here. Following these guidelines will help make your hike into and out of the Grand Canyon much safer and more enjoyable.

Dehydration

Hiking in the Canyon, everyone sweats around 0.5 to 1 quart of water and electrolytes (salts) each and every hour walking in the heat. This fluid/electrolyte loss can even exceed 2 quarts per hour if you hike uphill in direct sunlight during the hottest part of the day. Because inner Canyon air is so dry and hot, sweat evaporates instantly, making its loss almost imperceptible. This evaporation allows our bodies to lose heat and keep cool. **Do not wait until you start feeling thirsty to start replacing these fluids and**

Desert bighorns, surefooted masters of the inner Canyon's rugged landscape, sometimes fall victim to their precipitous habitat.

electrolytes. By the time you feel thirsty, you are already dehydrated.

Even this mild level of dehydration makes your body 10 to 20 percent less efficient, and this makes hiking a lot less fun. The more dehydrated you become, the less efficient your body becomes at walking and cooling. A slight to moderate fluid and electrolyte loss will lead to heat cramps and heat exhaustion (nausea, vomiting, headache, fatigue, fainting). A moderate to large fluid and electrolyte loss can lead to severe heat exhaustion (extreme dizziness, constant nausea and vomiting, shock, kidney damage), and possibly to heat stroke. Each year, inner Canyon rangers treat thousands of hikers for heat-related illnesses and injuries.

A normal hydrated adult should be able to urinate approximately 1 to 2 ounces of light yellow-colored urine every 2 hours. If you are urinating more frequently than this and your urine is clear in color, you may be over-hydrating and may need to cut back on your fluid intake. If your urine is dark in color [keep in mind that vitamins will turn urine yellow] and/or smells, you are probably dehydrated and need to drink more frequently.

Water Intake

Your body can absorb only about 1 quart of fluid per hour, so drink 0.5 to 1 quart of some type of electrolyte replacement drink (such as Gookinaid) each and every hour that you are walking in the heat. Carry your water bottle in your hand and drink small amounts often. The average adult should drink approximately 4 quarts of electrolyte replacement drink for every eig8 ht hours spent hiking in the heat. Remember to at least double your normal intake of food to help meet your energy and electrolyte needs.

Food Intake and Water Intoxication

Your body uses enormous amounts of energy (food calories) to keep you cool in the heat. Eating is your most important defense against exhaustion and water intoxication. Keeping yourself cool *and* hiking out of the Canyon takes a very large amount of energy. Heat will reduce your appetite; it seems all you crave is water. So you must force yourself to eat adequate amounts of food to keep up with the demands of Grand Canyon hiking. Be sure that you eat a lot more than you normally do.

Eat small amounts of complex carbohydrates (breads, fruits, crackers, grains, low-fat energy bars) throughout the day about every half hour. While hiking, you should avoid foods that are high in fats and proteins, because these foods take a long time to digest and will tend to unsettle your stomach in the heat. If you do not eat enough food to meet your energy needs, you end up burning your fat and muscle tissues to meet those needs. This is very inefficient and creates metabolic waste products that are guaranteed to make you feel ill in the heat.

Eating adequate amounts of food will also help guarantee that you are replacing the electrolytes that you are sweating out. If you replace the water but not the electrolytes, you can develop a serious and dangerous medical condition known as *hyponatremia* (water intoxication) which, if left untreated, can lead to seizures and possibly death. Don't use salt tablets to correct the problem; they will make you nauseous.

You need at least two to three times your normal food intake (4,000 to 5,000 calories) to meet your energy needs while hiking in the Grand Canyon. If you have food, eat it. If you have extra food, share it. If you do not have food, ask other hikers if they have any extra food that they will share with you. Eating well helps you hike well.

Wait for the Shade

Walk uphill in the shade. You will overheat if you hike uphill in the direct sunshine. You will use up a lot of energy trying to stay cool, and you will sweat out much more water and electrolytes hiking in the sunshine than you will in the shade; your risk of heat-related illness increases dramatically. If you wait until shade hits the trail before leaving, you will make better time, feel better, and quite possibly even enjoy the hike out of the Canyon. This will leave you with enough time (in summer) to hike out of the Canyon before it gets dark. Flashlights are available for sale at Phantom Ranch for those hikers who did not have the foresight to bring one.

Stay Wet and Stay Cool

If you must hike uphill in the sunshine, keep yourself soaking wet to stay cool. This is one of the best things you can do for yourself. Whenever you are near water, make sure that you wet (actually soak) yourself down. If you hike while soaking wet, you will stay reasonably cool. Carry some extra water to wet yourself down again when your hair and clothing begin to dry (10 to 15 minutes). This will make a wonderful difference in how well you feel, especially at the end of the day. You will stay fresher longer, and you will reduce your fluid, electrolyte, and energy loss significantly.

Sit Down and Put Your Legs Up

Every 0.5 to 1 hour, take a 5 to 7 minute break. Such a break can flush out 20 to 30 percent of the metabolic waste products that have built up in your legs while hiking. Sit down and prop your legs up above the level of your heart and let gravity help drain these waste products out of your legs. Take this kind of serious break at least every hour. Eat some food, drink some fluids, and take this break time to really enjoy and appreciate the view. These efficient breaks can really recharge your batteries. In the long run, it won't slow you down.

Do Not Huff and Puff

If you can talk while you are walking, you are walking the perfect speed. When you huff and puff, your legs, digestive system, and your whole body do not get enough oxygen to function efficiently. Your energy reserves get used up very quickly with such anaerobic activity (without enough oxygen), and it creates a lot of waste products. These waste products make your legs feel heavy and make you feel sick.

Walking uphill at a pace that allows you to be able to walk and talk will guarantee that your legs and your body are getting the oxygen that they need to function efficiently (aerobically). Because your body will generate fewer of these metabolic waste products, you will be better able to enjoy your hike, and you will feel much better when you reach its end. It may seem like you are walking too slow, but at an aerobic pace your energy reserves will last many times longer, and you'll arrive at your destination feeling good.

Be Kind to Yourself

Do not exceed your normal level of physical activity or training. If you have heart problems, asthma, diabetes, bad knees, a bad back, or any other medical problems, please limit your exertion and especially your exposure to the heat. The altitude, the strenuous climbing, dehydration, and the intense inner-Canyon heat all combine to make any medical problem worse. Attempting to hike to the river and back in one day is harder than running a marathon in the heat. It is dangerous and, at the very least, no fun. Most hikers and athletes must train for this level of physical activity. If you have not, then please stay within your training, physical limitations, and abilities and do not attempt to hike to the river and back in one day.

EMERGENCIES

Hiking in the Grand Canyon can be dangerous, as numerous fatalities over the years attest. People do occasionally end up with sprained ankles, broken bones, or other injuries that stop them in their tracks. Especially on some of the canyon's more remote wilderness trails, where help is far removed, solo hiking is not recommended.

Hikers must keep in mind that ranger patrols outside of the Corridor Use Area are infrequent. Some trails are patrolled only a few times each year. Hikers must also be aware that rangers are not babysitters. They have many responsibilities and others may need their assistance. If they are available, and you do not have a serious medical emergency, they will help you to help yourself if you get into trouble. In the Corridor area, hikers should note that mule evacuations are *not* available. Helicopter evacuations are for serious medical emergencies only, and the victim incurs the cost of the evacuation, which can exceed $1,200.

Every hiker in the Grand Canyon should carry a signal mirror. In the event of an emergency, use your mirror to continually flash points on the rim and passing aircraft. Ideally, someone will see your flashes and report them. If there are three or more people in your party, leave one person to care for the victim and send at least one other up to the rim for help. Mark the exact location on a topo map and have a clear description of where the victim is located and of the extent of the injuries. At the victim's location, mark a large "X" on the ground, using sleeping bags, tents, or other equipment, so that the helicopter can find the location from the air.

Solo hikers assume the greatest risks. Even a minor injury can become a life-threatening emergency; there is no companion to administer first-aid, to offer extra water and food, or to go for help. If you are hiking solo and get into trouble, use your signal mirror, try to find a shady place, and remain calm. If you are on a trail, other hikers will likely soon find you. If you are at the river, flag down a raft; boatmen are well-trained to handle emergencies. If you left your itinerary with someone at home (which you should always do), they will report to the Park Service that you are overdue when you fail to contact them.

Dark walls of Vishnu schist, marbled with intrusions of pink Zoroaster granite, typify the abyss of Granite Gorge. Photo by John Rihs.

GEOLOGIC PROFILE OF THE GRAND CANYON

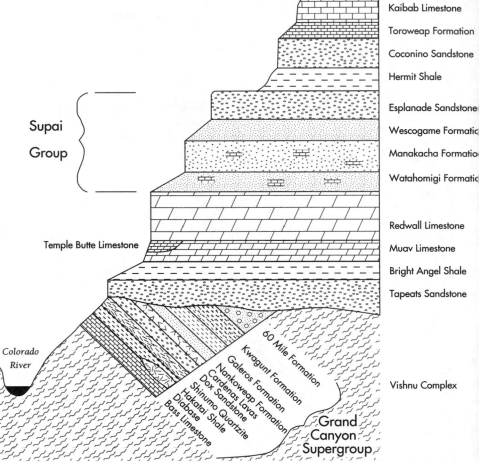

Kaibab Limestone

Toroweap Formation

Coconino Sandstone

Hermit Shale

Esplanade Sandstone

Wescogame Formation

Manakacha Formation

Watahomigi Formation

Supai Group

Redwall Limestone

Temple Butte Limestone

Muav Limestone

Bright Angel Shale

Tapeats Sandstone

Colorado River

60 Mile Formation
Kwagunt Formation
Galeros Formation
Nankoweap Formation
Cardenas Lavas
Dox Sandstone
Shinumo Quartzite
Hakatai Shale
Bass Limestone
Diabase

Vishnu Complex

Grand Canyon Supergroup

GRAND CANYON GEOLOGY

One need not be a geologist to appreciate the incredible scene of colorful, ancient rock layers that unfold from the rim of the Grand Canyon. The Canyon's rocks—sedimentary, metamorphic, and igneous—are displayed in raw grandeur, unmasked by a mantle of vegetation. At first glance, the rocks display a scene of sheer visual delight. Yet they also tell a story of the Earth's past, from the uplift, erosion, and metamorphosis of ancient mountain ranges to the ebb and flow of oceans and deserts. It's a story of the evolution of life on Earth, from the simple life forms of bacteria and blue-green algae to fish, reptiles, and plants.

The Grand Canyon is situated near the western edge of the Colorado Plateau physiographic province, which includes parts of Utah, Arizona, Colorado, and New Mexico. Covering an area of about 130,000 square miles, the Colorado Plateau is dominated by horizontal layers of sedimentary rocks— rocks deposited by wind and water. The plateau lies at high elevations relative to the low deserts to the west and south, and the region abuts the higher country of the Middle and Southern Rocky Mountains to the north and east.

Despite its name, the Colorado Plateau is not a single elevated surface. Indeed, many of its landscape features are flat, but the landscape is punctuated with many plateaus that have either been uplifted above the surrounding land by folding or faulting or have been isolated by erosion. Aside from the plateaus that characterize the Colorado Plateau landscape, this region is canyon country, containing some of the most notable canyons in the world.

The region is semi-arid to arid, thus little soil or vegetation has developed. Although precipitation is scant and unpredictable, it often comes abruptly and violently, hammering the fully exposed rock layers, stripping away loose fragments ranging from sand grains to boulders, and transporting these materials downhill. Canyons are formed as loose material is carried away by running water (erosion). The transported sediments have tremendous erosive power, abrading and scouring the bottom of a drainage. As the drainage deepens, rock layers above lose their supporting foundation. Moisture loosens the cement that binds sedimentary rock, water seeps into fractures, freezing and thawing cycles pry the rock apart, and gravity carries the loosened fragments to the canyon floor, all part of the processes of weathering. Over time, canyons become deeper through erosion and wider through weathering. As canyons extend their headwaters in a process called "headward erosion," they gather more runoff and, thus, erosion proceeds at a greater rate. Erosion dissects the flat-lying sedimentary rock layers of the Colorado Plateau, leaving the levels of plateaus, mesas, and buttes standing in relief above a maze of canyons.

Rock layers on the plateau respond differently to the effects of weathering and erosion. Hard rock layers such as limestone, sandstone, schist, and granite resist erosion and stand in relief, while softer layers such as shale, siltstone, and mudstone are subdued into slopes and terraces. In the Grand

Canyon, alternating hard and soft rock layers have formed a "stairstep" type of topography. Cliffs alternate with slopes and terraces colored in shades of red, tan, gray, and black, making the setting of the Canyon so uniquely beautiful. Although in-depth knowledge of Grand Canyon's rock layers is not prerequisite to hiking here, learning to recognize the rocks can greatly help hikers gauge their progress on the hike in or, especially, on that grind back to the rim.

Deep within the Grand Canyon are some of the world's most ancient rocks. Throughout much of its length, the Colorado River in the Grand Canyon is confined in the dark-walled abyss of Granite Gorge, what John Wesley Powell referred to as "our granite prison" during the epic 1869 Powell Expedition. These somber, convoluted, black-and-gray cliffs are composed of the 1.7-billion-year-old Vishnu Complex rocks, including the Vishnu schist, Brahma schist, and Rama schist and gneiss. The Vishnu rocks are composed of shales and volcanic materials that were subjected to great heat and pressure during an ancient mountain-building episode. Fractures in the Vishnu were later intruded by molten magma that was to become the Zoroaster granite, which forms great swirls of pink rock that marble the dark walls of Granite Gorge. The Vishnu creates a significant barrier to foot travel in the Grand Canyon. The rock is hard, yet it provides unstable footing. Most trails follow canyons that have carved through this barrier. The exception is the South Kaibab Trail, which descends 1,000 feet through the Vishnu on a trail blasted and carved into the great cliffs.

Lying atop the Vishnu in isolated locations in the Canyon are the layers of the Grand Canyon Supergroup of rocks, ranging from 1.2 billion to 800 million years old. These layers contain sandstone, limestone, shale, and volcanic rocks. Of the eight layers of the Supergroup, the Cardenas lavas, Dox sandstone, Shinumo quartzite, Hakatai shale, and Bass limestone are most widespread. These rocks form broad slopes and low cliff bands and occur in significant outcrops along trails, including Nankoweap, Tanner, New Hance, North Kaibab, South and North Bass, and Thunder River. Following deposition, these layers were broken along faults and uplifted into a series of north- to south-trending mountain ranges. Over time, erosion subdued these mountains. About 250 million years later, a sea advanced over the region and began depositing sands that would become the Tapeats sandstone atop the tilted strata of the Supergroup.

Powell was the first to recognize the Great Unconformity, where horizontal beds rest on top of the angular beds of the Grand Canyon Supergroup. This unconformity represents a gap of 250 million years of Earth history. The unconformity can be seen to best advantage from the New Hance Trail and from the Tonto Trail between Horseshoe Mesa and Red Canyon.

The remaining rock layers in the Grand Canyon rest in the same horizontal sequence in which their materials were deposited, from the rim of the inner gorge to the plateau rims. These rocks represent another 300 million years of the advance and retreat of seas, sandy deserts, coastal lagoons, and low-lying swamps.

The 550-million-year-old Tapeats sandstone generally forms the rim of Granite Gorge beginning in the eastern Grand Canyon. This coarse-grained, brown sandstone was laid down in shallow coastal waters and in dunes along the ancient beach. It forms a low, ledgy cliff ranging from 100 to 300 feet high, and in places such as Deer Creek and Muav Canyon, the Tapeats has been incised into spectacular narrows.

Lying atop the Tapeats is the colorful Bright Angel shale, a slope-forming layer composed primarily of green, gray, and brown mudstones. The Bright Angel contains the fossil remains of worms, trilobites, and brachiopods that indicate deposition in calm sea waters, 540 million years ago, farther from shore than the Tapeats. The Tonto Platform, a prominent feature in the eastern Grand Canyon, is composed of the Bright Angel shale.

Overlying the Bright Angel shale is the typically low, ledgy gray cliff of Muav limestone, forming the foot of the great Redwall limestone cliff above. It takes some practice to differentiate between these two limestone layers, but the low ledges of the Muav usually set it apart from the more massive Redwall. The dolomites, limestones, and siltstones of this formation were laid down offshore in a shallow sea 530 million years ago. Many vigorous springs emerge from near the contact of the Muav and Bright Angel shale, including Tapeats, Thunder, Deer, and Roaring springs.

Occasional outcrops of the cliff-forming, reddish purple Temple Butte limestone can be found overlying the Muav. Temple Butte materials filled erosion channels on the Muav surface 370 million years ago. One of the better places to observe the Temple Butte limestone is on the North Kaibab Trail above Roaring Springs Canyon.

Perhaps the most dramatic rock layer in the Grand Canyon is the Redwall limestone, lying roughly halfway between the rim and the river throughout much of the Canyon. It surfaces at river level in Marble Canyon, where Powell likened its water-polished surface to that of marble. Farther downcanyon, the Redwall forms the highest continuous cliff band in the Canyon, ranging from 400 to 650 feet high, making it *the* major barrier to inner Canyon travel. Where Supai rocks overlie the Redwall, the cliffs are stained a deep red. Redwall-bounded mesas and buttes, isolated by erosion that has stripped away the Supai cap thousands of years ago, have an orange or pinkish hue. Those buttes and cliffs eventually lose the red veneer and revert to the natural gray color of the Redwall.

The Redwall is composed almost entirely of calcium carbonate, the cement that binds other sedimentary rock layers. Hence this rock is highly resistant to erosion in the dry climate of the Grand Canyon. Brachiopod, crinoid, and bryozoan fossils indicate the Redwall was deposited in a warm ocean environment some 330 million years ago. The Redwall usually represents the second most rigorous and sustained steep grade on Grand Canyon trails. There are few breaks in the great cliff band, and most trails take advantage of slumps and faults to pass through this barrier.

The red beds of the Supai Group—the Esplanade sandstone and Watahomigi, Manakacha, and Wescogame formations—overlie the Redwall limestone. These red rocks were deposited about 300 million years ago in a swampy, low-lying environment. Fossils of plants and mudcracks are common in the siltstone layers, and cross-bedding in the sandstones is typical of windblown sand. The upper layer, the Esplanade sandstone, forms a broad terrace beginning in the central Grand Canyon and stretching downriver for much of the remaining distance to Lake Mead. The Esplanade terrace is entirely absent in the eastern Grand Canyon. The Supai Group, generally about 600 to 700 feet high, forms slopes of siltstone and low cliff bands of sandstone. Trails generally traverse this formation, which is prone to rockslides, often for considerable distances while en route to the break in the Redwall cliff.

Lying above the Supai is a bright red slope composed of siltstones that generally host a great variety and density of woodland vegetation. This slope, the Hermit shale, was laid down in swamps and lagoons 280 million years ago. From the top of the Hermit shale to the rim lies a sequence of cliffs representing the three remaining rock layers in the Canyon, and the ascent and descent of these cliffs provides the greatest sustained vertical relief on Grand Canyon trails.

The towering cliff of the Coconino sandstone is second only to the Redwall in its prominence in the Canyon. The advance of great sand dunes in a vast desert 270 million years ago is recorded in the cross-bedded cliffs of this resistant, tan-colored sandstone. Numerous species of small vertebrates inhabited the Coconino desert long before the dinosaurs and left fossil footprints in the sand; look for them on trailside slabs on the Hermit Trail.

The Toroweap formation lies atop the Coconino and is often difficult to differentiate from the overlying Kaibab limestone. Composed of sandstones and limestones, the Toroweap represents the advance and retreat of another sea from the west. Layers of the Toroweap that have weathered into slopes support a rich diversity of vegetation, including isolated groves of Douglas-fir below the South Rim.

The final layer capping both rims of the Grand Canyon is the Kaibab limestone, forming ledges and cliff bands below the rims. The Kaibab was deposited in a warm, shallow sea 250 million years ago and it includes fossils of brachiopods, crinoids, and mollusks.

Subsequent layers of sediments piled up another 8,000 feet of rock formations over the Grand Canyon region, but only two formations overlying the Kaibab limestone remain in isolated locations in the Park; the remainder have long since been stripped away by erosion. Remnants of the mudstones and siltstones of the Moenkopi formation occur about 0.5 mile south of Buggeln Hill on the South Rim and on Cedar Mountain near Desert View. Cedar Mountain is capped by the even younger rocks of the Shinarump conglomerate, rocks common north of Marble Canyon into southern Utah.

Deposition continued in the Grand Canyon region until about 70 million years ago. Yet after all the sedimentary rock layers were in place, there was still no Grand Canyon, no Kaibab or Coconino plateaus, and not even a Colorado Plateau. Compression of the Earth's crust from the east and west

Views from the Tonto Trail above Hanie Creek Canyon stretch past the angular beds of the Grand Canyon Supergroup and the head of Granite Gorge to the distant Palisades of the Desert.

resulted in a 20-million-year mountain building episode known as the Laramide Orogeny. This compression buckled the Earth's surface; the Rocky Mountains were born, and the Colorado Plateau was uplifted en masse thousands of feet above sea level.

The compressive forces reactivated old faults present in the pre-Cambrian layers of the Vishnu Complex and Grand Canyon Supergroup, and horizontal rock layers were folded in many places in the Canyon. Some of these folds are monoclines, where horizontal rock layers were squeezed upward but level off at a higher elevation. The East Kaibab Monocline is the most obvious example, since it folded rocks upward so they now rest 3,000 feet above corresponding rock layers to the east. The Kaibab Plateau was a large dome elevated above the surrounding landscape, its rock layers rising steeply along the eastern flanks of the dome, thanks to the East Kaibab Monocline, and dipping gently downward toward the south.

Beginning about 20 million years ago, tensional forces within the Earth began to stretch apart the crust of western North America, creating the basin and range topography west of the Colorado Plateau. These tensional forces also fractured the Kaibab Plateau, resulting in numerous prominent faults. Many tributary canyons were later formed in these fault zones as the fractured rock was readily removed by erosion. Other larger faults to the west would separate the Kaibab Plateau from the Kanab, Uinkaret, and Shivwits plateaus, and separate the Colorado Plateau from the Basin and Range province along the Grand Wash and Hurricane faults on the west. This period of faulting uplifted the Colorado Plateau to its present height and set the stage for large-scale erosion, but at that time, there still was no Grand Canyon.

The course of the Colorado River through the Grand Canyon is a puzzle geologists have yet to solve. The river follows a logical course through Marble Canyon along the edge of the Kaibab Plateau. But why, beyond the confluence with the Little Colorado River, does the river turn west and flow *through* the obvious barrier of the plateau? Various hypotheses have been offered throughout the last century, only to be refuted by emerging evidence. We now know that originally the Colorado River did not follow its present course, carving its canyon through the Kaibab Plateau as the plateau was slowly uplifted, as Powell suggested.

In the 1960s, geologists theorized that it followed its present course through Marble Canyon, but then flowed toward the Gulf of Mexico via the Little Colorado River drainage. However, evidence to support that theory has yet to surface. Another theory suggests that the river flowed *around* the Kaibab Plateau, before uplift and erosion isolated it as the highland it is today, and hence north into Utah. Geologists have determined that the Gulf of California opened up about 4 to 5 million years ago, and its drainage began carving farther north in the process of headward erosion. This theory suggests that the ancestral lower Colorado River drainage eventually captured the north-flowing river as its drainage carved northward, diverting the Colorado River toward the gulf.

The one thing geologists can agree on is that the Colorado River has been carving the Grand Canyon for about 6 million years. A phenomenal amount of erosion has taken place in that time, carving a canyon that is in places more than 5,000 feet deep and 10 miles wide. As the river sliced its gorge through the Kaibab Plateau, it separated the plateau into what we now consider two distinct landforms: the Kaibab Plateau to the north and the Coconino Plateau to the south. Both plateaus are remnants of a once continuous surface.

The Kaibab Plateau, due to its high elevation relative to the surrounding landscape, receives considerable precipitation. Runoff and groundwater are relatively abundant on the plateau, and the flow of water follows the southward dip of the rock layer's bedding planes, flowing into the Grand Canyon. With vertical relief of 5,000 to 6,000 feet from the North Rim to the river, more erosion takes place in these north side drainages, and these side canyons are typically deep and long. The erosional outliers of the ancestral plateau—the buttes and mesas for which the Canyon is famous—are most prominent on the north side of the river, where greater erosion has taken place.

Groundwater beneath the Coconino Plateau flows south also, but this flow takes it away from the Canyon. Few springs and perennial streams flow in South Rim tributary canyons. Erosion of South Rim canyons is more limited due to groundwater movement and the availability of surface water, and these canyons are considerably shorter and less well-developed than those of the North Rim.

Although the Grand Canyon is seemingly a timeless landscape, it is apparent that great changes have shaped it into the magnificent canyon we see today. Geologic processes are constantly at work here, though they are largely imperceptible to the visitor. Rocks continue to fall, slides and slumps carry material toward the canyon bottoms, and the canyons grow wider. Flash floods scour canyons and transport this material toward the river, deepening their gorges. The powerful waters of the river grind this material into sand and silt and ultimately carry it away.

GRAND CANYON VEGETATION

Grand Canyon vegetation, consisting of more than 1,400 species, is as diverse and spectacular as its layers of colorful rocks. Yet one need not be a botanist to appreciate the flora of the Canyon. Colorful spring wildflowers, the shade and shelter of pinyon-juniper woodland and groves of mesquite, thickets of stiff brush, and gardens of spiny cacti all play an important role in a Grand Canyon backcountry experience.

The flora of the Grand Canyon reflects the diversity of environmental conditions here, a diversity rivaled by few other locations in the country. Elevations in Grand Canyon National Park range from 9,165 feet on the Kaibab Plateau to 1,200 feet at the western end of the Canyon at Lake Mead. Within the nearly 8,000 feet of vertical relief demonstrated in the Grand Canyon are plant associations ranging from cool, moist forests of spruce and fir similar to forests in the Middle and Northern Rocky Mountains to desert scrub associations representing species from the Mojave and Sonoran deserts. Canyon vegetation is relatively dense for a desert area and is largely unaffected by past disturbance, being much richer than most other locations on the Colorado Plateau, with few exotic species present.

Grand Canyon's location in northwest Arizona is on the fringes of three major desert regions: the Great Basin Desert of Nevada and western Utah; the Mojave Desert of southern Nevada and southeastern California; and the Sonoran Desert of the lower Colorado River, extreme southeastern California, and southern Arizona. Plant species from the three deserts intermix here in an association that is unique to the Grand Canyon.

The wide variations in elevations in the Grand Canyon result in an equally diverse variation in climate. Desert species are limited in their upward distribution by cold seasonal temperatures, while upland species can only survive in the inner Canyon where moisture, soil cover, shelter from excessive sunlight, and temperatures are favorable.

Vegetation in the Grand Canyon is roughly separated into belts or life

A parklike forest of tall ponderosa pines covers much of Powell Plateau.

zones depending on elevation, available moisture, and climatic conditions. Within each life zone you find a common association of plants, although life zone boundaries are often indistinct and overlapping. The intricate topography of the Grand Canyon creates an abundance of microclimates that affect the distribution of plants as much as elevation does. Thus, you may find inner Canyon species thriving on the hot, dry edge of the south-facing North Rim, and groves of Douglas-fir and white fir occupying sheltered alcoves below the north-facing South Rim.

The high elevations of the Kaibab Plateau at the North Rim support vast stands of conifer forest. The plateau is a gently undulating surface characterized by low, rolling ridges, shallow draws, and large spreads of grassy meadows, or parks. Soil cover is well-developed, masking the underlying Kaibab limestone.

Above 8,500 feet in the Canadian Zone, Engelmann spruce and white fir dominate on ridges, north- and northeast-facing slopes, and around the margins of meadows. Mixing into this subalpine forest are subalpine fir and Colorado blue spruce. The understory in these shady forests is noticeably scarce, sometimes absent. The few species occasionally present in the understory are also common in northern forests, such as Oregon grape, common juniper, bracken fern, mallow ninebark, and snowberry.

In more open locations and on west- and south-facing slopes, Douglas-fir joins the forest, and ponderosa pine will be found on the sunniest, driest sites. Groves of quaking aspen are common on the plateau, and these trees put forth a memorable display of golden foliage in early autumn.

The Transition Zone ranges from about 8,000 feet to the rim, and in this zone ponderosa pine dominates, often forming pure stands of open, parklike forest. Climatic conditions are warmer in this zone, and considerable sunlight reaches the needle-carpeted forest floor. Understory shrubs are much more diverse here, though they seldom form thickets. Gambel oak, a shrub or small tree, is common in the ponderosa forest, and its foliage displays the rich autumn colors of yellows and oranges. Rocky Mountain maple prefers more sheltered sites, typically on shady slopes below the rim, and is often overlooked until early autumn frosts turn its foliage a brilliant crimson. New Mexican locust, a tall thorny shrub, wild rose, snowberry, and elderberry are also common associates of the ponderosa forest. As you approach the rim, more drought-tolerant shrubs appear, including curl-leaf mountain mahogany, manzanita, cliffrose, and sagebrush.

Despite the high elevations, seldom does the ponderosa forest reach the North Rim. Hot Canyon updrafts and a southern exposure create the "rim effect"—a microclimate on the very rim and there outliers of the upland forest mix with pinyon, juniper, and shrubs from the inner Canyon. The exception is the east rim of the Kaibab Plateau, at places such as Point Imperial and along the road to Cape Royal. Here the forest extends to the rim and well into the sheltered canyons below.

The South Rim lies at an average elevation of 7,000 feet and is consequently warmer and drier than the North Rim. Soils here are less well developed than on the North Rim, with Kaibab limestone bedrock often extending above the surface. Colorado pinyon and Utah juniper woodlands dominate the vegetation on the South Rim. These trees attain an average height of about 20 feet, forming an open woodland of gnarled, drab green trees that spread across the rolling surface of the Coconino Plateau. Gambel oak and cliffrose are also common here, and ponderosa pine makes an occasional appearance, sometimes forming pure but isolated stands.

The Coconino Plateau rises gently but steadily from the Grand Canyon Village area to the Coconino Rim near Grandview Point. There, above 7,200 feet, is the largest pure stand of ponderosa pine on the South Rim. The South Rim drops steadily east of Grandview Point, then rises gently to attain its highest elevation of 7,498 feet at Navajo Point near Desert View. You would expect a ponderosa pine forest to be present here, but the Coconino

Rim to the west creates enough of a rain shadow that Navajo Point supports only an open woodland of pinyon and juniper. Much of the South Rim lies within the Upper Sonoran Zone, and its pinyon-juniper woodlands are typical of the Southwest and Intermountain regions, where these woodlands are more widespread than any other forest type.

The upper cliffs of the South Rim face north toward the Canyon. Headward erosion of the South Rim's canyons have cut back into the Coconino Plateau, resulting in the scalloped outline of the rim. Many of the alcoves at the head of these canyons are protected by cliffs on the west, south, and east from excessive heat and sunlight, and thus retain greater moisture and are cooler than their surroundings. The microclimates in these alcoves support, in many places, stands of Douglas-fir and, in a few locations, white fir— trees of the North Rim, growing well below their usual elevation.

The Upper Sonoran Zone extends well into the upper reaches of the inner Canyon, with a diversity of shrubs and small trees far greater than on the rim. This life zone generally extends down to the top of the Redwall limestone, to elevations between 4,500 and 5,000 feet. Where conditions are favorable, however, plants of this zone reach well below the Redwall, particularly in canyons below the North Rim.

Tributary canyons north of the river often reach 8 to 10 miles toward the North Rim, compared with the abrupt canyons of the South Rim, most of which average only 3 miles in length. More moisture is available in North Rim canyons, both in the form of precipitation and groundwater. Cool air drainage from the uplands of the Kaibab Plateau and the sheltering influence of canyon walls have allowed a greater diversity of Upper Sonoran Zone vegetation to develop in those canyons. Microclimates in North Rim tributaries occasionally bring Douglas-fir and ponderosa pine down to the top of the Redwall. Sheltered North Rim tributaries also host dense thickets of brush that create additional challenge to navigation on some trails.

Species related to the pinyon-juniper woodland are considerably more diverse in the Grand Canyon than elsewhere on the Colorado Plateau. Shrubs and small trees are variable in their distribution, but after hiking any three or four Grand Canyon trails, you will have encountered most of them. Common below both rims are cliffrose, fernbush, alder-leaf mountain mahogany, roundleaf buffaloberry, mock orange, Apache plume, Gregg ceanothus, velvet, fragrant, and single-leaf ash, pale hoptree, Utah serviceberry, banana yucca, greasebush, gooseberry, Fremont barberry, and occasionally, brickellbrush. More common in brushy canyons and slopes of the North Rim are manzanita, Knowlton hophornbeam, silktassel, and scrub live oak. Moist and sheltered sites, such as Dripping Spring, often host the small tree netleaf hackberry.

Agave, or century plant, is widespread from the rims to the river. The narrow, stiff, spine-tipped leaves of this succulent plant resembling a cactus, form a low rosette that persists for several years until the plant channels its energy into producing a tall flowering stalk, covered with many small yellow blooms in spring. After flowering, the plant dies, yet will re-

The spring blooms of banana yucca are a common sight in the inner Canyon. Photo by John Rihs.

main erect for many more seasons.

Plants of the Upper Sonoran Zone are limited in their distribution by the cliff, slope, and terrace topography of the inner Canyon. The slopes and ledges of the Toroweap formation, between the cliffs of the Kaibab limestone and Coconino sandstone above and the Hermit shale and the slopes and terraces of the Supai Group below, support the best development of Upper Sonoran vegetation.

The great barrier Redwall limestone cliff of the inner Canyon generally separates the woodland and desert scrub plant associations, particularly below the South Rim. Once you have descended past the Redwall, you have finally reached true desert. Yet these desert slopes aren't nearly as barren as they appear from a distance.

Below the Redwall limestone in the eastern Grand Canyon, the soft Bright Angel shale has eroded into a broad terrace lying atop the resistant Tapeats sandstone. This terrace—the Tonto Platform—lies at elevations averaging 3,700 feet and represents the upper reaches of the Lower Sonoran Zone. The dominant shrub here is blackbrush, a species of the Great Basin and

Mojave deserts. Often growing in pure, evenly spaced stands, this shrub gives the Tonto Platform a gray caste when observed from a distance. Washes and drainages that bisect the platform often host four-wing saltbush and rabbitbrush along their banks, plus occasional shrubs from the pinyon-juniper woodland. Moisture is seasonally concentrated in washes. The canyon walls provide some relief from the desiccating desert sun, and cool air drainage from the plateaus at night lead to the development of greater plant diversity in these locations.

Other shrubs occur on the Tonto Platform, but are not as abundant as blackbrush. These include mormon tea; banana yucca, forming a rosette of dagger-like leaves 2 to 3 feet above the ground; the taller soaptree yucca, growing from a "trunk" to heights of 4 feet or more; shadscale; greasebush; broom snakeweed; turpentine broom; and in sheltered niches, saw grass. Various cacti inhabit the Tonto Platform, including beavertail, several species of prickly pear, hedgehog, and fishhook cacti. Cactus blooms are among the most delicate, beautiful, and conspicuous of the Grand Canyon's wildflowers.

From the rim of the Tapeats sandstone to the Colorado River is the inner gorge, in places more than 1,000 feet deep. This is the "canyon within the canyon" where hot, dry, desert conditions prevail. Much of the inner gorge is flanked by the dark walls of Vishnu Complex rocks, which absorb heat during the day and radiate it during the night. Plants of the inner gorge represent species from the Mojave and Sonoran deserts, though Sonoran Desert flora is most prevalent in the far western reaches of the Canyon. The inner gorge has served as a corridor for hot desert plant species to penetrate deep into the Colorado Plateau.

Plants here are sparse and grow widely scattered. Common are mormon tea; the gray foliage of brittlebush, which in spring paints the harsh desert landscape with its large yellow blooms; the tall Engelmann prickly pear cactus; California barrel cactus, often attaining heights of 3 to 4 feet; and small trees—catclaw acacia, with a sharp curved spine on its branches, and honey mesquite, with a longer, straight spine. In the western reaches of the Canyon grow ocotillo from the Sonoran Desert, and creosote bush and white bursage from the Mojave.

Wildflowers bloom unpredictably and in varying degrees of density each year, depending primarily on winter and spring precipitation. Most bloom in the spring, yet others bloom in late summer and early autumn following the monsoon season. Although Grand Canyon wildflowers are sporadic in their distribution, there are several species that are common along Canyon trails. Among these are specklepod locoweed, Indian paintbrush, blue flax, various species of penstemon, scarlet gilia, groundsel, globe mallow, hairy fleabane, hymenopappus, white cryptantha, and longleaf phlox.

Riparian woodlands occur along the course of the Colorado River and perennial streams, and hanging gardens are found on canyon walls at seeps and springs. Vegetation in the Riparian Zone is dependant on a continuous supply of surface water or groundwater. These desert oases are vitally important to both hikers and Canyon wildlife, where their greenery and cool water offer a welcome refuge from the harsh desert nearby.

Common plants of hanging gardens include maidenhair fern, scarlet monkeyflower, golden columbine, and giant helleborine orchid. Larger springs and streams host Hooker evening primrose, giant reed grass, horsetail, willow, boxelder, California redbud, seep-willow, Fremont cottonwood, canyon wild grape, and arrow weed.

Cottonwoods are noticeably absent along the Colorado River, but the riverbanks support abundant growth, often forming impenetrable thickets. Prior to the completion of Glen Canyon Dam in 1963, seasonal floods scoured the riverbanks and replenished sandy beaches, and most of the river's riparian ribbon was confined near the high-water mark. The dam eliminated seasonal flooding and discharge is now more uniform, allowing riparian growth to reach the water's edge. Common on Colorado River beaches are thickets of exotic tamarisk and native coyote willow. Farther back from the river's edge you find seep-willow and arrow weed. The margin between the Riparian Zone and the surrounding desert scrub is abrupt; often only a few feet separate willows from barrel cactus and brittlebush.

HISTORY

Archaeologists know that humans have dwelt in and utilized the cavernous depths of the Grand Canyon sporadically for at least the past 4,000 years. The discovery of a fragment of a Paleo-Indian projectile point suggests occupation of the Grand Canyon by big-game hunters as early as 10,000 years ago. Yet why would anyone choose to hunt, gather food, and even live in the forbidding, unforgiving landscape of the Grand Canyon? In the words of Lt. Joseph C. Ives, during his exploration of the lower Colorado River in the Grand Canyon in 1857, the Canyon is "...a profitless locality..." that "...shall be forever unvisited and undisturbed..."

People of the Desert, or Archaic, Culture, however, found an abundance of food and materials here. They left behind ceremonial split-twig animal figurines throughout the Canyon in Redwall limestone caves. These figurines have been radiocarbon dated and are between 5,000 and 3,200 years old. Archaeological evidence shows that these people hunted large and small animals, and collected various fibers for clothing and basketry, and wild plants and seeds for food. Yet little more is known about these people. Archaic-style rock art and projectile points that have been found in the Canyon has led archaeologists to believe that people of the Archaic/early Basketmaker culture occupied the Canyon until about A.D. 500.

By that time, small groups of Kayenta Anasazi—the Navajo name for "ancient ones"—migrated into the Canyon from the southeast. Occupying the far western reaches of the Park, north of the Colorado River, were the

Virgin Anasazi, people who migrated from the northwest. As their culture evolved from hunting and gathering to farming, both on the river deltas and on the rims, their population increased. From about A.D. 1000 to A.D. 1150, the Anasazi culture bloomed in the Grand Canyon. More than 3,500 Anasazi sites are known in the Canyon, and archaeologists believe the total number of sites in the Canyon could approach 50,000.

Anasazi granaries in the Grand Canyon were typically constructed of fitted stones in hidden alcoves in the cliffs. Yet dwelling sites have been discovered in open locations, such as those on the Bright Angel and Unkar deltas. This may suggest that the Grand Canyon provided a more secure haven for the Anasazi than the canyons to the north in the Four Corners region, where dwelling sites were well hidden in defensible locations.

Roughly at the same time the Anasazi began using the Grand Canyon, another farming culture, the Cohonina, began to occupy areas of the South Rim in the western reaches of the Canyon. People of the Cohonina Culture placed more emphasis on gathering wild foods than did the Anasazi, and they roasted the abundant mescal (agave) in pits throughout the inner Canyon. Mescal roasting pits are the most frequently observed archaeological sites along Canyon trails. The existence of these contemporary cultures in this arid land was marginal, and a severe drought in the late 1100s forced them to abandon the region. No one knows what became of the Cohonina, but the Anasazi moved eastward to more favorable environs. Today's Hopi people are thought to be descendants of the Anasazi. The village of Oraibi, on the Third Mesa of the Hopi Indian Reservation, was established around A.D. 1200, and it bears the distinction of being the oldest continually occupied village in North America.

By the 1300s, Cerbat peoples—the Hualapai and Havasupai—filtered into the canyons of the South Rim. Primarily hunter/gatherers, much like those of the ancient Desert Culture, these people also engaged in seasonal farming at places, including Indian Garden and Havasu Creek, where the Havasupai live today. Like the Cohonina, they roasted agave in pits throughout the Canyon. During that same period, Southern Paiutes began seasonal hunting and gathering forays into the Kaibab Plateau and North Rim canyons. Today descendants of these people live near Fredonia on the Kaibab Paiute Indian Reservation.

The Hopi, meanwhile, visited the Canyon on ceremonial treks to their sacred salt mines and to the Sipapuni, a circular travertine dome in the Little Colorado River canyon, from which the Hopi believe they emerged from the underworld. They also established trade routes to the Havasupai, and other routes for gathering the sacred Douglas-fir. Hopi people descended into the Grand Canyon via Tanner Canyon, and they used a route to Horseshoe Mesa, where they gathered blue-green copper ore for use as pigment.

These cultures lived undisturbed for centuries until Europeans arrived on the scene. Following Spain's conquest of Mexico, the Spaniards launched several expeditions into the northern territories in search of the fabled Seven Cities of Cibola, reputed to contain vast riches. In 1540 one such expedition

These ruins are all that remain of Louis Boucher's (the "Hermit") cabin in Boucher Creek canyon.

searched in vain for the seven cities. This expedition included Francisco Vásquez de Coronado, Pedro Tovar, and García Lopez de Cardenas, whose names are now memorialized in the Grand Canyon. While at the Hopi pueblos, soldiers were told of a great river lying to the west, and sent a detachment, aided by Hopi guides, to find it. After twenty days of travel they reached the South Rim of the Grand Canyon, at an undetermined point thought to be somewhere between Desert View and Moran Point, and became the first Europeans to gaze into its depths.

The Hopi showed no inclination to lead the Spaniards into the Canyon. Instead, the Spaniards spent several days unsuccessfully attempting to reach the river. In an account recorded by the expedition's historian, Pedro de Castañeda, he writes: "What appeared to be easy from above was not so, but instead very hard and difficult." This echoes the sentiments of Grand Canyon travelers to this day. Unsuccessful, the empty-handed expedition returned, and the Grand Canyon remained unvisited for another 200 years.

Spanish missionary priests filtered into the region in search of Indian tribes, to convert to Christianity and place under the authority of the king of Spain. One missionary, Francisco Tomas Garcés, with the aid of Indian guides, explored the Grand Canyon in 1776 from its mouth to the upper canyons. Garcés referred to "Rio Colorado" (Red River) in his journals, and much like the soldiers of the 1540 expedition, he considered the Grand Canyon more in terms of a barrier to travel, rather than recognizing its scenic attributes.

While some trappers, most notably James O. Pattie in 1826, likely entered the Grand Canyon in the years to come, the Grand Canyon region remained part of Mexican territory until 1848, and was largely unexplored. When the United States acquired the territories that would become Arizona and New Mexico, military expeditions were dispatched to fill in the blank spots on the maps. In 1857, an expedition led by Lt. Joseph C. Ives explored the lower Colorado River to determine to extent of navigable water for steamboats. Although they reached the head of navigation below the Grand Canyon, they continued into Ives's "Big Cañon" and were the first whites to record their observations. John S. Newberry, a geologist with the expedition, noted that the Canyon displayed "the most splendid exposure of stratified rocks that there is in the world." Ives's reports portrayed the Canyon landscape as dark and forbidding, and thus did little to attract attention to the Canyon for more than a decade.

The name of Major John Wesley Powell, Civil War veteran, geologist, and ethnographer, is almost synonymous with the Grand Canyon. His well-orchestrated yet daring expeditions through the Canyon by boat in 1869 and 1871 opened the book of the Grand Canyon for all to read. The expeditions mapped the course of the river and the Canyon; named, measured, and explored many tributaries and prominent features; and studied and recorded the cultures of the native peoples of the region. Facing the hardships of poor shelter, a meager and spoiled food supply, and the unknown hazards of the river itself within the Grand Canyon's "granite prison," the expedition nevertheless made great scientific contributions that led to further exploration. Prior to Powell's expeditions, the Canyon had no name in general usage. Powell's constant reference to the name "Grand Canyon" led to its eventual acceptance.

Geographical and geological surveys of the Grand Canyon followed in the 1870s and 1880s, at which time the Canyon became widely recognized not only for being "the best geological section on the continent," but for its beauty and majesty as well. Photographs, drawings, and paintings from these expeditions at last brought public awareness to the magnificence of the Canyon.

From 1880 to 1881, geologist Clarence Dutton led a geological expedition to the Grand Canyon that resulted in his naming of many Canyon features for architectural forms and for temples and gods of eastern religions. From 1902 through 1905, Francois Matthes, a topographer for the USGS, created the Vishnu, Bright Angel, and Shinumo quadrangles. Matthes also perpetuated the practice began by Dutton and is credited with naming such features as Krishna Shrine, Walhalla Plateau, and Wotans Throne.

While many remote outposts of the West were being opened up by railroads and homesteaded by settlers following the Civil War, northern Arizona lagged behind. By 1882 the Atlantic & Pacific Railroad finally pushed across northern Arizona, connecting Williams and Flagstaff with points east. Settlers, prospectors, ranchers, and loggers then began filtering into the region. After the early 1880s, cattle and sheep were grazed on the rims, timber was cut on the Kaibab Plateau to supply Mormon settlements to the north, prospectors explored the far reaches of the inner Canyon hoping to make a big strike, and tourists began to discover the Canyon's wonders. The first hotel in the Grand Canyon was established at Diamond Creek in 1884, and stagecoaches from the railroad at Peach Springs carried passengers 20 miles to the Farlee Hotel until it closed in 1889.

It was the prospectors who deserve credit for opening up the Canyon. With burros or on foot, innumerable prospectors roamed the Canyon from the 1870s to the 1890s. Hundreds of claims were filed, most of them on deposits of asbestos and copper. Burros were released by prospectors to multiply and ensure a reliable supply of pack animals to haul ore to the rim. The burro population eventually mushroomed to about 2,000 animals, which had a significant impact on vegetation and water sources, and competed with the native bighorn sheep for forage. The last burros were removed from the Grand Canyon in 1981.

Although the prospectors' burros are gone from the Grand Canyon, prospectors did leave a lasting legacy. Many of the trails used today were constructed by prospectors to haul ore to the rim. The distances and difficulties of hauling ore to the railroad produced limited financial returns, and there were few productive ore deposits. Eventually, most prospectors moved on, but a few stayed.

Meanwhile, tourists were making the journey to the Canyon in increasing numbers. The remaining prospectors, who knew the Canyon intimately, discovered new wealth in the burgeoning tourist trade. They guided visitors into the Canyon on their trails and housed them at tourist camps and, later, in hotels. Many of today's trails bear the names of the men who blazed them.

John Hance improved an old Indian trail down Hance Creek from the South Rim in 1883, to access his asbestos claims on the north side of the river. This trail, known as the Old Hance Trail, was obscured by rockfall, so Hance built the New Hance Trail into Red Canyon in 1894. He guided tourists into the Canyon via this trail on horses, mules, and foot, and housed them in tents at Hance Ranch, his "hotel" on the rim near Grandview Point.

Ben Beamer prospected near the Little Colorado River in 1890, and he built a stone cabin near the confluence using materials from a nearby Anasazi ruin. The Beamer Trail from Tanner Canyon to the confluence bears his name.

William Wallace Bass came to Arizona for his health in 1883. He discovered the Grand Canyon soon after and stayed. Bass constructed a camp on the South Rim, built a road to Ashfork around 1890, and located numerous mining claims in the Canyon. He built a trail down to the river, and established a tent camp along Shinumo Creek, where he, his wife, and two children tended a vegetable garden and fruit orchard, irrigated via a ditch from Shinumo Creek.

Bass also improved the old Indian trail up White Creek to Muav Saddle and the North Rim, and became the first to guide tourists from rim to rim.

Bass ran a stage line for his guests from the railroad at Williams and Ashfork and, later, from Bass Station near Bright Angel Lodge when the railroad reached the South Rim in 1901. Guests stayed on the rim at Bass Camp (today's South Bass Trailhead) in tent cabins. On trans-Canyon trips accommodations were provided at Shinumo Camp. Tourists and their mounts crossed the river via a cable car Bass constructed near the mouth of Bass Canyon. W. W. Bass loved the Grand Canyon, and when he died in 1933, his ashes were laid to rest atop Holy Grail Temple, thereafter known as Bass Tomb.

Other notable trail builders of that time included Seth Tanner, Louis Boucher, and Peter Berry. Tanner improved an old Hopi route above the canyon that now bears his name to access mining claims near the river. The Tanner Trail bears the dubious distinction of being one leg of the legendary Horsethief Trail, used by horse thieves, together with the Nankoweap Trail, to transport stolen stock between Utah and Arizona. John D. Lee, who established Lees Ferry across the Colorado River in 1871, reportedly buried gold somewhere near the Tanner Trail, but the treasure has never been found. In 1928, a distillery was discovered near the Tanner Trail, thought at the time to be a bootlegger's cache serving the speakeasy trade on the South Rim. More likely, the still was abandoned by prospectors.

Louis Boucher, another prospector, established a camp at Dripping Spring around 1891. He blazed a trail down into Long (Boucher) Canyon, where he filed on a copper claim. He built cabins there and planted an orchard of some 75 fruit trees alongside the perennial waters of Boucher Creek. Despite his moniker, "the Hermit," Boucher was no more of a loner than other prospectors, and he entertained occasional tourists at his canyon cabins. Ruins of one of Boucher's cabins still stand near Boucher Creek, but evidence of his orchard has been erased by time.

Of all the late nineteenth-century trailblazers, Pete Berry left handiwork that survives almost as if it were built yesterday. Berry was not an engineer, but his Grandview Trail, built in 1892, is a superb example of enduring trail construction, the likes of which are seldom seen today. Log cribbing supports the trail where it passes along the face of sheer cliffs, and stone riprap was used to form a lasting trailbed on portions of the trail. Berry built this trail to handle a steady stream of mule traffic that packed out the rich copper ore from his Last Chance Mine on Horseshoe Mesa. Several adits and shafts pockmark the surface of Horseshoe Mesa to this day, though only the ruins of Berry's stone cabin, various mining relics, and slopes strewn with blue-green copper ore remain to remind us of the richest mine of the time in the Grand Canyon.

By 1897, Berry built the Grandview Hotel on the South Rim, not far east of Grandview Point, and soon the hotel became the base of operations for trail riding visitors to the Grand Canyon. A stage line served the hotel from Flagstaff three times a week, and for the rough, all-day trip, stage fare was $20.

Before Berry came to Horseshoe Mesa, he and the brothers Ralph and

Niles Cameron reconstructed the Bright Angel Trail, an old Havasupai trail, into Indian Garden in 1891. By 1902, that trail was extended to the river. The Camerons held claims on that trail, and it was controlled as a toll route.

In 1901, after the Santa Fe Railroad had taken over the Atlantic & Pacific line, a spur was extended from Williams to the South Rim. The railroad was to change the Grand Canyon forever. Although the Grand Canyon Railroad was originally intended to transport ore from inner Canyon mines, as these mines proved unprofitable, the railroad began its long history of transporting tourists. (The Grand Canyon Railway still carries visitors from Williams to the South Rim.) Tourists then had the luxury of a smoother and less costly ride to the Grand Canyon, and the Bright Angel Hotel (established in 1896) at the end of the track offered overnight accommodations. The appeal of the more distant Grandview Hotel waned, but Berry stayed on there serving meals for passengers of Fred Harvey stage trips along the rim until 1908.

Perhaps the most grandiose scheme ever conceived in the Grand Canyon was a survey in 1889 to ascertain a proposed route for an inner Canyon railroad, a scheme that fortunately never materialized. A survey party led by chief engineer Robert Brewster Stanton left Green River, Utah, and its flotilla of flimsy boats was beset with disaster soon after. Boats were lost in rapids, and three members of the party, without life preservers, drowned in Marble Canyon. Stanton decided to abandon the river, caching their remaining supplies in a Redwall limestone cave about 100 feet above the river, just downriver from the mouth of South Canyon. The survey party returned the following winter, this time with sturdier craft and life preservers, and they retrieved their cache from "Stanton's Cave." Unbeknownst to Stanton's party was the collection of 4,000-year-old split-twig figurines that lay deeper inside the cave, and these went undiscovered until 1934.

As tourists came in greater numbers, so did noted conservationists John Muir, John Burroughs, and Theodore Roosevelt. The fledgling conservation movement was gaining impetus during the early twentieth century, and with increased visitation came an increase in interest to preserve one of the world's greatest scenic wonders. Theodore Roosevelt was so moved by his visit to the Grand Canyon in 1903 that he, as President of the United States, signed a bill in 1906 proclaiming the Grand Canyon Game Reserve. He believed, however, that only national park status would protect the Grand Canyon. The passage of the Act for the Preservation of American Antiquities by Congress opened the door for Roosevelt's proclamation of Grand Canyon National Monument in 1908. Following the establishment of the National Park Service in 1916, Grand Canyon finally gained national park status in 1919. The new park, however, was administered by the Forest Service until the Park Service assumed administration in 1920.

As tourism increased, hotel accommodations blossomed on the South Rim. Tourists entered the inner Canyon on mule, horse, and on foot, and Ralph Cameron charged a $1 toll for each person to use his Bright Angel Trail. To avoid tolls and conflicts with Cameron, the Santa Fe Railroad extended a road out to Hermits Rest between 1910 and 1912. From there they constructed the Hermit Trail, an excellent trail that employed some of Berry's construction designs. The railroad built Hermit Camp deep in Hermit Canyon, and this elaborate trail camp was the focal point of the inner Canyon tourist trade until 1930.

After a lengthy legal battle, Cameron finally relinquished control over the Bright Angel Trail in the mid-1920s, when the Park Service took possession of Cameron's invalid mining claims and shut down his distillery at Indian Garden. The Park Service then began trail construction in earnest. They built the South Kaibab Trail from Yaki Point to The Tipoff in 1925 and by 1927, completed the North Kaibab Trail through Roaring Springs Canyon, replacing the old trail through upper Bright Angel Canyon. In 1928, the Black Bridge was erected, connecting the North and South rims by trail.

Rust's Camp was established in Bright Angel Canyon in 1903, during initial construction of the North Kaibab Trail. Theodore Roosevelt used the camp in 1913, and today Phantom Ranch occupies the site, and remains as the sole enclave of civilization in the inner Canyon.

In 1928, construction began on a road connecting Williams to the Grand Canyon. Construction on the road from Cameron to Desert View was begun in 1932 and paved by 1937. A dirt road from Kanab, Utah, offered access to the North Rim as early as 1919. But until the completion of the Navajo Bridge across the Colorado River near Lees Ferry in 1928, access from the South Rim to the North Rim was via a roundabout, 600-mile route through Nevada and Utah to the road from Kanab.

Meanwhile, construction proceeded on Muav Cabin in 1925, and the Park Service constructed the Powell Plateau and Thunder River trails in 1926. Later, Civilian Conservation Corps crews built the Clear Creek and River trails in the 1930s.

Water has always been a precious commodity on the rims, and the railroad water cars that provided water to the South Rim eventually proved inadequate to meet the needs of an increasing number of tourists. In 1932, the first water pipeline became operational, transporting water from Indian Garden to the rim with the aid of a pump station. Yet even that pipeline could not keep up with the demands for water. After several starts and stops, including a monumental flood in 1966, a trans-canyon pipeline was finally completed. Water from Roaring Springs, near the North Rim, flowed through the new pipeline by 1970, crossed the river supported by the Silver Bridge, and up to the Indian Garden pump station by gravity flow. From Indian Garden, water is pumped to holding tanks on the South Rim. Another pump station located below Roaring Springs provides water to the North Rim.

Much like the fledgling administration in 1920, the Park Service today is faced with many challenges. Annual Park visitation now exceeds 5 million people, and most of these visitors come to the South Rim, in private automobiles. Noise, air pollution, and congestion are major issues being addressed by the Park Service. Future plans call for the reduction, if not elimination, of private vehicles on the South Rim, to be replaced by a public transportation system. The balance between freedom of movement and preservation of Park resources and the atmosphere of the Canyon now weighs in favor of mass transportation.

Overflights of tour aircraft have dramatically increased, averaging 80,000 per year in 1996. The Park Service is actively pursuing measures that would cap, if not reduce, the number of noisy aircraft plying the skies over the Grand Canyon. Perhaps the mission of the Park Service best explains the challenges its rangers face: To preserve the natural and historical values within national parks, while providing for the enjoyment of the landscape in a manner that will leave it unimpaired for future generations.

THE SOUTH RIM

OVERVIEW

When most people envision the Grand Canyon, images of the South Rim come to mind. After all, the South Rim is the most photographed part of the Canyon, and calendars, postcards, and magazine articles have planted South Rim panoramas in our minds. The vast majority of Park visitors come to the South Rim, for ample reasons. The South Rim offers an abundance of visitor services, it is easily accessible, and its vistas are among the finest in the Park.

Panoramas of the Grand Canyon unfold to their greatest dimensions from the South Rim. Most often, air quality in the desert Southwest, including the Grand Canyon, is among the best in the nation. Night sky viewing is excellent. A visual range of 243 miles has been observed at the Grand Canyon, and it is not unusual to clearly see plateaus and the dome of Navajo Mountain in southern Utah from the South Rim, more than 100 miles distant.

Hikers come to the South Rim in large numbers for many of the same reasons. Most trailheads are easily accessible via paved roads. There are more trails below the South Rim than elsewhere in the Park. These trails include eight major trails that reach into the inner Canyon from the rim, and the long Tonto Trail, segments of which can be used to devise a variety of extended backpack trips.

Tributary canyons here are much shorter than those on the north side of the Colorado River. Trails, as well, are shorter, affording one-day access to the river. Since South Rim canyons are so abrupt, they tend to be open and without the confining walls typical of North Rim labyrinths. Thus, vistas are tremendous and far-ranging. Many veteran hikers prefer South Rim trails for their quick access into the depths of the Canyon and for their memorable vistas.

So much of the South Rim is claimed by roads and other developments that there are few opportunities for day hikes on the rim. Most South Rim day hikers must descend into the Canyon and, of course, hike back out. Most hikers don't seem to mind, however, since the magnetic attraction of the inner Canyon lures tens of thousands of day hikers onto South Rim trails each year.

SOUTH RIM OVERVIEW

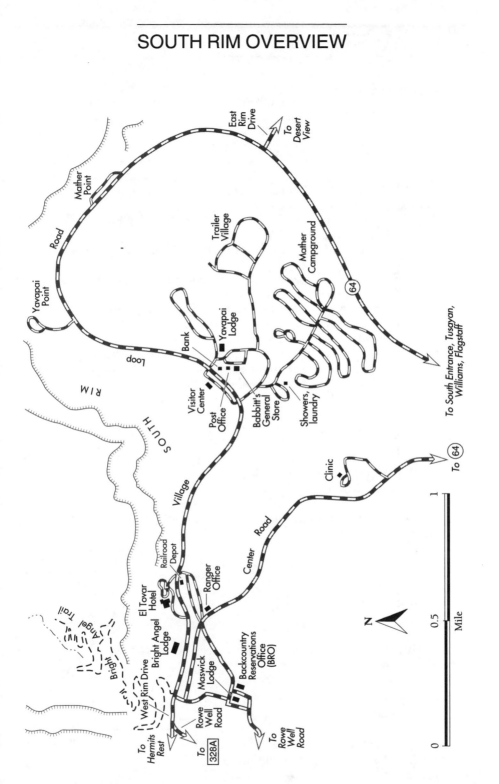

1   TANNER TRAIL

General description:	A rigorous rim-to-river backpack of three or more days, following one of the South Rim's more difficult trails.
Distance:	15.2 miles round-trip.
Difficulty:	Very strenuous.
Average hiking times:	5 hours to reach the river; 7 to 8 hours to return to the rim.
Type of trail:	Unmaintained; fair to good condition.
Trailhead elevation:	7,400 feet.
Low point:	2,650 feet.
Elevation gain and loss:	+250 feet; -5,000 feet.
Water availability:	Available only at the Colorado River, 9 miles from the trailhead.
Suggested cache points:	Seventyfive Mile Saddle or top of the Redwall below Cardenas Butte.
Optimum seasons:	March through May; September through November.
Use Area codes:	BB9, Tanner, at-large camping.
Management zone:	Primitive.
Topo maps:	Desert View USGS quad (Cape Solitude quad also required for Beamer Trail); Trails Illustrated Grand Canyon National Park.

Key points:
    0.0   Lipan Point parking area.
    1.9   Seventyfive Mile Saddle.
    3.5   Top of Redwall below Cardenas Butte.
    7.5   Junction with Beamer Trail; stay left.
    7.6   Tanner Beach, Colorado River.

Best day hike destinations: Seventyfive Mile Saddle is a fine destination for a 3.8-mile, round-trip day hike. The 7-mile round-trip to the top of the Redwall below Cardenas Butte offers dramatic river and Canyon views.

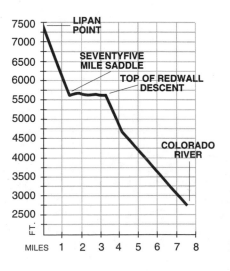

Finding the trailhead: Follow East Rim Drive to the Lipan Point turnoff, 2.3 miles west of the Desert View entrance station and 19.6 miles east of the Arizona Highway 64/Village Loop Road junction.

Follow the spur road for 0.5 mile to the Lipan Point parking area on the

South Rim. The trail begins below the parking area, at the beginning of the loop at the road's end. No facilities are available at Lipan Point.

The hike: The Tanner Trail, following an ancient Indian route later improved by nineteenth-century prospectors, surveys an unusual landscape in the eastern Grand Canyon. Along the lower reaches of the trail, the soft rocks of the Grand Canyon Supergroup have eroded into a broad, open valley at the river's edge, rather than the confined, cliff-bound setting typical of the inner gorge.

This unmaintained trail, recommended only for seasoned Grand Canyon hikers, is relentlessly steep, rocky, shadeless, and waterless until you reach the Colorado River. The tread is well worn and generally easy to follow, and the route offers access in one long day to one of the most scenic beach campsites in the Canyon. Vistas of the eastern Grand Canyon and lower Marble Canyon are superb, and the river is in view for much of the trip.

The openness of the terrain at the river affords ample opportunities for day hiking forays. The Escalante Route offers downriver access, and the Beamer Trail offers access to Lava Canyon Rapids and to the mouth of the Little Colorado River.

The hike out to the rim makes the Tanner Trail seem even longer and is best accomplished over two days, using one of the many excellent campsites between the top of the Redwall and Seventyfive Mile Saddle.

Colorado River from the Tanner Trail.

TANNER TRAIL

See Map on Page 75

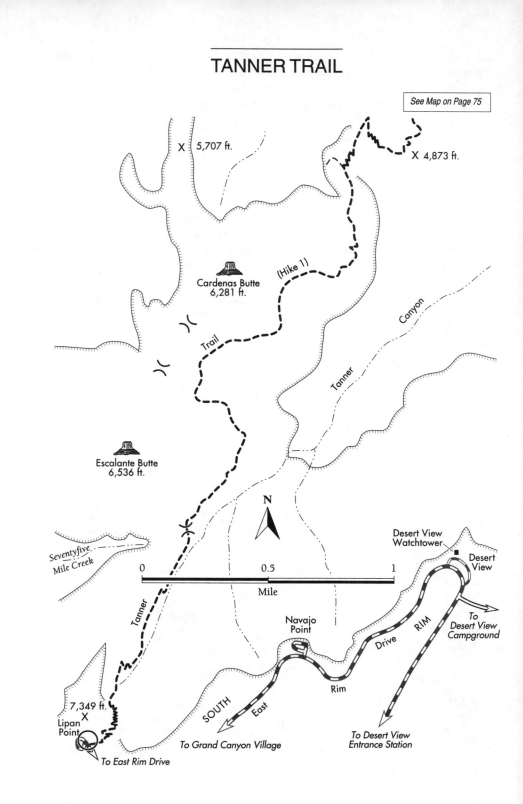

X 5,707 ft.

X 4,873 ft.

Cardenas Butte
6,281 ft.

(Hike 1)

Trail

Tanner

Canyon

Escalante Butte
6,536 ft.

N

Seventyfive
Mile Creek

0   0.5   1

Mile

Tanner

Desert View
Watchtower

Desert
View

To
Desert View
Campground

Navajo
Point

Drive

RIM

Rim

7,349 ft.
X
Lipan
Point

SOUTH   East

To Grand Canyon Village

To Desert View
Entrance Station

To East Rim Drive

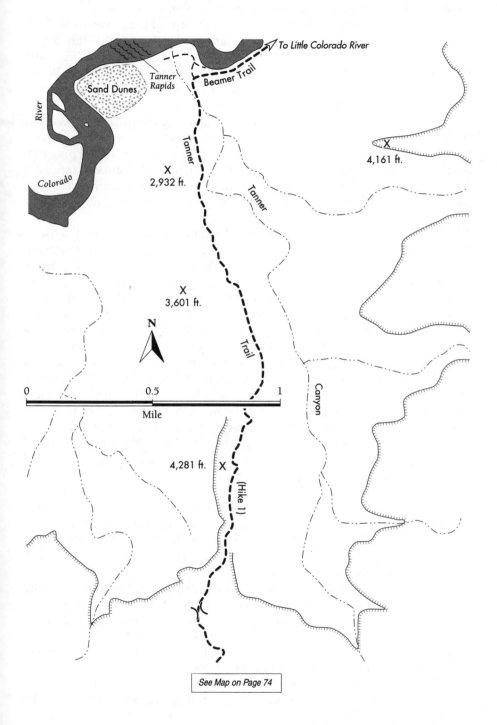

To Little Colorado River

Tanner Rapids

Beamer Trail

Sand Dunes

River

Colorado

Tanner

Tanner

X
2,932 ft.

X
4,161 ft.

X
3,601 ft.

N

Trail

Canyon

0   0.5   1
Mile

4,281 ft. X

(Hike 1)

See Map on Page 74

The trail begins several yards east of, and below, the loop at the road's end at Lipan Point. From the information sign, the trail begins a deceptively moderate descent into the pinyon-juniper woodland.

Far-ranging vistas from the rim here stretch beyond the towering walls of the Palisades of the Desert, bounding Tanner Canyon on the east to the broad plain of the Marble Platform, the Vermilion Cliffs, Echo Cliffs, and the dome of Navajo Mountain, 100 miles distant in southern Utah. Below you are the bold red crags of Escalante and Cardenas buttes, with the broad river silently meandering beyond.

Soon you leave the rim and follow switchbacks down the exceedingly steep and rocky terrain of the upper west arm of Tanner Canyon. This is one of the steepest rim descents in the Canyon, so be prepared for the hike out. A scattering of Douglas-fir here among the pinyons and junipers suggest a cooler, moister microclimate on the north-facing slopes. Common trailside shrubs in the woodland include Utah serviceberry, roundleaf buffaloberry, sagebrush, and snowberry.

The knee-jarring descent leads you through the boulders and slabs of Kaibab limestone and into the realm of the bulging, cross-bedded walls of Coconino sandstone. Typical of most trails through the Coconino, the grade here becomes even steeper. Here the woodland rapidly opens up, and the gnarled pinyons and junipers compete for precious moisture on the thin, sandy soils, sharing space with gooseberry, pale hoptree, and mormon tea.

The trail continues to grow steeper and rockier as you descend below the Coconino, onto the red, boulder-littered slopes of the Hermit shale and finally onto the red, ledgy slopes of Supai Group rocks. After hiking about 1 hour from the trailhead, you reach the ridge dividing Tanner Canyon and Seventyfive Mile Creek at 5,800 feet. From here the trail quickly descends east into the narrow wash of Tanner Canyon, then traverses out of the wash to a blocky, knife-blade saddle at the head of Seventyfive Mile Creek canyon. Fine views from the sandstone parapet at the saddle stretch into the somber upper reaches of Granite Gorge and are framed by the convoluted Redwall cliffs of Seventyfive Mile Creek.

From the saddle, a pleasant, though lengthy, Supai traverse ensues. Several yards from the saddle you pass a few inviting campsites, beyond which the narrow tread leads into an expansive bowl separating Escalante and Cardenas buttes. This grassy bowl, perched on the rim of the Redwall, offers many fine camping areas among the scattered boulders, shrubs, and pinyons and junipers that stud the basin.

The trail ascends moderately as it curves northeast and begins to exit the bowl. This ascent leads into another, smaller bowl lying beneath the splintered red sandstone crest of Cardenas Butte. You will find additional campsites here. An ascending traverse of this bowl leads to the shoulder of a minor ridge, which you quickly descend to the wooded bench below, negotiating a brief scramble among boulders en route.

You pass more inviting campsites as you wind among the pinyons and junipers that dot the bench. Soon you reach an unmarked junction at the

Looking north along the Colorado River from the Beamer Trail.
Photo by John Rihs.

top of the Redwall descent, about 2.5 hours below the rim. The Tanner Trail turns right here, but few hikers can resist the left fork, which leads about 50 yards to a dramatic overlook on a wooded bench at the north end of the Cardenas Butte ridge. The bench is often used as a camping area and a water cache point, and is the goal of a rewarding day hike.

The position of the bench, on a ridge deep within the inner Canyon, affords inspiring vistas. The silent whitewater of Tanner Rapids courses far below. There, at River Mile 68.5, the Colorado River abandons its southward course and begins to flow generally westward through the Grand Canyon, carving an improbable gorge through the Kaibab Plateau.

Rather than being confined in its usual inner gorge, the river both up and downstream from Tanner Beach flows through a broad, open valley, owing to the soft, erodible rocks of the Grand Canyon Supergroup, most notably, the Dox sandstone that dominates the riverside landscape. The open, spacious landscape at Tanner Beach is unique in the Grand Canyon, making the Tanner area a popular destination.

The view extends upriver to Lava Canyon Rapids, beyond which the canyon walls, there composed of Tapeats sandstone, once again enclose the river. The bold face of the Palisades of the Desert to the east jut skyward from the river to the rim. Spanning 4,000 feet of vertical relief, the wall also represents nearly 1 billion years of Earth history, from the Dox sandstone to the Kaibab limestone.

The Palisades and, farther north, the Desert Facade contrast their sheer

77

walls with an array of erosion-isolated buttes lying between the river and the North Rim. Prominent among them are Chuar and Kwagunt buttes and Nankoweap Mesa. Just east of the North Rim stands the blocky crag of Siegfried Pyre, a striking landmark in the eastern Grand Canyon. To the northwest are landmarks more familiar to Grand Canyon hikers, including Vishnu Temple, the isolated wooded platform of Wotans Throne, and the North Rim point of Cape Royal.

From the overlook, backtrack to the Tanner Trail and begin your descent through a break in the gray Redwall limestone cliff. The trail is rocky and gravelly and extremely steep with a slippery tread. A few half-hearted switchbacks make a weak attempt at easing the bone-jarring grade. As you descend, you may notice that blackbrush, squaw currant, and other coarse desert shrubs have supplanted the woodlands from above.

A descending traverse follows the initial plunge off the rim, then switchbacks guide you down to a red saddle, where scattered boulders and gnarled junipers offer minimal shelter for a pair of trailside campsites. From the saddle you descend into a minor draw beneath the fluted, greenish walls of Bright Angel shale. After leaving the draw the trail curves north and begins a lengthy, steadily descending traverse of open slopes and ridges, still high above Tanner Canyon.

At length you reach a saddle at 4,350 feet on the long ridge leading to the river. The distant roar of Tanner Rapids becomes audible here, and the river finally seems much closer, though you must endure another hour or so of steep downhill hiking before you can plunge your feet into its refreshing waters. A moderate, view-packed descent ensues from the saddle, following the open ridge above broken Tapeats sandstone cliffs.

Only sparse desert shrubs, primarily shadscale, mormon tea, and snakeweed, dot these slopes, along with the spiny, grizzly bear prickly pear and hedgehog cacti. Once you drop off the ridge, the trail descends steeply, following a winding course among blocks of Tapeats sandstone. The grade moderates beyond the Tapeats, and here you begin a protracted descending traverse upon steep, red Dox formation slopes above the dry, rocky bed of Tanner Canyon wash.

Low catclaw shrubs scatter across the trailside slopes, but their sparse foliage offers no shade. Brittlebush, a coarse desert shrub with gray green leaves, also appears, indicating your advance into the hot, dry Lower Sonoran Zone.

At length, the trail descends very steeply off the slopes of the ridge and into Tanner Canyon wash, 3.9 miles and about 2 hours below the top of the Redwall. Ample cairns show the continuation of the trail on the opposite side of the wash. The river is close at hand now, and soon after leaving the wash, you rise to the cairned junction with the Beamer Trail, forking right (east). To reach the river, continue straight ahead, descending several yards to the broad beach that spreads out just upstream from Tanner Rapids.

Numerous campsites, fringed with tamarisk, willow, and arrow weed, can be found both up and down the beach. Even if a river party is camped here, there is enough space that the area seldom seems crowded. Keep in mind that the tall sand dunes west of Tanner Beach are off-limits to foot travel. Through revegetation, the Park Service is attempting to stabilize these dunes.

The hike can be extended by following the Beamer Trail to the mouth of the Little Colorado River. But do not attempt this 19-mile round-trip in one day—you will exhaust yourself and likely fall far short of your goal. Instead, consider camping partway to the Little Colorado; the beach next to Lava Canyon Rapids offers the last suitable camping area on the trail (Use Area BA9), and makes a round-trip day hike from there to the Little Colorado more feasible.

From its junction with the Tanner Trail, the Beamer Trail heads east, following the bluffs above the river for 0.2 mile, then descends to the beach. You then follow the sandy beach first northeast, then north above the river bank. The route skirts tangled thickets of tamarisk, willow, arrow weed, and mesquite for 3.5 miles to dry Palisades Creek wash, next to Lava Canyon Rapids.

There are no suitable campsites ahead, and camping is not allowed within 0.5 mile of the confluence of the Colorado and Little Colorado rivers due to that area's religious significance to the Hopi people. Tread lightly here out of respect.

The route continues along the river bank for 0.3 mile from Palisades Creek, then the obvious trail ascends the east wall of the Canyon, gaining 500 feet via switchbacks. After climbing above the Dox formation, you reach the Tapeats sandstone after 1 mile. The following 5 miles is a long, circuitous route leading into and back out of nearly twenty minor side drainages. The trail remains easy to follow and gains and loses insignificant elevation en route.

Low cliffs of Tapeats sandstone frame the inner gorge here as they do in few other places in the Grand Canyon. The bold cliffs of the square-edged buttes of first Temple, and later the towering mass of Chuar Butte, allow you to gage your progress on the 3- to 4-hour hike from Lava Canyon Rapids. Once Chuar Butte begins to dominate the landscape west of the river, the river begins a northeast bend. Soon, the canyon of the Little Colorado opens up from the east, a deep and narrow gorge nearly as dramatic as the Grand Canyon itself. Here the Little Colorado's striking aquamarine waters mix with the often muddy Colorado. A trail of sorts continues beyond Ben Beamer's stone cabin and into the canyon of the Little Colorado. Beamer was a late nineteenth-century prospector who fashioned his confined quarters from nearby Anasazi ruins.

If time allows, the gorge of the Little Colorado affords rewarding explorations. To return to Lipan Point, you must retrace your route, best accomplished over two day's time.

2 NEW HANCE TRAIL

General description:	A rigorous rim-to-river backpack of three or more days, following the South Rim's most difficult trail.
Distance:	14.8 to 16 miles round-trip.
Difficulty:	Very strenuous.
Average hiking times:	5 to 6 hours to reach the river; 7 to 8 hours to return to the rim.
Type of trail:	Unmaintained; poor condition.
Trailhead elevation:	7,040 feet.
Low point:	2,560 feet.
Elevation gain and loss:	+200 feet; -4,680 feet.
Water availability:	Seasonal water in Red Canyon, 5.1 miles; Colorado River.
Suggested cache points:	Below Coronado Butte saddle or at the top of the Redwall descent.
Optimum seasons:	March through June; September through November.
Use Area code:	BD9, Red Canyon, at-large camping.
Management zone:	Primitive.
Topo Maps:	Grandview Point and Cape Royal USGS quads; Trails Illustrated Grand Canyon National Park.

Key points:

- **0.0** New Hance trailhead.
- **1.2** Coronado Butte saddle.
- **2.9** Top of Redwall descent.
- **5.1** Red Canyon wash.
- **6.8** Colorado River.

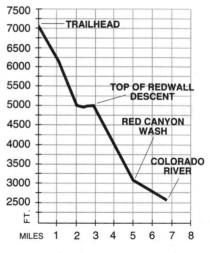

Best day hike destination: Strong hikers will enjoy the 7- to 8.2-mile round-trip to the top of the Redwall descent, where good views of Red Canyon and the river gorge unfold.

Finding the trailhead: No parking is allowed at the New Hance trailhead, which is prominently signed "No Parking" and "Tow Away Zone." Hikers must park at either Moran Point, 1.2 miles northeast, or alongside a gated fire road, 0.6 mile to the southwest, and walk to the trailhead. There is a turnout at the trailhead and hikers can pull out here and cache their packs before proceeding to either of the two parking areas.

The trailhead lies at the bottom of the grade between Buggeln Picnic Area and Moran Point, along East Rim Drive, 8.4 miles west of Desert View entrance station and 13.6 miles east of the Arizona Highway 64/Village Loop Road junction.

NEW HANCE TRAIL

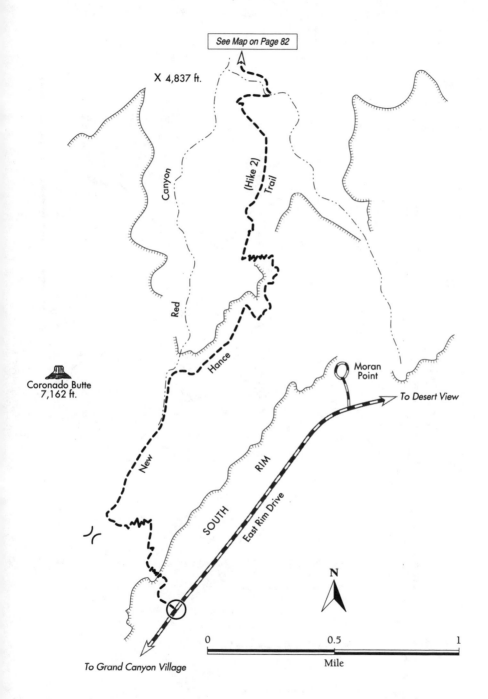

See Map on Page 82

X 4,837 ft.

Canyon

Red

Hance

(Hike 2) Trail

Coronado Butte
7,162 ft.

Moran
Point

To Desert View

New

SOUTH   RIM

East Rim Drive

To Grand Canyon Village

N

0   0.5   1
Mile

NEW HANCE TRAIL AND TONTO TRAIL

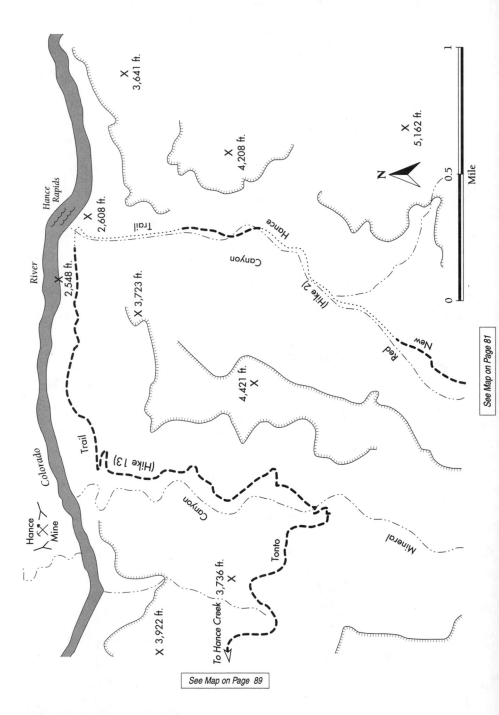

X 3,641 ft.

X 4,208 ft.

X 5,162 ft.

N

0.5 Mile 1 0

Hance Rapids

River

X 2,608 ft.

Trail

Trail

Hance

Canyon

X 3,723 ft.

2,548 ft. X

[Hike 2]

New

Red

4,421 ft. X

See Map on Page 81

Colorado

Trail

[Hike 13]

Canyon

Hance Mine

Tonto

Mineral

X 3,922 ft.

To Hance Creek 3,736 ft. X

See Map on Page 89

To reach the Moran Point turnoff, follow East Rim Drive 7.3 miles west from the Desert View entrance station or 14.6 miles from the AZ 64/Village Loop Rd. junction. The parking area lies 0.2 mile north of East Rim Dr.

Find the fire road by driving 9 miles west from the Desert View entrance station or 13 miles from the AZ 64/Village Loop Rd. junction. This dirt road branches south from East Rim Drive, 1 mile northeast of Buggeln Picnic Area, near the bottom of the grade, and 1.6 miles southwest of the Moran Point turnoff.

The hike: The New Hance Trail is an exciting, challenging, and very scenic route to the Colorado River, but it is also the South Rim's most difficult trail. Much of the trail is easy to follow, but you will encounter occasional route-finding problems, scrambling, and some exposure. The trail proceeds abruptly downhill from the rim to Red Canyon, an aptly named South Rim gorge walled by brick red slopes of Hakatai shale in its lower reaches.

Like many other side canyons in the Grand Canyon, Red Canyon follows the trend of a fault zone, here the Hance Fault. An abundance of shattered rock, rockslides, and slumps in the canyon attest to the dynamic geologic processes at work.

The trail ends at Hance Rapids on the Colorado River, just above the head of Granite Gorge. Here the varicolored rocks of the Grand Canyon Supergroup rise above the beach, where hikers will have the many fine campsites to themselves since the beach is inaccessible to river parties.

The New Hance Trail also offers the second shortest South Rim route to the river (longer than the South Kaibab Trail by 0.5 mile), but the difficulty of the trail demands that hikers have several other Grand Canyon hikes under their belt before attempting this one. Once a popular tourist trail around the turn of the century, nature has reclaimed much of the trail, and today only a few seasoned hikers follow this rugged route into the inner Canyon.

Hikers using this trail as part of a longer trek, on Hike 13 for instance, are advised to descend this trail, since routefinding is less problematic going downhill.

From either Moran Point or the fire road, follow the highway to the trailhead. The trail begins as a long-closed road, winding 0.2 mile northwest through pinyon-juniper woodland to the rim, where a backcountry information sign marks the beginning of the trail proper. You begin the descent off the rim through the Kaibab limestone, immediately enjoying views to massive Coronado Butte and into the colorful gaping maw of the Grand Canyon.

The narrow trail, invariably rough and rocky, descends steadily, often very steeply, through the Kaibab limestone via switchbacks upon north-facing slopes. During winter, snow and ice render this segment of the trail extremely dangerous. In dry weather, hikers should still proceed with caution.

Coronado Butte from the New Hance Trail.

Pinyon and juniper cloak the Kaibab ledges, and among this woodland grows a scattering of white fir, a conifer of the Canadian Zone common on the Kaibab Plateau but very rare below the South Rim. A profusion of shrubs also covers these sheltered slopes, including Utah serviceberry, alder-leaf mountain mahogany, Gregg ceanothus, mock orange, littleleaf mountain mahogany, and cliffrose.

The trail often follows the edge of narrow ledges, and occasional hand-and-foot scrambling over and around boulders is necessary. Once below the Kaibab, you reach a shady alcove in the red Toroweap formation rocks from where you enjoy fine views of Coronado Butte and to the tilted butte of Sinking Ship, both looming boldly to the west.

After several more short switchbacks, you traverse north to the top of the Coconino sandstone, then begin descending a series of steep, tight switchbacks, slab-hopping much of the way. Pay careful attention to the route of the trail as you descend through the Coconino; the way may be indistinct at times. As you approach the base of the Coconino, a very steep and slippery, but short, scramble leads you down to the resumption of the trail, and soon you reach the grassy slopes below and north of Coronado Butte saddle.

Pinyon, juniper, agave, mormon tea, cliffrose, and brickellbrush form a thick mantle on the trailside slopes here at 5,900 feet. Most notable, though, is the presence of a few ponderosa pines and Gambel oaks, far below their normal range.

Beyond the saddle, the trail turns north and becomes very steep and rocky as you descend through the Supai Group via the headwaters draw of Red Canyon. The trail passes through pinyon-juniper woodlands, repeatedly crisscrossing the rocky floor of the draw and at intervals traversing above both sides. The trail is obscure in places here, and at times scrambling over boulders is necessary.

The partially shaded, knee-jarring descent leads you down through the Supai layer to a pouroff at the top of the gray Redwall limestone. From there, views extend into the cottonwood—shaded confines of Red Canyon far below. The trail ahead traverses the lower layers of the Supai for 1 mile, while you search for a break in the Redwall limestone. Several short but steep ascents and descents en route, plus two steep draws choked with boulders, will markedly slow your progress on this traverse. Several inner Canyon landmarks come into sharper focus from this stretch of the trail. Angels Gate, to the left of the wooded mesa of Wotans Throne, is a prominent Coconino sandstone spire to the northwest. Farther downcanyon you see the blocky tower of Zoroaster Temple and its massive neighbor, Brahma Temple.

At length you begin descending steadily, pass several fair campsites, then reach the upper layers of the Redwall at 4,850 feet, on the narrow crest of a fin projecting into the canyon away from the Redwall cliff band. Thus far, Red Canyon has appeared to be little different than any other South Rim canyon. Yet this unusual rocky fin may give you a hint that the canyon is indeed somehow different. Here, a section of the massive Redwall cliff has slumped into Red Canyon, weakened by movement along the Hance Fault. This slump provides passage through that barrier for the trail that John Hance forged in 1894. Farther on, you will see much more evidence of slumps and rockslides, processes that are the primary means of canyon widening and enlargement in the Grand Canyon.

Before you drop off the fin, pause to enjoy the views that will quickly fade as you enter the depths of Red Canyon. North of the river are the prominent towers of Vishnu Temple, Solomon Temple, and Wotans Throne, and the wooded point of Cape Royal on the North Rim. Typical of most Redwall descents, the trail here is steep and gravelly, with a slippery tread. An abrupt descent off the west side of the fin leads to a small campsite, where the grade moderates.

After one final switchback below the campsite, you begin a descending traverse across a broad slope of slump debris, its contours now covered in vegetation and softened by ages of erosion. Pinyon and juniper, growing here well below their usual range, are joined on the trailside slopes by squaw currant, apache plume, Utah serviceberry, single-leaf ash, pale hoptree, and alder-leaf mountain mahogany.

The traverse leads north, and you descend steeply to a narrow ridge littered with blocks and slabs, the fault-shattered remnants of Tapeats sandstone. The bright red slopes and thin ledges of Hakatai shale that embrace the lower canyon come into view as you descend northwest down the ridge, above Red Canyon's east fork. You gain a fine view of the Great Unconformity on the west wall of the canyon, where the tilted layers of the Hakatai shale are capped by the horizontal beds of Tapeats sandstone.

At length you pass beyond the reach of scattered junipers, then curve east around the shoulder of the ridge, heading through clumps of Apache plume that decorate the red slopes with their white spring blossoms and feathery summer fruits. Here the tread is firm, red, and crunchy as you head into the wash of the east fork of the canyon. After a brief traverse above several east fork pouroffs, you begin the final traversing descent into Red Canyon wash, its course below studded with tall Fremont cottonwoods. Upon reaching the wash, you will find seasonal water flowing about a hundred yards upstream.

The remaining 1.7 miles, most of it without a discernable trail, follows the wash down to the Colorado River. At first, the route passes over red slickrock and firm gravel, but shortly the route gives way to soft gravel among many boulders, and progress is slow and arduous. To pass the time as you follow the serpentine confines of the wash, notice that in numerous places the red Hakatai shale slopes above are buried beneath a mantle of rockslides, originating from the splintered Tapeats sandstone walls above.

Mesquite fringes the high water mark of the wash, and tenacious seep-willow adds its greenery to the flood-scoured wash bottom. About halfway to the river, large landslide boulders begin to choke the wash, forming impassable dry falls in two places. Careful attention is required here to find

The Colorado River from the mouth of Red Canyon, at Hance Rapids.

the trails that bypass these obstacles, first on the left (west), then on the right (east). Beyond the second dry fall, follow the trail as it carves a swath through mesquite thickets, eventually dropping back into the wash 0.5 mile from the river.

The wash, flanked by a sandy bench to the west and a mesquite-clad bench to the east, steeply enters the river like a boat ramp. Hance Rapids, where the river channel is filled with submerged boulders that floods have carried down Red Canyon, thunders away at your feet.

Many fine, mesquite-shaded campsites lie several yards east of the wash, just above the churning river. Open sites lie atop the sandy, mesquite-dotted bench west of the wash, offering good views up the Canyon past the thumb-like spire of Ochoa Point to Desert View Watchtower high above on the South Rim. Downcanyon views reach into the head of Granite Gorge's somber defile.

The variegated strata of the Grand Canyon Supergroup, capped by a wall of Tapeats sandstone, enclose the inner gorge here. Slopes and cliff bands colored in shades of red, gray, and brown include the Hakatai, Shinumo, and Dox formations. A dark gray diabase dike angles northeast through those ancient rocks on the north wall of the gorge.

Eventually, backpackers must retrace their steps to the trailhead, best accomplished over two days' time.

3 GRANDVIEW TRAIL—GRANDVIEW POINT TO HORSESHOE MESA

General description:	A rewarding day hike or backpack to a wooded mesa below the South Rim.
Distance:	6.4 miles round-trip.
Difficulty:	Moderately strenuous.
Average hiking times:	1.5 to 2 hours down to the mesa; 3 hours to return to the rim.
Type of trail:	Unmaintained; generally good condition.
Trailhead elevation:	7,420 feet.
Low point:	4,900 feet.
Elevation loss:	2,520 feet.
Water availability:	Miners Spring, 0.8 mile and 450 feet below Horseshoe Mesa.
Suggested cache points:	Base of the Coconino sandstone near the saddle at the head of Cottonwood Creek canyon.
Optimum season:	March through November.
Use Area code:	BF5, Horseshoe Mesa, designated campsite.
Management zone:	Threshold.
Topo maps:	Grandview Point and Cape Royal USGS quads; Trails Illustrated Grand Canyon National Park; Earthwalk Grand Canyon National Park.

Key points:

0.0 Grandview Point.

3.0 Junction with trail to Miners (Page) Spring on Horseshoe Mesa; continue straight ahead.

3.1 Junction with trail to Cottonwood Creek; stay right.

3.2 Junction with trail to designated camping area and toilet; backpackers will turn right here.

Finding the trailhead: The trail begins at Grandview Point, located at the end of an 0.8-mile spur road north of East Rim Drive. Find the Grandview Point turnoff 13.2 miles west of the Desert View entrance station and 8.7 miles east of the Arizona Highway 64/Village Loop Road junction. No facilities, except for garbage collection, are provided at Grandview Point.

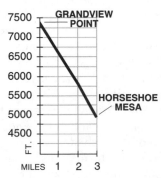

The hike: Wooded mesas are common in the mid to upper reaches of the inner Canyon, and when viewed from the canyon rims, many of them appear to be inviting destinations. Yet few of these cliff-bound "islands" are accessible to hikers. Horseshoe Mesa, perched atop the Redwall limestone halfway between the South Rim and the Colorado River, is one notable exception.

88

GRANDVIEW TRAIL—GRANDVIEW POINT TO HORSESHOE MESA

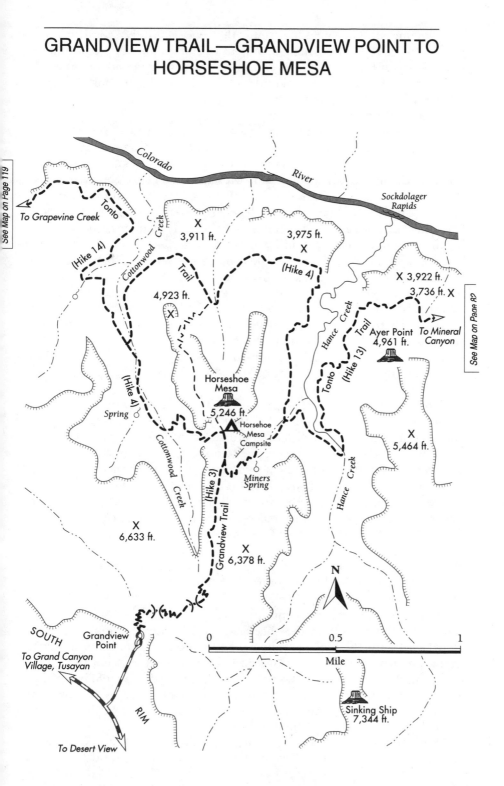

Following an ancient Indian route that was skillfully rebuilt by miner Pete Berry in 1892, the Grandview Trail to Horseshoe Mesa combines the rich history of the Grand Canyon mining era with tremendous inner Canyon scenery. The trip is suitable to any hiker in good condition as an introduction to Grand Canyon hiking, offering many of the rewards without the time and effort required for a rim-to-river trip.

Various mining relics, far-ranging vistas, and a scenic designated camping area, with sites for groups and smaller parties, combine to make Horseshoe Mesa an attractive destination for day hikers and backpackers alike. The Last Chance Mine on Horseshoe Mesa is listed in the National Register of Historic Places. The Grandview Trail (and all other Grand Canyon trails) are in the process of being listed. All relics present in this fascinating area, from the ruins of Pete Berry's cabin, to mining implements, and even rusting tin cans, have historic significance and tell a silent story of a bygone era in the Grand Canyon. Hikers should employ the same no trace practices in this area as they would in an archaeological site.

The trail begins at the north end of the Grandview Point overlook. About 50 yards below the point, look to your left and you may notice the inscriptions of early travelers on the trailside Kaibab limestone. The trail descends steadily over ledges of Kaibab limestone via a series of short, tight switchbacks. Bulging walls require care when passing with a bulky backpack. This shady stretch of trail is notoriously treacherous during winter when snow and ice coat the trail.

Broad Canyon vistas open up from the start, stretching up-Canyon to the Palisades of the Desert, and including a view of the Colorado River near Tanner Canyon. The Kaibab ledges are studded with tall, spindly pinyons and juniper. But soon you reach the steep slopes and thicker soils of the Toroweap formation, where the shrub cover quickly increases.

Views from these slopes stretch down the long trench of Grapevine Creek canyon, far below to the northwest. When you reach the brink of the Coconino sandstone cliff, the tread becomes paved with cobbles. You descend this stone riprap to a saddle clad with Gambel oak at the head of Grapevine Creek. Look back to the segment of trail you have just descended. There, Pete Berry constructed juniper-log cribbing to support the trail on the Coconino cliff. And today, more than 100 years later, Berry's work has solidly withstood the test of time.

From the saddle, the trail contours north just beneath a ridge of Coconino sandstone bluffs. Here in the shady confines of upper Grapevine Creek, Douglas-fir joins the ranks of pinyons and junipers on trailside slopes. The trail soon curves around the ridge and begins a steep descent through the Coconino via cobble-paved switchbacks. The layered strata of Sinking Ship, a 7,344-foot butte detached from the South Rim and tilted by the fold of the Grandview-Phantom Monocline, rises boldly above Hance Creek canyon beyond the notch below to the southeast.

Soon you reach that narrow notch on the divide separating Cottonwood Creek from Hance Creek. Despite the white Coconino sandstone blocks

Ruins of Pete Berry's cabin on Horseshoe Mesa.

that litter the slopes here, you have emerged from that formation onto the red slopes of the Hermit shale. This notch is a convenient location to cache water for the hike out.

The trail beyond the notch continues the moderately steep descent, and you will negotiate occasional switchbacks and lengthy traverses through the Supai rock layer ahead. The shady north-facing slopes en route support a vigorous woodland of pinyon and juniper and a varied assortment of shrubs that include mormon tea, cliffrose, Utah serviceberry, Gregg ceanothus, Wright silktassel, agave, littleleaf mountain mahogany, and Fremont barberry.

After bending north, you begin a long traverse high on the east wall of upper Cottonwood Creek canyon. Here, in response to increased sunlight and competition for scant moisture, the pinyons and junipers become widely spaced, stunted, and gnarled. This segment of the trail is quite rocky, with several minor rockslides to negotiate.

Eventually the high traverse ends where the trail merges with a broad red ridge. The red Supai summit of Horseshoe Mesa butte looms ahead to the north, and in the distance rises the stony spire of Vishnu Temple. You briefly follow the ridge north among small, spreading junipers, then quickly descend past the first of many adits that pierce the flanks of Horseshoe Mesa. Here the trailside slopes are decorated with the colorful blue and green rocks of azurite and malachite—fragments of the richest copper ore unearthed in the Grand Canyon.

Soon you pass a second tunnel, beyond which the faint trail signed for Page (A.K.A. Miners) Spring branches right. Bear left here and make one final brief descent to the narrow neck of Horseshoe Mesa. Here the trail to Cottonwood Creek branches left (see Hike 4), but you continue straight ahead, reaching the stone-walled ruins of one of Pete Berry's cabins within several yards.

A spur trail heads 100 yards east from the cabin, leading to a toilet and several fine campsites set in a woodland of junipers. The marked group campsite lies a short distance away to the north.

Views from the mesa are excellent, stretching southeast to the bold tower of Coronado Butte, east up the Canyon to the Palisades of the Desert, and northeast to the mountainlike buttes of Vishnu Temple, Rama Shrine, Sheba Temple, and The Tabernacle. The North Rim forms the horizon far above, and much closer rises the South Rim fringed with tall ponderosa pines.

The Grandview Trail continues north for 1 mile via the west arm of the mesa, then descends a thousand feet in 1 mile to the Tonto Trail. The vistas that unfold from the rim of the mesa's west arm are expansive, including the vast reaches of the Tonto Platform and the somber depths of Granite Gorge.

From Horseshoe Mesa, you must eventually backtrack to the trailhead.

4 *GRANDVIEW TRAIL LOOP*

General description:	A three- to four-day backpack below the South Rim, tracing a segment of the Tonto Trail. See Map on Page 89
Distance:	13.1 miles.
Difficulty:	Strenuous.
Average hiking times:	45 minutes from Horseshoe Mesa to Cottonwood Creek spring; 3 hours to Miners Spring trail junction above Hance Creek; 4 to 5 hours from that junction to return to rim.
Type of trail:	Unmaintained; fair to good condition.
Trailhead elevation:	7,420 feet.
Low point:	3,680 feet.
Elevation gain and loss:	4,000 feet.
Water availability:	Cottonwood Creek spring, 4.4 miles; Hance Creek, 0.75 mile via Tonto Trail from junction below Miners Spring; Miners Spring, 9.5 miles.
Suggested cache points:	Horseshoe Mesa or base of the Coconino sandstone near the saddle at the head of Cottonwood Creek canyon.
Optimum seasons:	March through June; September through November.
Use Area codes:	BF5, Horseshoe Mesa, designated campsite; BG9, Cottonwood Creek, at-large camping; BE9, Hance Creek, at-large camping.
Management zones:	Horseshoe Mesa, Threshold; other zones, Primitive.
Topo maps:	Grandview Point and Cape Royal USGS quads; Trails Illustrated Grand Canyon National Park; Earthwalk Grand Canyon National Park.

Key points:

0.0 Grandview Point.
3.0 Junction with trail to Miners (Page) Spring on Horseshoe Mesa; continue straight ahead.
3.1 Junction with trail to Cottonwood Creek; turn left.
4.4 Cottonwood Creek spring.
4.9 Junction with Tonto Trail; turn right.
6.3 Junction with Grandview/Horseshoe Mesa Trail; stay left.
9.0 Junction with trail to Miners Spring and Horseshoe Mesa; turn right.
9.5 Spur trail to Miners Spring.
10.1 Junction with Grandview Trail on Horseshoe Mesa; turn left.
13.1 Grandview Point.

Best day hike destination: The popular 6-mile round-trip to Horseshoe Mesa is a rewarding but rigorous day hike.

Finding the trailhead: See driving directions for Hike 3.

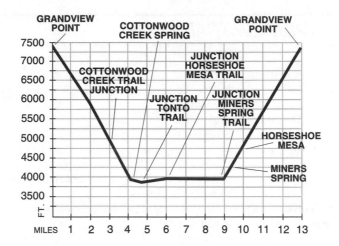

The hike: This memorable three-day circuit is an excellent, though brief, introduction to the spectacular Tonto Trail. The trip is a good choice for well-conditioned and experienced, first-time Grand Canyon hikers, and it offers many of the rewards of a Grand Canyon trek, save for a riverside campsite.

Two of the three perennial water sources are located at convenient intervals, with good camping areas nearby. Much of the trail is generally easy to follow, except a stretch of the Tonto Trail above Hance Creek canyon, where care must be taken to stay on course.

From Grandview Point, follow the Grandview Trail (see Hike 3) for 3.1 miles, descending 2,520 feet below the rim to the signed junction with the trail to Cottonwood Creek, and turn left (west). This trail briefly descends a precipitous side canyon on the west flanks of Horseshoe Mesa, winds past two mine tunnels, then begins the abrupt descent through a break in the Redwall limestone on an exceedingly steep and rocky grade via switchbacks. The tread is gravelly and constant attention is necessary to avoid a spill. The juniper woodland is left behind at the mesa rim, and coarse desert shrubs begin to dominate trailside slopes. Common trailside shrubs include four-wing saltbush, mormon tea, turpentine broom, brittlebush, and banana yucca.

Here the Redwall lacks its usual salmon hue and the trailside rock displays its natural gray color. Once you pass through the Redwall, the trail begins a northwestbound traverse upon steep slopes beneath the now salmon tinted Redwall cliffs that bound Horseshoe Mesa. Soon, one final but extremely steep and slippery descent leads down to the floor of Cottonwood Creek wash, where junipers reappear along its sheltered banks.

The trail is briefly faint and follows the wash for several yards down-canyon, then becomes distinct again after exiting the wash on the left. The trail ahead traverses toward the tall Fremont cottonwoods that hug the banks of a southwest-trending tributary. After a brief but steep descent, you reach the floor of that draw, where a trickling stream flows among the cottonwoods and thickets of seep-willow. Jump across the stream, rise to the north bank, and there you will find a pair of campsites beneath the arching branches of cottonwoods and a scattering of pinyon, juniper, and catclaw.

The stream emerges at a reliable spring about 175 yards up the draw. Another spring, shown on the Cape Royal quad in the northwest tributary of Cottonwood Creek, usually flows only during the winter and early spring.

This is a scenic campsite, with the bold cliffs edging Horseshoe Mesa rising to the east, the short, precipitous canyon of Cottonwood Creek behind you, and an array of colorful buttes in the north framing the distant North Rim.

From the spring draw, follow the brushy, rocky trail north above the west banks of the wash. Mormon tea and cliffrose grow thickly here, and tall Engelmann prickly pear stud the slopes above. After about 250 yards, drop into the often dry wash next to a massive, spreading cottonwood and cross to the opposite bank. The trail ahead passes more good campsites and crosses the wash three more times. After 0.5 mile, at 3,680 feet, you reach the cairned junction with the Tonto Trail, perched atop the rim of the Tapeats sandstone.

The westbound Tonto leads to Grapevine, Boulder, and Lonetree canyons, and eventually to the South Kaibab Trail (see Hike 14). A boot-worn path descends into Cottonwood Creek's narrow Tapeats sandstone gorge. Several excellent campsites are located there, and the creek is often flowing.

You, however, turn right at the junction, cross the wash for a fifth and final time above the lip of a pouroff, then skirt the rim of a 20-foot cliff above the wash. The Tonto Trail is a narrow, but usually obvious, path that remains reasonably level for the following 4.2 miles to the junction above Hance Creek. The Tonto Platform ahead is a pleasant change of pace from the vertical environs above, and its gently rolling surface is clad in a sea of blackbrush, mormon tea, snakeweed, and a variety of cacti.

As you follow Cottonwood Creek's rim at a nearly constant elevation, its gorge, flanked by the brown cliffs of the Tapeats, grows increasingly deeper. After the trail curves around the platform beneath the west arm of Horseshoe Mesa, views open up into the dark, Vishnu-bound lower reaches of Cottonwood and Granite Gorges, but the river remains unseen. Swirls of pink Zoroaster granite streaking through the contorted, dark gray beds of Vishnu schist comprise the rugged walls of the inner gorge. And a continuous array of colorful, cliff-bound buttes and spires are in view throughout your trek across the Tonto Platform.

After cresting a broad ridge above Cottonwood Creek canyon, the trail bends southeast toward the draw separating the two arms of Horseshoe Mesa. About 100 yards before reaching the dry wash of that draw, there is a junction indicated by a piece of drill steel and a cairn. The right fork ascends 1,000 feet in 1 mile to the rim of Horseshoe Mesa.

Resume your trek across the Tonto Platform after dipping into the wash beyond the junction, following a northeast course. The trail ahead curves

Angels Gate and Wotans Throne rise beyond the dark cliffs of Granite Gorge, as seen from the Tonto Trail.

around the east arm of Horseshoe Mesa, eventually topping a rise beside a boulder-stacked knoll, 0.9 mile from the previous junction. From here the trail begins a gradual descent toward the southeast, but the trail is obscure for 250 yards or so ahead. Careful scouting is necessary here to stay on course.

During your attempts at relocating the trail, pause to enjoy the view. Yawning Hance Creek canyon opens up far below to the east, as well as a fine view into the inner gorge and your first view of the Colorado River, from where the muffled roar of hidden Sockdolager Rapids emanates. The Tonto rim about 0.25 mile north affords an even better view. As you gaze up-Canyon, you can see where the Vishnu schist dips underground 2 miles upriver, just below Hance Rapids, beyond which the tilted strata of the Grand Canyon Supergroup embrace the gorge.

As you proceed southeast from the knoll, you should soon relocate the trail where the tread is cut by an eroded gully. Descend steadily for about 250 yards to the Tapeats sandstone ledge on the rim of Hance Creek canyon, then bend south and follow the rim, now on obvious tread. Gaping Hance Creek lies virtually at your feet, 800 feet below, flanked by the rugged, dark walls of Vishnu schist. From this exciting stretch of trail you also gain views to Sinking Ship, Coronado Butte, and to the cool ponderosa pine forests atop the South Rim.

The Tonto Platform begins to pinch out as you proceed south along the flanks of Hance Creek canyon. The trail clings to the Tapeats rim, with

Relics of the Grand Canyon's nineteenth-century mining era can be found near Horseshoe Mesa.

steep and colorful slopes of Bright Angel shale rising above. Blackbrush, that ubiquitous Tonto shrub, has now been replaced brittlebush, rabbitbrush, and four-wing saltbush, but mormon tea, also common on the Tonto, persists.

As you continue farther south, the Tapeats rim becomes less abrupt and the trail begins traversing steep slopes away from the cliff edge. You dip in and out of numerous minor draws and, at length, reach the steep and rocky wash emanating from the eastern flanks of Horseshoe Mesa.

The Tonto Trail curves east beyond the wash, but keep an eye out for an unsigned right-branching trail within several yards of crossing the wash, at 3,760 feet. This is your trail, leading past Miners Spring en route back to Horseshoe Mesa.

No camping is allowed between this junction and the mesa. Good campsites and perennial water can be found in Hance Creek (Use Area BE9, at-large camping) by following the Tonto Trail ahead for 0.75 mile.

To close the circuit, bear right at the junction and proceed southwest up the draw. The trail ascends a moderate grade southeast of the wash and heads into the Redwall-bound amphitheater. The confines of the amphitheater hosts a microclimate that is reflected in an abrupt change in the diversity of vegetation. Here, not far above the Tonto Platform's limited assemblage of coarse shrubs, you will see an abundance of bunchgrasses, single-leaf ash, Utah serviceberry, cliffrose, Apache plume, catclaw, and juniper.

After 0.25 mile, you dip into the boulder-strewn wash then ascend steeply via the northwest slopes of the drainage. The rocky spire of Vishnu Temple, and its companion butte Rama Shrine, which displays a gentle crest of red Supai rocks, forms a dramatic backdrop during your ascent back to the mesa.

As you approach the foot of the salmon-tinted Redwall cliff, you mount a rocky rib and meet the spur trail signed for Page Spring (Miners Spring) next to a rusty wheelbarrow dating back to Pete Berry's time. That spur leads 175 yards south into a cliff-bound draw. There, in a small alcove decorated with maidenhair fern, perennial water drips from the ceiling in a steady rain to nourish the shallow pool on the alcove's floor.

From that junction, two long, steep switchbacks lead to the foot of the Redwall, where you pass a mine tunnel complete with a nineteenth-century ore car and various other relics. Beyond the tunnel, the trail crosses the colorful slopes of a mine dump, then you begin to rise via a series of short, steep, and rocky switchbacks carved into the Redwall cliff. There is some exposure on this stretch where the walls bulge out into the trail, and at times you will be scrambling hand-and-foot to negotiate rockbound pitches.

At length you top out on Horseshoe Mesa and intersect the Grandview Trail, 1.1 miles from the Tonto Trail, at 4,960 feet. Turn left here and retrace your steps for 3 long, steep miles back to Grandview Point.

5 SHOSHONE POINT

General description:	An easy day hike to a glorious South Rim viewpoint.
Distance:	2 miles round-trip.
Difficulty:	Easy.
Average hiking time:	40 to 60 minutes round-trip.
Type of trail:	Dirt road.
Trailhead elevation:	7,190 feet.
High point:	7,300 feet.
Elevation gain:	110 feet.
Water availability:	None available.
Optimum season:	April through November.
Topo maps:	Phantom Ranch USGS quad; Trails Illustrated Grand Canyon National Park; Earthwalk Grand Canyon National Park.

Key points:

 0.0 Shoshone Point Road.
 1.0 Shoshone Point.

Finding the trailhead: Find this unsigned trailhead along the north side of East Rim Drive, 3.5 miles east of the Arizona Highway 64/Village Loop Road junction and 1.25 miles east of the prominently signed Yaki Point turnoff.

If you are approaching from the east via Desert View, note your odometer reading at the Grandview Point turnoff. You pass a picnic area on the north side of the road 2.7 miles west of the Grandview Point turnoff and reach the Shoshone Point Road and small parking area 6.3 miles west of the turnoff to Grandview Point.

The hike: The majority of South Rim viewpoints offer easy and short, yet often crowded and noisy, access from their paved parking lots. Seldom does the viewer enjoy quiet solitude when gazing across the vast depths of the Grand Canyon. Shoshone Point is a notable exception. Anyone willing to walk a 1-mile, nearly level dirt road will enjoy the opportunity to contemplate this great canyon in relative solitude.

Perched high on the South Rim on a point dividing Grapevine and Cremation canyons, Shoshone Point offers one of the finest vistas available from the South Rim. The view encompasses much of Hike 14, affording an excellent overview to hikers planning to take that trip.

If your time and energy allow you to hike only a few short trails on the South Rim, the trip to Shoshone Point, combining a walk through cool pine forests with truly dramatic vistas of the eastern Grand Canyon, should be at the top of your list.

Your solitude, however, may be disrupted at times at the point. The picnic

SHOSHONE POINT

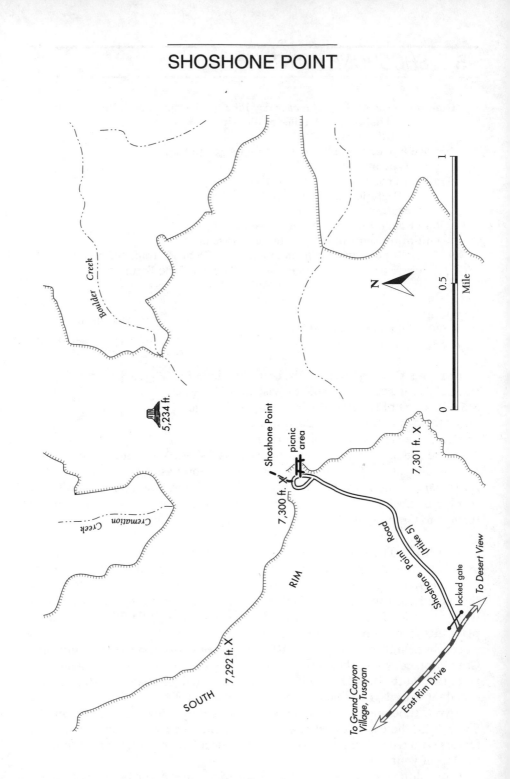

area at the road's end is an occasionally popular spot for weddings, family gatherings, and other festivities. The site is available for day use by fee and permit from May 15 to October 15—contact Park Headquarters at (520) 638-7761 for the information sheet on Shoshone Point. Before and after those dates, you'll likely have Shoshone Point to yourself.

Begin your walk at the locked gate on the Shoshone Point Rd. The road rises imperceptibly up a shallow draw beneath the shade of tall ponderosa pines. Gambel oaks and occasional pinyons and junipers mix into the ranks of the pine forest.

Typical of either Canyon rim, the forest signals your approach. The pines quickly diminish and are supplanted by a woodland of pinyon and juniper. Shortly after entering this woodland, the road edges close to the east rim of the point, and soon you reach the loop at the road's end, where you find picnic tables, a large fire pit, fire grills, portable toilets, and garbage cans, facilities well-used by permitted visitors who drive the dirt road in season.

A well-worn path ascends north beyond here, then descends another 150 yards among gnarled pinyons and over slabs of Kaibab limestone out to the point, where an unobstructed vista of the Grand Canyon unfolds, far from the crowds, noisy buses, and exhaust fumes of other South Rim viewpoints.

Up-Canyon to the east you can see the foaming torrent of Hance Rapids, but elsewhere the river is blocked from your view by the Tapeats sandstone rim of the inner gorge. On the skyline beyond the rapids is Desert View Watchtower, and your eyes follow the east rim of the Canyon past the towering walls of the Palisades of the Desert to the distant Marble Platform and the Echo Cliffs.

Part of that view is obscured by the pyramidal crag of Vishnu Temple, one of the Canyon's most striking peaks. From Powell Plateau in the northwest, past Point Sublime to Cape Royal and Wotans Throne in the northeast, the forest-fringed North Rim and an incredible array of colorful buttes, mesas, and spires spread out before you.

Virtually at your feet, the broad, dry wash of the east fork of Cremation Creek winds northwest and disappears into its Tapeats sandstone narrows above Granite Gorge. The switchbacks of the South Kaibab Trail through the Redwall limestone are clearly visible west of Cremation's broad desert basin. Clear Creek canyon, with its own tortuous Vishnu gorge, winds northeast beyond the invisible river, gathering its waters from its many-fingered canyons that reach up to the forested rim of Walhalla Plateau.

Lying far below is the wash of Boulder Creek, north of the point. To the east are the depths of Grapevine Creek, one of the South Rim's most extensive canyons. Other prominent features below the South Rim to the east of the point include Horseshoe Mesa, Sinking Ship, Coronado Butte, and the distant red buttes of Escalante and Cardenas looming above the Tanner Trail.

While you are on the point, you may notice a grove of Douglas-fir clinging to the foot of the Kaibab cliff below the picnic area. More of these Canadian Zone trees can be seen to the west, occupying the Toroweap

Vishnu Temple, Wotans Throne, and Cape Royal on the North Rim rise in the distance beyond Boulder Creek Canyon and Granite Gorge, from Shoshone Point.

formation slopes westward toward Yaki Point, between drought-tolerant bands of pinyon and juniper.

After enjoying the tremendous vistas, retrace your steps to the trailhead.

6 SOUTH KAIBAB TRAIL TO BRIGHT ANGEL CAMPGROUND

General description:	A backpack of two or more days, following one of the most popular trails in the Grand Canyon.
Distance:	13.8 miles round-trip.
Difficulty:	Strenuous.
Average hiking times:	4 to 5 hours down to the campground; 6 to 7 hours to return to the rim.
Type of trail:	Maintained; excellent condition.
Trailhead elevation:	7,200 feet.
Low point:	2,460 feet.
Elevation loss:	4,740 feet.
Water availability:	Colorado River, 6.4 miles; Bright Angel Creek, 6.7 miles; piped drinking water at River Ranger Station, 6.7 miles, and at Bright Angel Campground, 6.9 miles.
Suggested cache points:	O'Neill Butte saddle; top of the Redwall descent; at The Tipoff (conceal your cache well).
Optimum seasons:	March though June; September through November.
Use Area code:	CBG, Bright Angel, designated campground.
Management zone:	Corridor.
Topo maps:	Phantom Ranch USGS quad; Trails Illustrated Grand Canyon National Park; Earthwalk Bright Angel Trail or Grand Canyon National Park .

Key points:
- **0.0** South Kaibab trailhead.
- **1.4** Cedar Ridge.
- **4.4** Tonto Trail junction; continue straight ahead.
- **4.6** The Tipoff.
- **5.0** Panorama Point
- **6.1** Junction with River Trail; bear right.
- **6.3** Black (Kaibab) Bridge spanning the Colorado River.
- **6.7** Junction with Bright Angel Trail opposite River Ranger Station; stay right.
- **6.9** Bridge at junction with spur trail to Bright Angel Campground; turn left.

Best day hike destinations: The 2.8-mile round-trip to Cedar Ridge is the most popular day hike in the Park, offering far-ranging views and a good introduction to Grand Canyon hiking. The 6-mile round-trip to the top of the Redwall descent offers even better views, including the cottonwood-shaded oasis of Bright Angel Creek.

Finding the trailhead:
Find this well-signed trailhead by driving 1.1 miles east on East Rim Drive from the Arizona Highway 64/Village Loop Road junction to the Yaki Point turnoff, also signed for Kaibab Trail. Follow this spur road north for 0.3 mile, then turn left where the sign points to the trailhead. After another 0.25 mile, you reach the trailhead parking lot. Seasonal drinking water, toilets, garbage collection, and a pay telephone are available here.

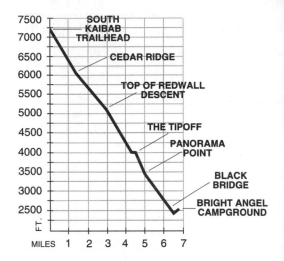

If you are approaching from the east, follow East Rim Dr. west from the Desert View entrance station for 20.75 miles to reach the Yaki Point turnoff.

(Note: Due to congestion and overcrowding at the South Kaibab trailhead, this area may be closed to private vehicles in the near future. At that time, hikers must then use the Kaibab Shuttle bus to reach the trailhead. For more information on shuttles, see "Planning Your Trip" and check with the Backcountry Reservations Office for current schedules.)

The hike: Much like the Bright Angel Trail, the South Kaibab Trail is a must-do for Grand Canyon visitors wishing to see the Canyon from the inside out. Hikers flock to this excellent trail in a steady stream for much of the year. Although the majority of trail users are day hikers making the rewarding trip to Cedar Ridge, thousands of overnight users also follow this trail each year en route to Bright Angel Campground and Phantom Ranch.

The trail offers the shortest, fastest access to the Colorado River of any Grand Canyon trail, and many first-time Canyon hikers use this trail to reach the campground, then return to the rim via the longer, less rigorous Bright Angel Trail.

Park Rangers advise that hikers avoid ascending the South Kaibab Trail during the hot summer months. The trail is steep, shadeless, and unlike the Bright Angel Trail, no drinking water is available. **DO NOT attempt to hike from the rim to the river and back in one day!** It is much farther and far more strenuous than it looks from above, and many hikers who attempt the trip become seriously ill due to heat, exhaustion, and dehydration.

Since this is a ridgetop trail, a continuum of tremendous vistas unfold with every step of the way, from the rim to the river. Interpretive signs along the trail offer insights into Grand Canyon geology.

Mule trains returning from Phantom Ranch use the trail daily. When you

SOUTH KAIBAB TRAIL TO
BRIGHT ANGEL CAMPGROUND

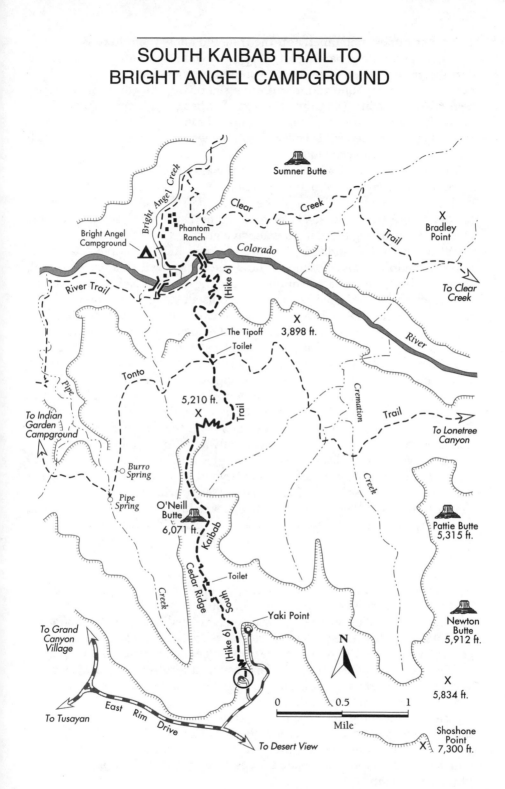

Sumner Butte

Bright Angel Creek

Clear Creek

Phantom Ranch

Bright Angel Campground

X Bradley Point

Colorado

To Clear Creek

River Trail

(Hike 6)

The Tipoff

Toilet

X 3,898 ft.

River

Tonto

Pipe

5,210 ft. X

Trail

Cremation

Trail

To Lonetree Canyon

To Indian Garden Campground

Creek

Burro Spring

Pipe Spring

O'Neill Butte 6,071 ft.

Kaibab

Pattie Butte 5,315 ft.

Cedar Ridge

Toilet

Creek

South

(Hike 6)

Yaki Point

Newton Butte 5,912 ft.

To Grand Canyon Village

N

X 5,834 ft.

To Tusayan

East Rim Drive

To Desert View

0   0.5   1

Mile

Shoshone Point 7,300 ft. X

encounter mules, step quietly off the trail and allow them to pass.

From the trailhead parking lot, follow the wide trail north past the mule corrals for several yards to the pinyon and juniper-clad South Rim. Here, next to a pay telephone and interpretive signboard, the South Kaibab Trail begins its plunge into the Grand Canyon. A series of wide switchbacks leads down through the gray cliff band of Kaibab limestone at a moderate grade. In winter, when the trail is covered with snow or ice, the wide trail is still reasonably safe and easy to follow.

At the foot of the Kaibab cliff, you traverse north upon the steep red slopes of the Toroweap formation. Here pinyons and junipers reappear, along with an occasional Douglas-fir in sheltered recesses. Pipe Creek canyon lies far below the trail, and shady alcoves at the canyon's head also support Douglas-fir, growing there in an extensive grove.

Where the trail rounds the shoulder of Cedar Ridge, you reach the sparkling Coconino sandstone, then follow the rocky trail steadily downhill, switching back from one side of the ridge to the other. O'Neill Butte, capped by a block of red Esplanade sandstone, looms ahead as you stroll down the red slopes of Hermit shale to the broad, pinyon- and juniper-studded platform of Cedar Ridge at 6,550 feet, pass the solar dehydrating toilets, and reach the dramatic vista point, the goal of most day hikers on the trail.

A boot-worn trail leads 300 yards northwest to the point of the ridge, which affords even broader panoramas. Pipe Creek canyon lies far below to the west, and one can visually trace the course of the Tonto Trail as it traverses that creek's basin en route to Indian Garden. The Devil's Corkscrew on the Bright Angel Trail is visible as it descends from the hanging valley of Garden Creek into the dark Vishnu schist hallway of lower Pipe Creek.

The broad, blackbrush-studded basin of Cremation Creek spreads out below to the east of your vantage. Far beyond rises the barrier wall of the Palisades of the Desert, and Desert View Watchtower can be seen capping the eastern end of the South Rim. The forest-fringed North Rim backdrops your Canyon vista, and to the northeast, the erosion-isolated mesa of Wotans Throne and the slender spire of Vishnu Temple rise in bold relief.

A pair of switchbacks on the South Kaibab Trail lead you on a steady descent from Cedar Ridge for 0.4 mile down to O'Neill Butte saddle, another good destination for a day hike. Beyond the saddle the grade steepens as the trail traverses the boulder-strewn Supai slopes, first east, then north of O'Neill Butte. The pinyon-juniper woodland steadily diminishes and fades out entirely by the time you crest a ridge, where the grade abates. The now-gentle trail leads north along the narrow ridgeline en route to the break in the Redwall limestone cliff below. The scattered shrubs of cliffrose, mormon tea, four-wing saltbush, yucca, and clumps of bunchgrass comprise the sparse groundcover on this open ridge.

After reaching the northern point of the ridge at 5,200 feet, 3 miles from the trailhead, you abruptly descend via switchbacks toward the rocky notch below. En route a memorable view of the Colorado River unfolds, beyond which lie the cottonwood-shaded oases of Bright Angel Campground and Phantom Ranch.

The switchbacks of the South Kaibab Trail as it passes through the Coconino sandstone en route to Cedar Ridge.

After reaching the rocky notch, a series of steep switchbacks plunge through the break in the Redwall limestone. As you approach the foot of the 500-foot descent, the trail cuts through a purple outcrop of Temple Butte limestone, then you emerge onto the broken cliffs of the Muav limestone, where a descending traverse begins. This traverse leads steadily downhill, dropping another 500 feet en route to the Tonto Trail junction, along the western flanks of Cremation Creek's broad desert basin.

As the wide trail approaches the brushy expanse of the Tonto Platform, the painfully obvious Tipoff toilet building comes into view, the solar panels on its roof glistening in the sun. When you reach the interpretive sign at the Muav limestone/Bright Angel shale interface, look upward to the crest of the limestone ridge to the southwest. There you will see a rare natural arch in the Redwall limestone.

The grade abates at 4,000 feet on the blackbrush flats of the Tonto Platform, and soon you pass the signed westbound Tonto Trail, then within moments meet the eastbound Tonto Trail (which affords access to the toilet), leading to Cremation, Grapevine, and Cottonwood creeks (see Hike 14). Proceed straight ahead on the wide South Kaibab Trail to The Tipoff—the rim of the inner gorge. An emergency telephone is located a few yards east of the trail here.

The trail ahead follows the steepest and greatest sustained descent yet, dropping nearly 1,600 feet in 1.7 miles to the Colorado River. Unless your legs are already sore, you will likely breeze through this segment in less than 1 hour. This exciting stretch of the trail first drops through a broken cliff of Tapeats sandstone, then traverses bright red slopes of Hakatai shale en route to a gravelly saddle littered with slabs and blocks of Tapeats sandstone. Beyond the saddle, you curve northwest down to the shoulder of a ridge where, at 3,600 feet, a fine view of the Colorado River and the twin bridges spanning its turbulent waters unfolds at Panorama Point.

The trail ahead follows a steep grade as you descend switchbacks through the variegated rock formations of the inner gorge, the Bass limestone, Brahma schist, and outcrops of granitic rocks. The Black Bridge (or Kaibab Bridge) comes into view as you clamber down to the junction with the River Trail, at 2,640 feet.

Since this bridge has a solid walkway, and mules can't see the river below them, mule trains use it to cross the river, both coming and going from Phantom Ranch. A few final switchbacks beyond the junction lead to a 50-yard-long tunnel—the portal to the bridge's south abutment. If a mule train preceded you across the bridge, you may wish to wait briefly for the bridge's swaying to subside.

Stretching 440 feet across the river, and 78 feet above the low water line, the construction of the Black Bridge in 1928 was no easy task. Notice the eight heavy, 1.5-inch steel cables that support the bridge. These 550-foot cables, weighing more than 1 ton each, were carried here on the shoulders of Havasupai Indian laborers via the South Kaibab Trail.

After you reach the north abutment of the bridge, anchored in pink

Views of Pipe Creek canyon and Granite Gorge unfold along the South Kaibab Trail. The well-worn trail to Plateau Point lies at center.

Zoroaster granite, follow the dusty trail west above the delta of Bright Angel Creek, passing trails leading to the beach, and traversing above the ruins of an Anasazi dwelling site first discovered by the Powell Expedition in 1869. At 2,460 feet, 0.4 mile from the bridge, the Bright Angel Trail joins from the left, opposite the buildings of the River Ranger Station. Drinking water, toilets, and a pay telephone can be found there.

Continue straight ahead into the mouth of Bright Angel Canyon, traversing above the vigorous, cottonwood-lined creek opposite Bright Angel Campground. After walking 0.2 mile from the last junction, you finally reach the steel bridge spanning Bright Angel Creek at the entrance to the campground, at 2,480 feet. The 32 campsites, with a capacity of 90 people, are strung out along a 250-yard spur trail above the west banks of the large creek.

Despite the somewhat congested atmosphere of the campground, it is nonetheless a beautiful site, and is an excellent location for an overnight stay whether you are here for the first time or are a trail-hardened Grand Canyon veteran. The campsites are shaded by tall, spreading Fremont cottonwoods, and thickets of willow and seep-willow afford a modicum of privacy between sites. Each site features a picnic table, pack poles, and ammo cans for food storage. Be sure to protect your food supply during your stay here, both day and night. Use the ammo cans, and hang your *empty* packs on the pack poles. Piped drinking water is provided year-round at two locations in the campground. There is a centrally located bathroom, featuring running water and flush toilets. Don't forget your swimsuit, since soaking in the creek's cool waters is a popular pastime during summer's oppressive heat.

Views are limited by the confining cliffs of granite and dark schist that embrace the campground. You can see but a short distance up Bright Angel Canyon and across the inner gorge bounded by colorful cliffs and terraces.

In contrast to the creek's ribbon of riparian greenery, the convoluted cliffs above support a sparse assemblage of desert growth only a few yards away. Engelmann prickly pear, mesquite, agave, mormon tea, and brittlebush maintain a tenuous foothold on the rocky slopes above.

Rangers offer evening interpretive programs at the Phantom Ranch amphitheater adjacent to the Phantom Ranger Station. Phantom Ranch offers a snack bar, where cold beer and "the best lemonade in the Canyon" are available.

There is much to do from a base camp at Bright Angel Campground. Leisurely activities include a soak in the cool waters of the creek, or an evening stroll down to the river. Short day hikes can be taken to the fine viewpoints along the first 1.5 miles of the Clear Creek Trail or into the tortuous gorge of The Box via the North Kaibab Trail. Ambitious hikers often make the all-day, 13-mile round-trip to Ribbon Falls via the North Kaibab Trail, located deep within Bright Angel Canyon.

To return to the South Rim, consider following the Bright Angel Trail. Whichever trail you take back to the rim, attempt to get a pre-dawn start during summer to beat the heat.

7 BRIGHT ANGEL TRAIL TO BRIGHT ANGEL CAMPGROUND

General description:	A very scenic two- to four-day backpack along Grand Canyon's most popular trail.
Distance:	18.8 miles round-trip.
Difficulty:	Strenuous.
Average hiking times:	5 to 6 hours down to the campground; 7 to 8 hours to return to the rim.
Type of trail:	Maintained; excellent condition.
Trailhead elevation:	6,820 feet.
Low point:	2,450 feet.
Elevation loss:	4,360 feet.
Water availability:	Available May through September at Mile-and-a-half Resthouse and Three Mile Resthouse; year-round at Indian Garden Campground (4.6 miles), River Ranger Station (9.2 miles), and Bright Angel Campground (9.4 miles).
Suggested cache points:	Caching water on this trail is not necessary.
Optimum seasons:	March through June; September through November.
Use Area codes:	CIG, Indian Garden, designated campground; CBG, Bright Angel, designated campground.
Management zone:	Corridor.
Topo maps:	Grand Canyon and Phantom Ranch USGS quads; Trails Illustrated Grand Canyon National Park; Earthwalk Bright Angel Trail or Grand Canyon National Park.

Key points:
- **0.0** Bright Angel trailhead.
- **1.5** Mile-and-a-half Resthouse.
- **3.0** Three Mile Resthouse.
- **4.6** Indian Garden Campground and junction with westbound Tonto Trail.
- **4.9** Junction with eastbound Tonto Trail; stay left.
- **7.8** River Resthouse.
- **9.0** Silver Bridge spanning the Colorado River.
- **9.2** River Ranger Station.
- **9.4** Bridge at the entrance to Bright Angel Campground; turn left.

Best day hike destinations: This is the most heavily used trail in the Park, and each day countless hikers follow the trail as far as their time and energy allow. Various destinations on this trail offer something for every hiker.

Mile-and-a-half Resthouse is a good turnaround point for first-time Grand Canyon hikers. Three Mile Resthouse affords fine canyon views. Indian Garden offers drinking water and picnic tables in the shade of tall, spreading cottonwoods. The 12.2-mile round-trip to Plateau Point will appeal to strong day hikers. The point affords excellent views of the Colorado River in Upper Granite Gorge.

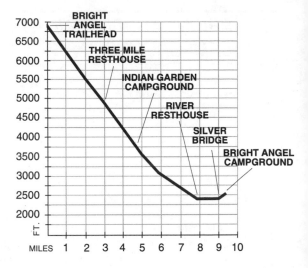

Finding the trailhead: The Bright Angel Trail begins just west of Bright Angel Lodge on the South Rim at the West Rim Drive interchange. No parking is available at the trailhead. Hikers must park at either the public parking lot adjacent to Maswik Lodge, 0.2 mile south of Bright Angel Lodge, or park in one of the large parking areas south of the railroad tracks between Bright Angel Lodge and the train depot.

To reach the Bright Angel Lodge area and the West Rim Dr. interchange, follow the Village Loop Road, which begins at the Arizona Highway 64/East Rim Drive intersection, for 2.75 miles to a Y junction in Grand Canyon Village. Bear right at that junction onto a one-way road, prominently signed for El Tovar and Bright Angel Lodge. Follow the road past the train depot and hotel complex for another 0.6 mile to the West Rim Dr. interchange. Here you turn left (south) to reach the public parking areas within another 0.2 mile.

The hike: The Bright Angel Trail is not only the most popular trail in the Park, it is also one of the most beautiful. From the pinyon-juniper woodlands near the rim to parched desert flats, well-watered oases rich with canyon wild grape and cottonwood groves, spectacular narrows, perennial steams, deep gorges, and a memorable walk along the river, this trail combines some of the Grand Canyon's finest scenery.

Although the number of backpackers using the trail is strictly regulated through the permit system, expect the company of innumerable day hikers on the trail at least as far as Indian Garden.

Rather than making the hike back to the rim from Bright Angel Campground in one long, strenuous day, consider spending the night en route at Indian Garden Campground at the halfway point between the rim and the river.

Mule trains use this trail each day to descend into the Canyon en route to Plateau Point and Phantom Ranch. As a result of this heavy downhill traffic, the trail is rougher than the South Kaibab Trail and the tread has developed a corrugated surface.

The trail begins immediately north of the West Rim interchange, a short

BRIGHT ANGEL TRAIL TO BRIGHT ANGEL CAMPGROUND

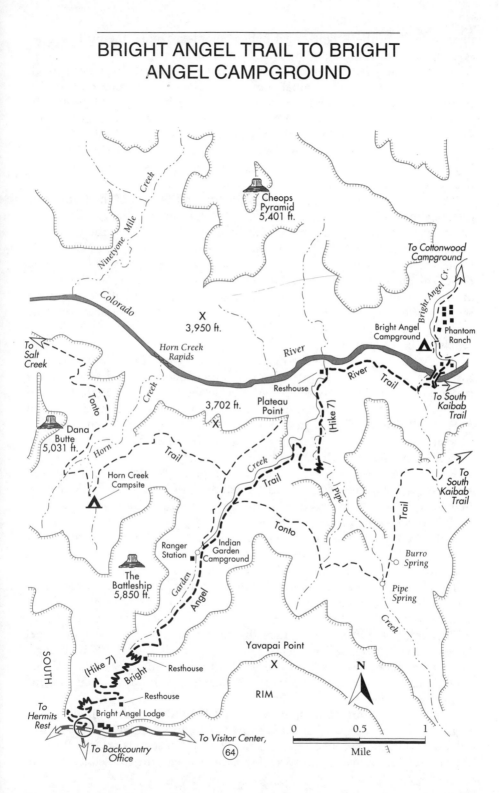

Cheops
Pyramid
5,401 ft.

To Cottonwood
Campground

Ninetyone Mile Creek

Colorado

X
3,950 ft.

Horn Creek
Rapids

River

Bright Angel Cr.

Bright Angel
Campground

Phantom
Ranch

To Salt
Creek

Tonto

Creek

Resthouse

River   Trail

To South
Kaibab
Trail

Dana
Butte
5,031 ft.

Horn

Trail

3,702 ft.

X

Plateau
Point

(Hike 7)

Creek

Trail

Pipe

To
South
Kaibab
Trail

Horn Creek
Campsite

Tonto

Trail

Ranger
Station

Indian
Garden
Campground

Burro
Spring

The
Battleship
5,850 ft.

Garden

Angel

Pipe
Spring

Creek

Yavapai Point

SOUTH

(Hike 7)

Bright

Resthouse

X

N

RIM

Resthouse

Bright Angel Lodge

To
Hermits
Rest

To Backcountry
Office

To Visitor Center,
(64)

0   0.5   1

Mile

113

distance west of the Bright Angel Lodge complex. Follow the trail as it descends below the rim, avoiding two right-branching spurs of the Rim Trail within the first several yards. Beyond the first switchback, you pass through a tunnel carved into the Kaibab limestone. Look for a pictograph panel, believed to be of Havasupai origin, just above the trail beyond the tunnel.

Although the Bright Angel Trail follows a canyon route, excellent views are nevertheless enjoyed from the beginning. Far below lies Indian Garden, an oasis surrounded by the blackbrush flats of the Tonto Platform. The Plateau Point Trail, nearly as wide as a road, appears as a white scar across the Tonto Platform, beyond Indian Garden.

The Bright Angel Fault, a prominent feature in this part of the Canyon, is one of many faults in the Grand Canyon that have altered the generally flat-lying layers of sedimentary rock. It stretches northeast from the Coconino Plateau to the Kaibab Plateau. Garden Creek below you and the distant trough of Bright Angel Canyon were eroded along this zone of shattered rock. The cliffs that bound the headwaters amphitheater of Garden Creek are noticeably offset by movement along the fault. The cliffs to the west were uplifted nearly 200 feet relative to the cliffs east of the canyon. The resulting break in the cliff bands has been used by humans for centuries to reach the inner Canyon.

After two long switchbacks through the Toroweap formation, you pass through a second short tunnel then reach the Coconino sandstone. Here a series of short, moderately steep switchbacks leads down through the fault-controlled break in the Coconino cliff. Garden Creek's drainage has carved a steep gully in this break, through which the trail descends among a jumble of shattered blocks. A scattering of Douglas-fir appears in the cool, shady microclimate that prevails at the base of the gully.

Beyond the switchbacks, a steadily descending traverse of steep, red Hermit shale slopes leads down to Mile-and-a-half Resthouse, tucked away in a shady recess. Seasonal drinking water, toilets, and an emergency telephone are available here.

With the bold, Esplanade-capped tower of The Battleship looming over the canyon ahead, another series of long, moderately descending switchbacks takes you through the steep red slopes and ledges of the Supai layer to Three Mile Resthouse, perched atop the Redwall limestone cliff. This resthouse offers the same amenities as the resthouse above, plus a tremendous inner Canyon vista. A path leads for several yards to an unobstructed viewpoint. From here, you can visually trace the cavernous course of Bright Angel Creek, carved seemingly arrow-straight along the line of the Bright Angel Fault, as it reaches far back toward the North Rim. An array of varicolored buttes and towers, including Sumner Butte, Cheops Pyramid, and Brahma Temple, punctuate the middle distance.

You leave the pinyon-juniper woodland behind at the resthouse, then begin a final series of switchbacks, known as Jacob's Ladder, in this lengthy, forty-switchback descent from the rim. The trail descends steeply through the fault-broken Redwall. Midway down the descent, the trail edges close to

Bright Angel Campground, shaded by spreading cottonwoods, lies alongside the cool, perennial waters of Bright Angel Creek.

a pouroff in the Redwall cliff, stained white with salts precipitated from the rock layers above.

Beyond Jacob's Ladder, the trail opens up into the increasingly broad Garden Creek basin, and you follow a moderately descending grade above the creek's usually dry course. Shortly you pass a spur trail leading to the Indian Garden Ranger Station, and soon thereafter reach the spur trail leading into Indian Garden Campground at 3,800 feet, 4.6 miles from the South Rim. Campsites here are more open than those at Bright Angel Campground, but each site features an awning for shade and a picnic table, pack poles, and ammo boxes for food storage. Toilets and piped drinking water are nearby.

Just below the campground, the Bright Angel Trail follows above the cottonwood-lined banks of Garden Creek and soon reaches a water fountain, trailside benches, and toilet. A few yards beyond these improvements, the westbound Tonto Trail branches left, heading for Plateau Point and Hermit Creek (see Hike 15).

The springs that emerge at Indian Garden watered seasonal Havasupai garden plots for centuries. When Ralph Cameron occupied the site in the early 1900s, he also maintained a garden, and he is credited with transplanting cottonwood shoots he gathered at Cottonwood Creek near Horseshoe Mesa. Those shoots have since grown into the tall, spreading trees that now provide welcome shade to heat-weary hikers.

As you continue down the Bright Angel Trail, you soon pass the pumphouse that provides water to the South Rim via the 15-mile, trans-canyon pipeline from Roaring Springs. Shortly thereafter the signed eastbound Tonto Trail branches right, but you continue the gradual descent along the course of Garden Creek. Vines of canyon wild grape spread across the canyon floor like ivy and redbud trees at the trailside cast occasional shade.

Soon, Tapeats sandstone cliffs begin to embrace the canyon, blocking views of the parched, brush-studded Tonto Platform above. The trail closely follows the east banks of Garden Creek, and the music of its waters is amplified by the low brown cliffs that bound these narrows. The creek is often hidden from view by thickets of willow and canyon wild grape. Scattered Fremont cottonwoods arch their fluttering green canopies overhead.

At length, you rock-hop the small creek twice and soon follow the creek's bend to the east. Shortly before leaving the creekside, you may be tempted into a detour by the deep, inviting pool just below, cupped in the Tapeats sandstone slickrock.

After leaving the creek, the trail leads to a minor saddle on a granite rib overlooking the narrow depths of Pipe Creek canyon. From there a moderately descending traverse leads south to a slickrock draw, then southeast to the Devil's Corkscrew. This series of switchbacks descends a moderate grade for 200 feet to the floor of Pipe Creek, usually dry at this point. Within moments you cross the creekbed opposite an old mine tunnel and soon thereafter, the pencil-thin waterfall of Columbine Spring emerges from the west wall of the canyon, its waters supporting a rich hanging garden of maidenhair fern, golden columbine, and scarlet monkeyflower.

The occasionally rocky trail follows the sinuous canyon ahead, descending gently. You cross the creekbed two more times before reaching the mouth of perennial Garden Creek, entering from a slot canyon on the left. Beyond that confluence, you continue down along the now-flowing creek, fringed by a riparian ribbon of cottonwood, willow, and seep-willow that contrast their green foliage with the somber, convoluted walls of Rama schist that rise above.

At length, after crossing the creek two more times, you reach River Resthouse (no water), a shady refuge at the mouth of Pipe Creek. Just beyond it, a spur trail branches left, quickly leading down to the Colorado River. Here, at 2,450 feet, the River Trail begins, and you follow it east, staying well above but in full view of the river. Views up and down Granite Gorge are dramatic from your vantage here in the depths of the Grand Canyon. The trail generally traverses the foot of the inner gorge's schist and granite walls, where the tread is firm. At times, though, the mildly undulating trail crosses sandy stretches that will interrupt your steady progress.

Typical of the Lower Sonoran Zone of the inner gorge are coarse desert shrubs, clinging to the rock walls and ledges wherever they can gain a foothold. Look for mormon tea, brickellbrush, soaptree yucca, brittlebush, and mesquite.

After strolling above the river for 1.1 miles, you reach the Silver Bridge spanning the Colorado River. The longer Black Bridge lies a short distance upriver. The open grate of the walkway allows you to gaze at the riffling river beneath your feet. The bridge also supports the trans-canyon water pipeline from Roaring Springs to the South Rim.

You exit the bridge and emerge onto the Bright Angel Creek delta, then amble past the Park Service mule corrals, a sewage treatment plant, toilets, piped drinking water, and a pay telephone, and finally pass between the River Ranger Station on the right and a private residence on the left. Just ahead lies the steel bridge spanning Bright Angel Creek, and beyond it you join the North Kaibab Trail and turn left.

The entrance to Bright Angel Campground is another 0.2 mile up the trail (see Hike 6 for more information about the campground).

After your stay at the campground, retrace your steps to return to the South Rim.

General description:	An extended backpack trip of four to six days deep within the Grand Canyon.
Distance:	18.4 miles round-trip from Bright Angel Campground.
Difficulty:	Strenuous.
Average hiking times:	5 hours each way from Bright Angel Campground.
Type of trail:	Unmaintained; good condition.
Trailhead elevation:	2,640 feet.
High point:	4,240 feet.
Elevation gain and loss:	+550 feet; -1,100 feet.
Water availability:	Bright Angel Campground; Clear Creek, 9.2 miles.
Suggested cache points:	The wash between Bradley and Demaray points at roughly the halfway point between Clear Creek and the North Kaibab Trail.
Optimum seasons:	March through June; September through November.
Use Area codes:	CBG, Bright Angel, designated campground; AK9, Clear Creek, at-large camping.
Management zones:	Bright Angel Campground, Corridor; Clear Creek, Threshold.
Topo maps:	Phantom Ranch USGS quad; Trails Illustrated Grand Canyon National Park; Earthwalk Grand Canyon National Park.

Key points:
- **0.0** Bright Angel Campground.
- **0.25** Phantom Ranch.
- **0.7** Clear Creek Trail junction; turn right (east).
- **1.3** First overlook.
- **1.6** Second overlook.
- **2.5** Sumner Wash.
- **6.6** Zoroaster Canyon wash.
- **9.2** Clear Creek campsites.

Best day hike destinations: Hikers taking a layover day at Bright Angel Campground will enjoy the 2.6- and 3.2-mile, round-trip hikes to the vista points on this trail high above Bright Angel Creek.

Finding the trail: The signed Clear Creek Trail branches east from the North Kaibab Trail 0.7 mile north of Bright Angel Campground and 6.4 miles southwest of

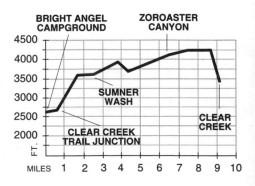

CLEAR CREEK TRAIL

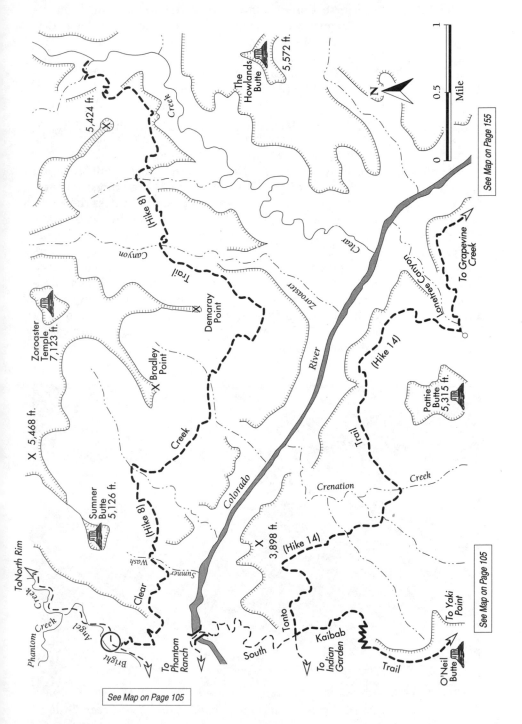

The Howlands Butte 5,572 ft.

5,424 ft. X

Creek

(Hike 8)

Canyon

Trail

Trail

Clear

Zoroaster

Zoroaster Temple 7,123 ft.

Demaray Point X

Bradley Point X

X 5,468 ft.

To Grapevine Creek

Lonetree Canyon

(Hike 14)

Pattie Butte 5,315 ft.

River

Creek

Sumner Butte 5,126 ft.

(Hike 8)

Crenation

Creek

Trail

Colorado

X 3,898 ft.

(Hike 14)

To North Rim

Wash

Sumner

Clear

Phantom Creek

Angel

Bright

Creek

To Phantom Ranch

South

Tonto

Kaibab

To Indian Garden

O'Neil Butte

Trail

To Yaki Point

N

0.5   1
Mile
0

See Map on Page 155

See Map on Page 105

See Map on Page 105

(below) Cottonwood Campground.

The hike: The Clear Creek Trail, built by the Civilian Conservation Corps in the 1930s, is the North Rim's counterpart to the Tonto Trail. From its beginning at Bright Angel Creek above Phantom Ranch, this long, dry, shadeless trail affords memorable Grand Canyon panoramas from its serpentine, undulating course on the Tonto Platform. Since this is a constructed trail, unlike much of the Tonto Trail that evolved through ages of use, the Clear Creek Trail is well-defined and easy to follow.

At the trail's end lies perennial Clear Creek and several fine cottonwood-shaded campsites set in the canyon's dark-walled gorge. Among the attractions of this trail are cross-country side trips upcanyon to Cheyava Falls, Grand Canyon's highest, and downcanyon to the Colorado River.

The most direct access to this trail is via the South Kaibab Trail. Since you must follow the waterless Clear Creek Trail east from its beginning for nearly 2 miles before you can legally establish a camp, most hikers pass their first night at Bright Angel Campground, then tackle this trail on the second day. Carry plenty of water for the long trek to Clear Creek—the only reliable water on the trail. Clear Creek is a fascinating, off-the-beaten-track destination that deserves several days of exploration—plan your trip accordingly.

From Bright Angel Campground, follow the North Kaibab Trail past Phantom Ranch into the increasingly narrow gorge of Bright Angel Canyon. After 0.7 mile you reach the signed Clear Creek Trail at 2,650 feet, branching right (east) at the mouth of the first minor side drainage. Follow the steadily ascending, moderately steep Clear Creek Trail over slopes hosting a scatter-

Dramatic views from the Tonto Platform unfold along the Clear Creek Trail.

ing of mormon tea, brittlebush, mesquite, tall Engelmann prickly pear, and beavertail cactus.

Views begin to expand with every step on the trail, stretching down the narrow confines of Bright Angel Canyon, past cottonwood-sheltered Phantom Ranch to the fluted gray walls of Granite Gorge and beyond to the cliffs and terraces that stair-step up to the South Rim.

The grade moderates when you crest a saddle at 2,950 feet, where even broader Canyon views open up. Then the trail leads steadily up to a switchback at Phantom Overlook (3,080 feet), perched on the canyon wall 550 feet directly above the ranch. Two steep switchbacks follow beyond the overlook, leading to the foot of the dark brown Tapeats sandstone cliffs. An eastbound traverse ensues, following the scalloped topography of the cliff band. You duck into alcoves and round several points, enjoying dramatic views with every step.

Since the trail hugs the rim of Granite Gorge, with cliffs plunging 1,000 feet from the trail to the Colorado River below, views both up and down the gorge are tremendous, including glimpses of the twin bridges spanning the river, the switchbacks of the South Kaibab Trail, and the River Trail, carved into the walls of the gorge. Once you reach the easternmost point, above Sumner Wash, pause to enjoy your final view of the river, then follow the trail north into the rocky draw ahead. Sumner Butte's gray Redwall battlements loom 1,500 feet above to the north. In the northeast the towering spire of Zoroaster Temple pierces the sky.

Soon you cross two minor, rocky drainages, then curve east and cross larger Sumner Wash over its floor of Tapeats sandstone, at 3,650 feet. Beyond this wash you enter the Clear Creek Use Area (AK9) and are free to camp where you wish. About 300 yards beyond the wash, the trail curves into a minor drainage. Two spartan campsites flank both sides. The trail ahead leads gradually uphill onto the Tonto Platform, a classic desert expanse studded with blackbrush, yucca, and mormon tea. Clumps of mesquite cling to the flanks of the draws that bisect the platform. The Clear Creek Trail involves many ups and downs ahead, but it takes a more direct route across the Tonto Platform than its meandering counterpart on the south side of the river.

After 1 mile from Sumner Wash, you reach a larger wash, draining the immense Redwall limestone amphitheater beneath towering Zoroaster Temple. Waterpockets in the Tapeats sandstone slickrock of the wash are your only source of water—if recent rainfall has filled them—between Bright Angel and Clear creeks. You pass a good campsite before bending northeast into the main branch of the drainage, then begin a steadily rising traverse skirting first Bradley Point, then Demaray Point. The broad panorama enjoyed from the trail encompasses much of the eastern Grand Canyon, providing one of the most expansive scenes of terraces, buttes, and cliffs obtained from any Grand Canyon trail.

At the shoulder of the ridge south of Demaray Point, 4.7 miles from the North Kaibab Trail, the trail begins a northeast course high above the dark

Hikers enjoy fine views of the Colorado River and the Bright Angel delta from the Clear Creek Trail.

Vishnu gorge of Zoroaster Canyon. As the trail gradually rises ahead, the immense amphitheaters and canyons of the large Clear Creek drainage opens up to your view, reaching far back toward the North Rim. You cross the dry wash of Zoroaster Canyon at 4,080 feet in the shadow of 7,123-foot Zoroaster Temple, then ascend steadily to the 4,200-foot ridge above.

Slowly, by increments, the trail leads closer to the rim of Clear Creek's gorge, undulating eastward until it finally curves north beneath a soaring Redwall butte. Here the trail reaches its highest point at 4,240 feet, and the floor of Clear Creek finally comes into view, its cool inviting waters luring you onward. The northbound traverse soon ends on the flanks of the shallow draw ahead, from where you begin a steep descent over red slopes of Hakatai shale, dropping 550 feet in a 0.5 mile into the cliff-rimmed tributary canyon below. Upon reaching the canyon floor, the trail swings southeast, mounts a minor rise, and finally ends alongside Clear Creek, a vigorous perennial stream. Scattered Fremont cottonwoods cast their shade over the good campsites here and a solar-dehydrating toilet lies nearby. (Note: Camping is not allowed downstream from the first major side canyon entering from the east, about 0.6 mile below the toilet).

Although the constructed trail ends here, there are side trip opportunities to keep you busy for several days. Most popular is the long, 10-mile round-trip down Clear Creek to the Colorado River. This trailless route follows the serpentine gorge, more than 1,000 feet deep in places, through one of the most spectacular stretches of Vishnu narrows in the Park. The route requires much boulder-hopping and wading, and you must downclimb a 15-foot slickrock pouroff 350 yards before reaching the river.

If time allows, don't miss the off-trail side trip to Cheyava Falls. Emerging from a Redwall limestone cave high on the east wall of Clear Creek, Cheyava free-falls for several hundred feet, making it Grand Canyon's highest waterfall. Unless the fall has been recharged in spring from the meltwater of a good snow year, Cheyava may be only a wet streak on the canyon wall.

From the toilet at the trail's end, you can reach the fall by boulder-hopping and bushwhacking your way up Clear Creek canyon. The creek will likely dry up about 0.5 mile up-canyon, so carry plenty of water—this is an all-day, 8-mile round-trip. For the first half of the hike, you travel through the varicolored rock layers of the Grand Canyon Supergroup, first the Hakatai shale, then the Shinumo quartzite, and finally the Dox sandstone. En route two major side canyons open up to the north; stay right at each juncture. Finally, you wind your way beyond the Tapeats sandstone's low brown cliffs, and as you approach the upper limit of the Bright Angel shale north of the red butte of Thor Temple, and just beneath the towering cliffs that plunge off the forested North Rim, you gain a good view of the falls, more than 1,000 feet above on the east wall of the canyon.

After enjoying this beautiful canyon, return the way you came.

9 HERMIT TRAIL

General description:	A backpack of three or more days, surveying a deep tributary canyon below the western reaches of the South Rim.
Distance:	15.2 miles round-trip to Hermit Creek campsite; about 18 miles round-trip to Hermit Rapids.
Difficulty:	Strenuous.
Average hiking times:	5 to 6 hours to Hermit Creek campsite and about another hour to Hermit Rapids; 7 to 8 hours to return to the rim.
Type of trail:	Unmaintained; generally good condition.
Trailhead elevation:	6,640 feet.
Low point:	2,840 feet at Hermit Creek campsite; 2,350 feet at Hermit Rapids.
Elevation loss:	3,800 feet to Hermit Creek campsite; 4,290 feet to Hermit Rapids.
Water availability:	Santa Maria Spring at 2.25 miles offers a trickling seep; Hermit Creek is perennial from the campsite to the river; the Colorado River.
Suggested cache points:	Hermit Basin; near Lookout Point on the Supai traverse; near Cathedral Stairs at the top of the Redwall.
Optimum seasons:	March through June; September through November.
Use Area codes:	BM7, Hermit Creek, designated campsite; BM8, Hermit Rapids, designated campsite.
Management zone:	Threshold.
Topo maps:	Grand Canyon USGS quad; Trails Illustrated Grand Canyon National Park; Earthwalk Grand Canyon National Park.

Key points:
- **0.0** Hermits Rest trailhead parking area.
- **1.5** Junction with Waldron Trail; stay right.
- **1.75** Junction with Dripping Spring Trail; bear right.
- **2.25** Santa Maria Spring.
- **6.4** Junction with eastbound Tonto Trail; bear left.
- **7.2** Junction with trail to Hermit Rapids; bear left to reach Hermit Creek campsite.
- **7.6** Hermit Creek campsite.
- **9.0** Hermit Rapids (via Hermit Creek campsite).
- **8.7** Hermit Rapids (via trail cited above).

Best day hike destinations: The 3.5-mile round-trip into the pinyon-juniper woodlands of Hermit Basin is a fine half-day trip below the South Rim. The 4.5-mile round-trip to the resthouse at Santa Maria Spring offers a good introduction to Grand Canyon hiking, in addition to dramatic views into Hermit Creek canyon.

Finding the trailhead: From late May through September, West Rim Drive is closed to private vehicles. During this time, a free shuttle bus offers access to Hermits Rest every 15 minutes from 7:30 a.m. to sunset each day. You can board the brown and white buses at the West Rim Drive interchange.

To find Hermits Rest when West Rim Drive is open, follow driving directions for Hike 7 to the West Rim Drive interchange, then proceed straight ahead on West Rim Dr. for 7 miles to the loop at the end of the pavement at Hermits Rest. A sign here points to Hermit Trail parking; follow the dirt spur road for another 0.2 mile down to the trailhead. Drinking water, toilets, garbage collection, a pay telephone, pop machine, snack bar, and curio shop are available at Hermits Rest.

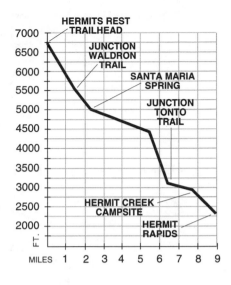

The hike: The scenic Hermit Trail is the usual next step for hikers who have already completed the Bright Angel and South Kaibab trails. Although this trail was abandoned in 1931 and the tread is generally rougher than the groomed Corridor trails, it remains easy to follow, with the exception of several rockslides on the Supai traverse.

This fine trip follows a trail constructed by the Santa Fe Railroad in 1912 and leads to pleasant Hermit Creek campsite located below the ruins of the railroad's tourist camp alongside the perennial waters of Hermit Creek. A route that follows remnants of a constructed trail leads downcanyon to the beach camp at the Colorado River next to the foaming waves of Hermit Rapids.

Since no camping is allowed above Hermit Creek campsite, you must hike out in one long day. Some hikers cache water near the top of the Redwall or in Hermit Basin for the hike out.

The abrupt cliffs of the South Rim have been softened by time below Hermits Rest, and the Hermit Trail takes advantage of this break, as it descends a moderate yet rocky grade through pinyon-juniper woodlands below the road's end. After dropping into a shallow draw, the trail switchbacks briefly through the Kaibab limestone, then begins a southbound traverse over red and gray Toroweap formation slopes. Pinyon and juniper are joined on the trailside slopes by a shrub cover of cliffrose, littleleaf mountain mahogany, and sagebrush. Exciting views begin to unfold here, reaching across the gaping red abyss of Hermit Creek canyon to the soaring cliffs that bound the wooded hanging valley of Hermit Basin.

The traverse ends upon reaching the sparkling sandstone of the broken

HERMIT TRAIL

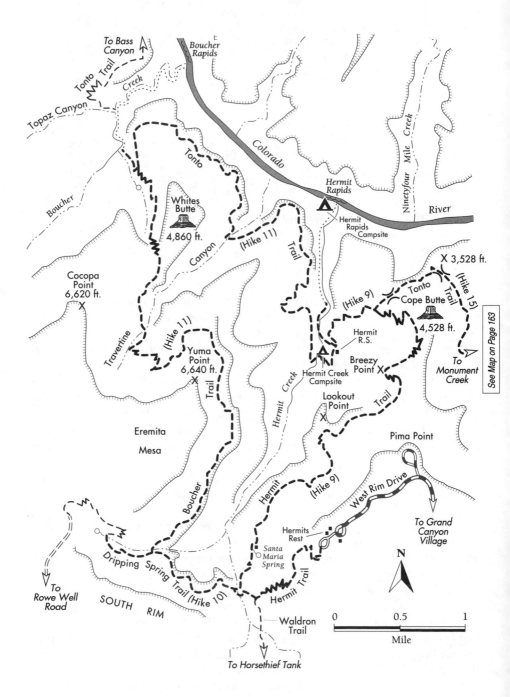

To Bass
Canyon

Boucher
Rapids

Tonto Canyon Trail

Tonto

Creek

Colorado

Boucher

Tonto

Hermit
Rapids

River

Whites
Butte
4,860 ft.

Canyon

(Hike 11)

Trail

Hermit
Rapids
Campsite

Ninetyfour Mile Creek

Cocopa
Point
6,620 ft.
X

X 3,528 ft.

(Hike 11)

Travertine

Tonto
Cope Butte
4,528 ft.

(Hike 15)

Trail

(Hike 9)

Yuma
Point
6,640 ft.
X

Trail

Hermit
R.S.

Breezy
Point X

To
Monument
Creek

Eremita

Mesa

Hermit Creek
Campsite

Hermit Creek

Lookout
Point
X

Trail

Pima Point

Boucher

Hermit

(Hike 9)

West Rim Drive

To
Rowe Well
Road

Dripping Spring Trail (Hike 10)

Santa
Maria
Spring

Hermits
Rest

Hermit Trail

To Grand
Canyon
Village

SOUTH RIM

Waldron
Trail

N

To Horsethief Tank

0   0.5   1
Mile

See Map on Page 163

126

Exciting views of Granite Gorge from the head of the Cathedral Stairs on the Hermit Trail.

Coconino cliff, and switchbacks ensue, leading steadily downhill over ledges and slabs. Reminiscent of the Grandview Trail, steeper pitches are paved with cobbles, allowing the tread to withstand the ravages of erosion. Keep an eye out for fossil reptile tracks on trailside slabs; they are more obvious here than along any other Canyon trail. Mats of scrub live oak join various other shrubs here. Along with abundant pinyon and juniper, the woodland of shrubs and small trees forms a drab green veneer that engulfs Hermit Basin and obscures much of the Canyon's upper rock layers, lending a softer appearance to the landscape.

After emerging onto the red slopes of Hermit shale that flank Hermit Basin, the trail begins a straightforward, steep, and rocky descent past the signed junction with the seldom-used Waldron Trail at 5,400 feet. Finally the grade moderates in the wash on the basin floor. At the junction here at 5,200 feet, you turn right. The trail ahead continues west to the Boucher Trail (Hike 11) and Dripping Spring (Hike 10).

From the junction, a brief series of short switchbacks lead down to the crossing of the dry wash, where the trail is funneled between two slickrock pouroffs. This marks the beginning of a 3-mile Supai traverse of steep slopes and ledges. Although the cavernous gulf of Hermit Creek canyon lies directly below the trail, the roundabout nature of the trail involves about three more hours of walking before you reach the canyon floor.

The trail ahead descends 250 feet in 0.5 mile, with the aid of a few switchbacks, to the Santa Maria Spring resthouse. This long, roofed shelter, draped by an arbor of canyon wild grape, offers a welcome refuge from the sun, particularly on the hike out. The spring, however, is a mere trickle. It offers enough water for a drink, but filling a bottle requires a long-term commitment.

Beyond the spring the traverse continues among pinyons and an array of shrubs, including scrub live oak, mock orange, fragrant ash, and single-leaf ash. The absence of junipers on the west-facing slopes here suggests a relatively cool, sheltered microclimate unfavorable to those trees.

About 0.8 mile from the spring, the trail bends east into two boulder-choked chutes that will briefly hamper your steady progress. Beyond the chutes, the trail descends abruptly via switchbacks, dropping 400 feet down to the Lookout Point ridge. A 0.4-mile traverse beyond the point leads to the greatest obstacle of all on this trail—a 0.5-mile traverse through the rocky jumble of slide debris. Boulder-hopping and the use of hands to maintain balance is necessary along this slow, rough segment. Keep an eye out for cairns; the route is sometimes obscure.

Once beyond that obstacle, you curve around Breezy Point and soon reach the top of the Redwall descent, where you can enjoy well-earned views of the Colorado River deep in Granite Gorge and of a colorful array of buttes and terraces stair-stepping up to the North Rim. The trail abruptly descends a pair of chutes through the Redwall limestone via the Cathedral Stairs. Steep at times, the gravelly trail drops in a series of short, tight switchbacks. Good views en route stretch up to the North Rim, and the river appears from time to time through the rocky notch south of Cope Butte.

Upon reaching the boulder-stacked alcove at the foot of the Redwall, the trail begins a long, steeply descending traverse beneath the Redwall crag of Cope Butte. The trail then descends steeply, via switchbacks, over boulder-studded slopes to the junction with the eastbound Tonto Trail (see Hike 15).

Bear left at the junction and descend the moderate grade across the Tonto Platform among its typical blackbrush and mormon tea shrub cover. The trail descends 200 feet in 0.8 mile to a junction signed for Hermit Rapids. That trail descends 0.2 mile into Hermit Creek and then follows the wash for 1.3 miles to the Colorado River. The left fork, signed for Hermit Creek, traverses southwest along the rim of Tapeats sandstone, passes the seldom-occupied Hermit Ranger Station, then curves into a draw below the stone-walled ruins of the Santa Fe Railroad's Hermit Camp, a tourist base camp that operated from 1913 to 1931.

After you exit the draw, a few final switchbacks lower you to a mesquite-studded bench, set against a low wall of Tapeats sandstone, where you find Hermit Creek campsite at 2,880 feet. This pleasant site offers a good base camp for explorations down Hermit Creek to the river and upcanyon into the Redwall narrows. Excellent views reach back to the soaring Redwall cliffs that embrace Hermit's cavernous defile and stretch above to the wooded fringe of Eremita Mesa and Yuma Point. The deep pool in Hermit Creek just below the campsite was a major attraction prior to the August 1996 flood

Camping on the beach at Hermit Rapids.

that washed it away.

The Tonto Trail continues from the camp up the west wall of the canyon, bound for Boucher Creek (see Hike 11). A point between Hermit Creek and Travertine Canyon, 2 miles via the Tonto Trail from camp, affords memorable views of the river in Granite Gorge.

To reach Hermit Rapids from the campsite, follow a well-worn, steep path along the east bank of the creek, into the Tapeats sandstone narrows below. After 250 yards you meet the constructed trail descending from the junction on the Tonto Platform above. Proceed downcanyon through the narrows, at first following remnants of constructed trail on ledges west of the creek, and farther on, segments of a boot-worn path. Don't become alarmed if you lose the trail; simply follow the canyon downstream. The Tapeats narrows end where the broken black walls of Vishnu schist outcrop. This part of the canyon is still narrow but much less confined. Beautiful exposures of sparkling mica schist may catch your eye along the way.

You meander back and forth across the stream, its banks lined with a ribbon of seep-willow and saw grass. After following serpentine Hermit Creek for 1.4 miles from the camp, you emerge onto the sandy, boulder-strewn beach just upstream from Hermit Rapids at 2,350 feet. Several excellent campsites, fringed by tamarisk and seep-willow, lie next to the mouth of Hermit Creek. The rocky beach alongside the rapids offer good, but open, camping areas—if you don't mind the thundering roar of the river.

From Hermit Creek, you must retrace your steps to the trailhead.

10   HERMITS REST TO DRIPPING SPRING

General description:	A rewarding day hike below the South Rim leading to an aptly-named spring.
Distance:	6.5 miles round-trip.
Difficulty:	Moderate.
Average hiking time:	4 to 5 hours round-trip.
Type of trail:	Unmaintained; generally good condition.
Trailhead elevation:	6,640 feet.
Low point:	5,150 feet.
Elevation gain and loss:	+400 feet; -1,600 feet.
Water availability:	Dripping Spring (must be treated before drinking).
Optimum season:	March through November.
Use Area codes:	No camping is permitted.
Topo maps:	Grand Canyon USGS quad; Trails Illustrated Grand Canyon National Park; Earthwalk Grand Canyon National Park.

See Map on Page 126

Key points:

0.0   Hermits Rest trailhead parking area.

1.5   Junction with Waldron Trail; stay right.

1.75   Junction of Hermit and Dripping Spring trails; bear left.

2.75   Junction with northbound Boucher Trail; stay left.

3.25   Dripping Spring.

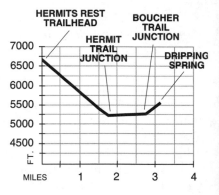

Finding the trailhead: Follow driving directions for Hike 9.

The hike: The hike to Dripping Spring via the Hermit Trail is one of the best day trips on the South Rim. The trail offers a good introduction to the nature of Grand Canyon trails, as well as dramatic vistas, and ends at an unusual spring, where water rains from the roof of an alcove at the base of the Coconino sandstone. Hikers should carry ample water for the round-trip, since Dripping Spring must be treated before drinking.

There are two alternative ways to reach the spring: via the Waldron Trail and via Louis Boucher's original Dripping Spring Trail. Those trails can be reached by following a confusing network of Park roads west from the Rowe Well picnic area, but they are seldom used. Finding the trailheads takes map reading skills, as well as driving skills on exceedingly rough and rocky four-wheel-drive roads. Contact the Backcountry Reservations Office for directions if you are determined to use one of those trails.

From the Hermits Rest trailhead parking area, follow the Hermit Trail (see Hike 9), descending 1,450 feet in 1.75 miles and about 1 hour to Hermit Basin. From the signed junction, bear left toward Dripping Spring and the Boucher Trail. The following mile of trail is an exciting stretch that undulates along the steep slopes of the red Hermit shale. The trail is, by necessity, funneled between the sheer, 1,200-foot Kaibab-Toroweap-Coconino cliffs above and the 800-foot Supai cliffs below.

With minor undulations, the trail curves into two prominent, shadowed amphitheaters that host a rich woodland of tall, spreading shrubs and small trees, such as pale hoptree, Utah serviceberry, alder-leaf mountain mahogany, Fremont barberry, mock orange, squaw currant, and single-leaf ash.

The Supai cliffs at the trail's edge plummet into the narrows of upper Hermit Creek canyon far below, lying in the near-perpetual shade of towering Redwall cliffs. The North Rim, cool and forested, rises in the distance behind innumerable buttes, towers, and terraces.

At length you enter the wooded lower reaches of the Dripping Spring draw, where you meet the northbound Boucher Trail (see Hike 11). Bear left at the junction and begin a moderate ascent west up the draw through an open woodland of pinyon, juniper, cliffrose, scrub live oak, fragrant ash, apache plume, and other shrubs. The draw ahead appears to dead-end in an amphitheater embraced by bulging, cross-bedded walls of Coconino sandstone, stained with veils of brown desert varnish. Soon you reach the head of the amphitheater, then curve into its sheltered alcove. Here, beneath the overhanging sandstone walls, you find Dripping Spring.

True to its name, the spring rains from the roof of the alcove, decorated with clumps of maidenhair fern, into a small, rock-framed pool fringed by the nodding blooms of scarlet monkeyflower. Other seeps, also fringed with ferns, emerge from the walls of the alcove, a few feet above the Coconino sandstone/Hermit shale contact zone. Ample shade is cast by the alcove's overhanging walls and by the thickets of shrubs and netleaf hackberry trees that surround it. Coconino cliffs rise 300 to 400 feet above this peaceful locale, where you will likely enjoy the aerial acrobatics of white-throated swifts and violet-green swallows, and perhaps hear the melancholy song of a canyon wren.

Louis Boucher maintained a tent camp and corrals on the bench below the spring from the 1890s to about 1912. Nature has since reclaimed the site, and now the bench hosts the spreading foliage of netleaf hackberry and redbud trees. (No camping is allowed here or elsewhere along the trail). Boucher's original trail continues east through the alcove beyond Dripping Spring, then ascends 800 feet in 1.25 miles to the remote trailhead atop the South Rim.

From Dripping Spring, return the way you came.

The Dripping Spring Trail traverses above the Redwall gorge of Hermit Creek Canyon.

11 BOUCHER CREEK TO HERMIT CREEK LOOP, VIA BOUCHER AND HERMIT TRAILS

General description:	A demanding loop trip of three [See Map on Page 126] to four days, tracing one of the most difficult South Rim trails.
Distance:	20.9 miles.
Difficulty:	Very strenuous.
Average hiking times:	7 hours to Boucher Creek; 3 to 4 hours to Hermit Creek campsite; 7 hours to return to the rim.
Type of trails:	Unmaintained; parts of Boucher Trail in poor condition; other trails in fair to good condition.
Trailhead elevation:	6,640 feet.
Low point:	2,800 feet at Boucher Creek; 2,330 feet at Boucher Rapids.
Elevation gain and loss:	4,550 feet.
Water availability:	Boucher Creek, 8.5 miles; Hermit Creek, 13.3 miles; the Colorado River at Boucher and Hermit rapids; Santa Maria Spring, which provides a trickling seep.
Suggested cache points:	Hermit Basin near the junction of the Hermit and Dripping Spring trails.
Optimum seasons:	March through June; September through November.
Use Area codes:	BN9, Boucher, at-large camping; BM7, Hermit Creek, designated campsite; BM8, Hermit Rapids, designated campsite.
Management zones:	Boucher, Primitive; Hermit, Threshold.
Topo maps:	Grand Canyon USGS quad; Trails Illustrated Grand Canyon National Park; Earthwalk Grand Canyon National Park.

Key points:

0.0	Hermits Rest trailhead parking area.
1.5	Junction with Waldron Trail; stay right.
1.75	Junction of Hermit and Dripping Spring trails; bear left.
2.75	Junction with Boucher Trail; turn right.
5.0	Overlook below Yuma Point.
6.3	Cross dry wash of Travertine Canyon.
7.0	Whites Butte saddle.
8.2	Junction with eastbound Tonto Trail; bear left.
8.5	Campsites at Boucher Creek.
8.8	Return to junction with eastbound Tonto Trail; turn left (north).
10.9	Cross dry wash of lower Travertine Canyon.
13.3	Hermit Creek campsite.
14.5	Junction with eastbound Tonto Trail; bear right.
18.7	Santa Maria Spring
19.2	Junction with Dripping Spring Trail; bear left.
19.4	Junction with Waldron Trail; bear left.
20.9	Hermits Rest trailhead parking area.

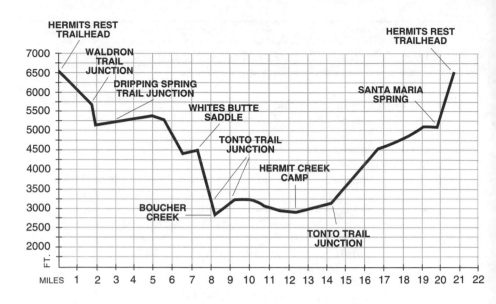

Best day hike destination: The 10-mile round-trip to the overlook below Yuma Point on the Boucher Trail offers some of the more memorable inner Canyon vistas.

Finding the trailhead: The trip begins at Hermits Rest at the end of West Rim Drive. To get there, follow the driving directions for Hike 9.

The hike: The rugged Boucher Trail demands a higher level of Grand Canyon hiking experience than the nearby Hermit Trail. Although the trail is generally easy to follow, there is considerable exposure in places, and you must downclimb at one point on this exceedingly steep and rocky trail.

Good campsites are available on the ridge below Yuma Point (dry), and at Boucher Creek and Boucher Rapids at the Colorado River, both with perennial water. You loop back to the trailhead via a spectacular cliff-hanging segment of the Tonto Trail and finally the Hermit Trail. Plan on spending your second night at either Hermit Creek or Hermit Rapids.

Louis D. Boucher, the Grand Canyon's "hermit," forged the trail into the Canyon in the 1890s. Alongside Boucher Creek he worked a copper mine, built a cabin, planted an orchard, and tended a garden. Much like Boucher's ruined cabin, segments of his trail have fallen into various stages of disrepair in the century since its construction.

The only drawback to the Boucher Trail is its location beneath the Dragon Corridor for tour aircraft. Each day a continuous procession of noisy helicopters and airplanes practice their brand of "eco-tourism" overhead.

From the Hermits Rest trailhead parking area, follow the Hermit Trail (see Hike 9) for 1.75 miles to the Dripping Spring/Boucher Trail junction in Hermit Basin and turn left onto that trail. After another mile of undulating travel above the head of Hermit Creek canyon (see Hike 10), you reach the Boucher Trail junction in the pinyon-juniper woodland.

Bear right onto the Boucher Trail, dip into the dry wash draining the Dripping Spring draw, then begin a lengthy Supai traverse high on the west wall of Hermit Creek canyon. This stretch of trail, with minor undulations, is infrequently used but is generally easy to follow. The tread is narrow and occasional rock slide debris is more of an inconvenience than it is a challenge. Vegetation en route consists of widely scattered pinyon and juniper and an assemblage of shrubs from various life zones in the Canyon. You would expect shrubs of the pinyon-juniper woodland, such as cliffrose and single-leaf ash. Also colonizing trailside slopes are shrubs typical of the Tonto Platform: blackbrush, mormon tea, broom snakeweed, and yucca. Most unusual is the tall Engelmann prickly pear growing upslope from the trail, a cactus common in the inner gorge.

Hermit Camp comes into view midway through this traverse, as well as the Tapeats sandstone narrows below the camp and the Hermit Trail above it. Expansive views reach to the North Rim, from the dark walls of the inner gorge past a dramatic array of varicolored cliffs, buttes, and towers. The vista encompasses a broad stretch of the Grand Canyon, from Powell Plateau in the northwest to Vishnu Temple in the northeast.

Even more expansive vistas unfold upon reaching the slickrock point below the headland of Yuma Point, 2.25 miles from the Boucher Trail junction. Here at 5,429 feet, the inner gorge opens up to reveal fine views of the Colorado River, including the churning whitewater of Granite Rapids and the shadowed gorge above it. This point is a rewarding destination for a

Memorable views of the Grand Canyon unfold from the Boucher Trail below Yuma Point.

memorable day hike. Campsites here invite backpackers to stay the night. Waterpockets in the slickrock below the trail may hold enough water for a small party soon after significant rainfall.

The traverse continues west of Yuma Point, leading you deeper into the headwaters amphitheater of Travertine Canyon. Once you reach the middle of the amphitheater, the inevitable descent begins—the second of three major descents en route. The 950-foot descent is steep, abrupt, and moderated by only a few switchbacks. Pay careful attention to the trail en route—it zigs and zags in unexpected directions. This is a rough, rocky descent through the cliff bands of the Supai layer. The tread ranges from rocky to gravelly and constant attention is necessary. One short but steep pitch midway down is stacked with boulders, presenting considerable exposure. Some hikers may feel more comfortable lowering their packs, then downclimbing the pitch.

At length you reach the dry wash of Travertine Canyon just above the Redwall limestone cliff. Notice the water-polished, marble-like limestone on the floor of the wash. J.W. Powell named Marble Canyon in 1869 for the similar exposures of polished Redwall limestone there. From the comparatively level terrain of Travertine Canyon's basin, follow the trail north along the top of the Redwall cliff, winding among the gray boulders of that formation. Soon the trail gradually rises over blackbrush-clad slopes, then crosses an expanse of needle-and-thread grass on the site of an old toilet paper fire, and finally you mount the 4,533-foot saddle south of red, Supai-crowned Whites Butte. Here you are confronted with the third and final descent, and now only 1.5 miles and 1,800 feet of elevation separate you from the pleasant campsites at Boucher Creek.

From the saddle, the very steep and gravelly trail drops into a narrow chute that affords passage through the Redwall. Clumps of saw grass are a notable addition to the common desert shrubs here. As its name implies, the leaves of this sedge are sharp and serrated, and can easily slice the hand of an unwary hiker. Once you pass below the gray Redwall and purple Temple Butte limestones, you begin a steep traversing descent of Muav limestone slopes. The draw deepens below you and soon cottonwoods appear on its floor, watered by a spring issuing from the walls of the draw. A large dome of reddish brown and gray travertine rises behind the spring and is seen to better advantage as you negotiate the final switchbacks through the Bright Angel shale to the cairned junction with the westbound Tonto Trail. After passing a day or two in Boucher Creek, you will return to this junction to finish the circuit.

Bear left at the junction onto the much wider, better-defined trail. Switchbacks lead you steadily down via ledges of Tapeats sandstone and into the draw 350 feet below. Upon reaching the draw, proceed west along the course of its often dry wash to the campsites along the banks of perennial Boucher Creek, at 2,700 feet, 0.3 mile from the Tonto Trail junction.

By the time you reach Boucher Creek, you have traveled through the entire sequence of Grand Canyon rocks (rocks of the Grand Canyon Super-

Fine views of Hermit Rapids unfold from the Tonto Trail between Boucher and Hermit creeks.

group are absent here), from the 250-million-year-old Kaibab limestone to the 1.7-billion-year-old Brahma schist, a member of the Vishnu Complex that composes the lower walls of Boucher Creek. A short distance down the canyon, Vishnu schist appears in outcrops and follows the meandering canyon to the Colorado River.

The campsites here are well worn by many years of use, but are a welcome refuge after the long trek. A scattering of mesquite and redbud decorate the boulder-strewn site, with space enough for two tents. Small Boucher Creek, bordered by willows, trickles by several yards away. The canyon here is confined, offering no broad views of the Grand Canyon but views of only your immediate surroundings. Boucher Creek is bounded by soaring cliffs on both sides, with the South Rim looming 3,700 feet above its headwaters amphitheater.

Just below the campsites and above the east bank of the creek are the ruins of Louis Boucher's stone cabin. All that remains are four stone walls and the fireplace. Remnants of his large orchard and garden have been erased by time.

There is no other suitable place to camp other than at the river alongside Boucher Rapids, 1.5 miles downcanyon. Even if you don't camp there, the walk down the wash to the rapids is a worthwhile sidetrip. To get there, follow the Tonto Trail into the boulder-strewn wash of Boucher Creek, where the tread disappears in the rocky debris. Follow the rocky and gravelly wash generally north, downstream. After 0.3 mile, Topaz Canyon opens up to the west. Cairns here show the route of the Tonto Trail (bound for Bass Canyon) as it ascends the west wall of the canyon.

Bear right and continue down the winding, somber-walled canyon. The creek is intermittent for the remaining distance to the river. The gravelly wash is littered with rocks and boulders, yet the walk down the canyon is trouble-free, seldom requiring rock-hopping. As you approach the river, the slickrock of Vishnu schist serves as the wash's floor and the muffled rumble of Boucher Rapids begins to fill the air. Suddenly you emerge onto the beach alongside the Colorado River, just above the riffle of Boucher Rapids.

Good but shadeless campsites, fringed by seep-willow and tamarisk, can be found here at 2,330 feet. Views are obstructed by the towering walls of the inner gorge, but you can see Pima Point looming 4,500 feet above to the southeast on the South Rim.

To reach Hermit Creek from Boucher Creek, return to the eastbound Tonto Trail and turn left (north). This trail is a pleasant change from the relentless downhill plunge of the Boucher Trail. The mildly undulating Tonto Trail leads first north above Boucher Creek, then east above Granite Gorge. The rolling expanse of the Tonto Platform here is several hundred feet lower in elevation than it is farther east, and between Boucher and Hermit creeks, the trail stays between 3,000 and 3,200 feet. The widely spaced shrub cover is dominated by ubiquitous blackbrush and also includes mormon tea, broom snakeweed, brittlebush, and prickly pear and hedgehog cacti.

The trail follows the Tapeats sandstone rim of the inner gorge, and fine

Boucher Rapids at the Colorado River opens up at the mouth of Boucher Creek Canyon.

views reach downcanyon to Boucher Rapids and upcanyon past the torrent of Hermit Rapids. As the trail begins to curve into Travertine Canyon, you pass an interesting gray knob of travertine on your left and enjoy a striking view up into that canyon's gaping, terraced amphitheater.

At length you reach lower Travertine Canyon's dry wash at 3,200 feet and cross just above a lone pinyon and a minor gorge carved through the travertine. You exit the wash via travertine ledges then begin a descending traverse above the canyon's deepening gorge in which springs support a verdant riparian ribbon far below. As you curve around the point dividing Travertine and Hermit Creek canyons, you traverse beneath an overhanging travertine cliff, 900 feet directly above Hermit Rapids. Views from here reach upriver past Granite Rapids to Zoroaster Temple and portions of the North Rim.

After curving around the point, you exchange views of Granite Gorge for views into gaping Hermit Creek canyon, overlooked by the tree-fringed points of Hermits Rest, Mojave, and Pima points on the South Rim. A long traverse of the western flanks of the canyon leads to a point opposite the Hermit Ranger Station and the rock-outlined ruins of Hermit Camp. Then you briefly descend into the Tapeats sandstone narrows below, jump across vigorous Hermit Creek, and ascend for several yards to the mesquite-fringed bench where you find Hermit Creek campsite.

To close the circuit, follow the Hermit Trail back to the South Rim (see Hike 9).

General description:	A memorable rim-to-river backpack of three to four days, tracing an historic trail from the westernmost South Rim trailhead in the Park.
Distance:	16 miles round-trip.
Difficulty:	Strenuous.
Average hiking times:	5 to 6 hours in both directions.
Type of trail:	Unmaintained; generally good condition.
Trailhead elevation:	6,652 feet.
Low point:	2,210 feet.
Elevation loss:	4,442 feet.
Water availability:	Available, briefly, in waterpockets in the slickrock on the Esplanade and in lower Bass Canyon following significant rainfall. The Colorado River provides the only perennial water.
Suggested cache points:	On the rim of the Esplanade.
Optimum seasons:	April through June; September through October. Rain and snow make the trailhead access road periodically impassable.
Use Area code:	BQ9, South Bass, at-large camping.
Management zone:	Primitive.
Topo maps:	Explorers Monument and Havasupai Point USGS quads; Trails Illustrated Grand Canyon National Park.

Key points:

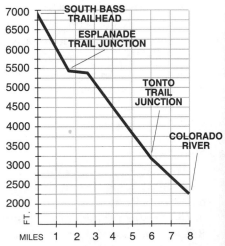

- **0.0** South Bass trailhead (Bass Camp).
- **1.7** Junction with Esplanade Trail; stay right.
- **2.7** Rim of the Esplanade.
- **5.9** Junction with westbound Tonto Trail; bear right.
- **6.0** Junction with eastbound Tonto Trail; bear left.
- **7.0** Junction with shortcut trail to westbound Tonto Trail; stay right.
- **7.8** Junction with trail to Bass Rapids beach; bear right.
- **8.0** Colorado River at Bass Rapids beach.

Best day hike destinations: Few day hikers make the long drive to the South Bass trailhead, but if you're one of the few, you'll enjoy the 5.4-mile round-trip to the rim of the Esplanade. Off-trail trips to Darwin Plateau and Spencer and Huxley terraces are rewarding, view-packed day trips for experienced hikers. However, please make an effort to avoid crushing the well-developed cryptobiotic soil crust on the Esplanade.

Finding the trailhead: Finding this remote South Rim trailhead is as much of an adventure as the hike itself. Roads are rough, rocky, and rutted in places and may become impassable after heavy rains and during winter. A high-clearance, four-wheel-drive vehicle is recommended. Expect a drive of 1.5 to 2.5 hours to reach the trailhead from either Tusayan or Grand Canyon Village.

Hikers approaching Grand Canyon from the south via Arizona Highway 64 need not enter the Park at the South entrance station. Drive to the top of the hill 0.3 mile north of the north end of the town of Tusayan, where you find a wide, gravel Forest Road 328, unsigned, branching left (west) from the highway. If you reach the turnoff to the Tusayan Ranger Station, you've driven 0.5 mile too far. Follow FR 328 west for 6 miles to the junction with Forest Road 328A and see directions below.

From Grand Canyon Village, there are two ways to reach the junction with FR 328: 1) When West Rim Drive is open (October through late May), drive 0.1 mile west of Bright Angel Lodge via West Rim Dr., then turn left onto southbound Rowe Well Road (signed). 2) When West Rim Dr. is closed, turn left at the West Rim interchange, adjacent to Bright Angel Lodge, and drive south for 0.2 mile to Maswik Lodge. From there, follow signs pointing to "Kennels," and negotiate a series of right-angle turns for 0.4 mile to Rowe Well Road, 0.5 mile south of the road's junction with West Rim Dr., then turn left.

Follow Rowe Well Rd. south; the pavement ends 0.6 mile south of West Rim Dr. After entering the Kaibab National Forest at 3.4 miles, the road becomes FR 328A. Follow this road across the railroad tracks three times, and at 4.4 miles from West Rim Dr. you will meet FR 328; turn right. The sign points to "Pasture Wash." All junctions ahead are prominently signed for either FR 328 or Pasture Wash—your destination.

You cross the railroad tracks a fourth and final time 0.1 mile from the junction, then begin a long, undulating course across the broad Coconino Plateau. The roadbed is in the Kaibab limestone, and like Grand Canyon trails through that formation, the surface is generally rocky and rough. Since the road lies about 3 to 5 miles south of the South Rim, there are few Canyon views as you pass through woodlands of pinyon and juniper and open flats clad in sagebrush and rabbitbrush.

After driving 15.8 miles from the FR 328/328A junction, you leave the Kaibab National Forest and enter the Havasupai Indian Reservation at a cattle guard. Continue ahead for another 1.8 miles, then turn right (north) onto a poor, narrow dirt road signed for Pasture Wash Ranger Station.

You reenter the Kaibab National Forest 0.9 mile from the last junction and reach the Park boundary after another 0.4 mile, at a rough cattle guard crossing and a gate (be sure to close the gate behind you). After passing the Pasture Wash Ranger Station (unstaffed), continue straight ahead on the narrow, rutted road. The road gently ascends the sagebrush-carpeted floor

SOUTH BASS TRAIL

See Map on Page 143

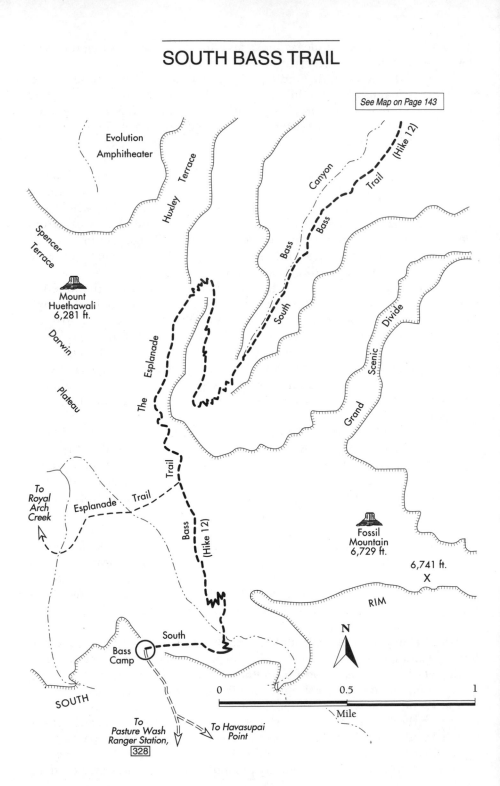

Evolution
Amphitheater

Huxley Terrace

Spencer
Terrace

Bass Canyon

Bass Trail (Hike 12)

South Bass

Mount
Huethawali
6,281 ft.

Darwin

Plateau

The Esplanade

Grand Scenic Divide

Trail

To
Royal
Arch
Creek

Esplanade Trail

Bass (Hike 12)

Fossil
Mountain
6,729 ft.

6,741 ft.
X

RIM

N

South

Bass
Camp

SOUTH

0   0.5   1

Mile

To
Pasture Wash
Ranger Station,
328

To Havasupai
Point

142

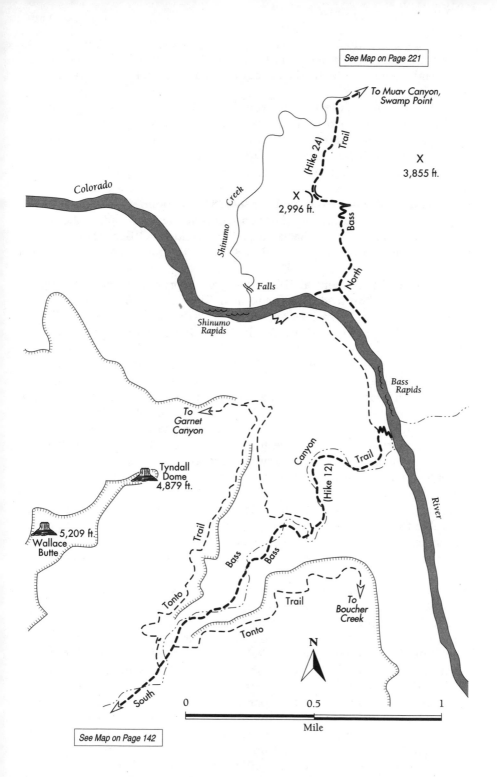

See Map on Page 221

To Muav Canyon,
Swamp Point

(Hike 24)

Trail

X
3,855 ft.

X
2,996 ft.

Bass

Colorado

Shinumo Creek

North

Falls

Shinumo
Rapids

Bass
Rapids

To
Garnet
Canyon

Canyon

Trail

(Hike 12)

Tyndall
Dome
4,879 ft.

River

Trail

Bass

Bass

5,209 ft.
Wallace
Butte

Tonto

Trail

To
Boucher
Creek

Tonto

N

South

0   0.5   1

Mile

See Map on Page 142

of Pasture Wash valley and soon begins to ascend into the pinyon-juniper woodland above, where the road becomes a narrow, rocky corridor through the trees.

Quite soon after entering the woodland, at a point 2.5 miles from the ranger station, the road becomes extremely rocky and rough. There is a single parking space here on the right side of the road, and hikers without a high-clearance vehicle can proceed no farther.

The narrow road ahead, with few places wide enough for vehicles to pass, provides a jarring ride for the remaining 0.9 mile to the loop at the road's end, 24.6 miles from the FR 328/328A junction.

Hikers arriving late in the day can camp at the trailhead, *if* they have obtained a permit from the Backcountry Reservations Office. There are also numerous places to camp along FR 328 within the Kaibab National Forest.

The hike: In the central Grand Canyon, a prominent ridge descends from the South Rim to the Colorado near River Mile 107. This ridge—the Grand Scenic Divide—marks an abrupt and dramatic division of Grand Canyon landscapes. To the east of this divide, the Canyon is filled with the colorful buttes, mesas, and towers it is famous for. West of this dividing ridge is a landscape where the stark simplicity of plateau rims, Esplanade terrace, and inner gorge dominates the Canyon's profile.

The South Bass Trail, descending from rim to river just west of the Grand Scenic Divide, is the most unusual and perhaps the most spectacular trail of the South Rim. The remoteness of the trail, combined with its unique scenery, easily justify the long drive to the trailhead. The trail, though long-abandoned, is in good condition and is generally easy to follow until you reach lower Bass Canyon, where ample cairns guide you down the meandering, trailless wash.

There is no reliable water on this trail until you reach the river. It is advisable to cache water on the Esplanade for the hike out. The Esplanade offers excellent, but dry, camping areas, which are useful on a two-day hike out from the river. The sandy beach at the Colorado River is one of the finest riverside campsites accessible by trail in the Canyon, but during the May through September river running season, you could be invaded by river parties during your stay here.

The South and North Bass trails can be combined by experienced canyoneers into a 21.5-mile, rim-to-rim trip that is the wilderness counterpart of the Bright Angel/North Kaibab route. Aside from the 242.5-mile car shuttle between trailheads, there is one minor problem with this route: There is no bridge across the river. To cross the river from one trail to the other, you must hitch a ride with a float party. You may get lucky and catch a ride across right away or you may have to wait until you meet an agreeable party. Your best chance of finding a ride is at the beach on the North Bass Trail, and it is advisable to hike from the North Rim to the South Rim anyway, since route-finding is easier while descending the North Bass Trail.

From the north edge of the trailhead parking area, the gravelly South

Hikers gaze into the depths of the Grand Canyon from Huxley Terrace, on a side trip off the South Bass Trail.

Bass Trail descends a moderate grade below the rim, traversing eastward through an open woodland of pinyons. The Kaibab limestone here has eroded into a broad slope, clad in sagebrush, Utah serviceberry, and Gambel oak. The broad Esplanade terrace, clothed in pinyon and scattered brush, spreads out far below to the north, bounded by the rocky dome of 6,281-foot Mount Huethawali.

Shortly, the trail descends more steeply via switchbacks into a wooded draw. From there you begin an exciting traverse; cliffs of Coconino sandstone plunge 300 feet from the edge of the trail. Grand views are enjoyed from this pinyon-shaded traverse, stretching west across the Esplanade to the east wall of Great Thumb Mesa and north across the 10-mile-wide gulf of the Grand Canyon to the North Rim. Remote Powell Plateau is prominent on the northwest skyline beyond Mount Huethawali.

The traverse terminates where a draw has carved a break in the Coconino cliff. Steep switchbacks lead down slanting ledges on the Coconino descent, where the way may be briefly indistinct. Junipers join the pinyons as you descend, as do a greater variety of shrubs, such as mormon tea, yucca, broom snakeweed, mock orange, Gregg ceanothus, turpentine broom, and alder-leaf mountain mahogany.

The grade moderates when you emerge onto the red slopes of the Hermit shale, which you follow on a descending traverse. Shortly thereafter you bottom out on the Esplanade, a rolling red bench thickly clad in pinyon, juniper, and a wide variety of shrubs that include Fremont barberry, scrub live oak, and blackbrush. The trail is rock lined at the cairned junction with the Esplanade Trail at 5,400 feet. Bear right, continuing gently down the wooded slopes to level ground, where you begin to skirt low, bulging walls of gray and salmon-tinted Esplanade sandstone. The trail crosses much slickrock as you curve around this sandstone wall. The way is indistinct at times and cairns are widely scattered.

Soon the trail leads out into the blackbrush flats and then forks. Follow either branch; they both rejoin after about 200 yards. You will surely notice that the soil on the Esplanade terrace supports a very well-developed cryptobiotic crust, which looks like dark, jagged mountain peaks projecting a few inches above the ground. Although camping and cross-country travel on the Esplanade is inviting, hikers must make the extra effort to avoid crushing this delicate crust. It takes many years to redevelop.

After skirting the foot of Mount Huethawali, you eventually reach a cairn at Benchmark 5376 on the rim of the Esplanade. Bass Canyon, deep and precipitous, opens up far below. Pause here long enough to absorb the dramatic vista; it will fade from view by increments as you descend into the canyon below. Between Powell Plateau in the northwest to the North Rim in the north, an array of soaring towers project skyward from the shadowed depths of Shinumo Amphitheater. These are the westernmost towers in the Grand Canyon. Downcanyon the landscape assumes a more symmetrical

The Ross Wheeler, *abandoned here in 1915, lies above the beach on the South Bass Trail.* Photo by John Rihs.

profile. Use your topo map to locate such prominent features as Dox Castle, Evans Butte, Guinevere and King Arthur castles, and Holy Grail Temple. On the latter, the ashes of William Wallace Bass were spread from an airplane in 1933, hence the temple has become known as Bass Tomb.

The descent off the Esplanade begins via rocky switchbacks leading down a northeast-trending draw. Then the trail curves south and you follow a long traverse upon shadeless, rubbly Supai slopes, descending with the aid of occasional switchbacks. Typical of the Supai layer, the trail is quite rocky, so expect to be boulder-hopping part of the time.

After curving into the head of Bass Canyon, steep switchbacks lead down to the top of the Redwall limestone. The break in the Redwall cliff here is in the upper gorge of Bass Canyon, sliced by the Bass Fault. The Redwall descent follows the drainage of Bass Canyon. You will likely be halfway through the Redwall before you realize that you're descending it. The gorge is not without obstacles, however. A jumble of Supai boulders fallen from above choke the draw, so the route is part trail, part rock-hop. Also, the trail is very brushy here. The stiff branches of scrub live oak will be constantly tearing at your arms and legs, slapping you in the face, and may snag your gear if it is not firmly lashed to your pack. The gorge is also home to much saw grass—avoid reaching out to its serrated, knife-sharp leaves.

You eventually emerge from the brushy gorge and begin a lengthy, steadily descending traverse on the east flanks of the increasingly broad canyon. Here in the upper reaches of the Lower Sonoran Zone, blackbrush is the dominant groundcover. Evenly spaced, the blackbrush gives the canyon's slopes a dark gray caste. At length you dip into Bass Canyon's dry wash, cross it, and resume the downcanyon trek on the west side. Soon you approach the cairned junction with the westbound Tonto Trail at 3,200 feet, a long, waterless dead-end trail leading to Royal Arch Creek.

Beyond the junction, you drop back into the wash through the upper layers of the Tapeats sandstone, cross to the east side, and meet the eastbound Tonto Trail after 0.1 mile. That segment of the Tonto is its longest, stretching 28.75 miles to Boucher Creek. Slate Creek and Turquoise Canyon offer only intermittent water along that segment, which should only be followed by experienced canyoneers with ample planning, preferably during spring.

By now, mormon tea, yucca, and a scattering of catclaw clothe the nearby slopes, signaling your arrival into the hot, dry environment of true desert in the Lower Sonoran Zone. The trail crosses to the west side of the wash again within several minutes of the previous junction. Here layers of Bass limestone and dark, nearly black layers of Hakatai shale bound the wash beneath the low brown walls of Tapeats sandstone. You can't help but notice the prominent arch of the Wheeler Fold that rises ahead, a short distance downcanyon. Soon, you cross the wash for a fourth time, at the very foot of the fold. Pause here on the black rocks of the fold, which you can see rising up the opposite canyon wall, and ponder the compressive forces that bent these rock layers on edge.

Several minutes beyond the fold you make a fifth wash crossing over black slickrock, where, shortly following significant rainfall, you may find water in the numerous waterpockets. The topo map shows a spring immediately north of this crossing in the slickrock gorge just below. Like many springs shown on maps, it seldom flows.

Cairns guide you across the slickrock to a trail segment that drops back into the wash below the gorge to a sixth crossing. Follow the trail above and south of the meandering wash for 250 yards, then drop quickly to the seventh crossing, ascending the west side over a tread of green Bass limestone. Several yards beyond the crossing, avoid a faint, cairned shortcut that branches left, uphill, to the westbound Tonto Trail.

As you continue, thorny mesquite trees begin to appear, and the green foliage of seep-willow fringes the banks of the wash. The trail leads through the sand and rocks of the wash until you emerge onto the light gray slickrock of the Bass limestone just above a low pouroff. Although trails follow above both sides of the pouroff, hikers should be sure to take the right-hand trail above the east side of the wash after crossing it for the eighth time.

You can sense the Colorado River, though you cannot see it, as you wind down the slopes above the wash to a ninth and final crossing over its dark granodiorite floor. The trail then proceeds briefly above the rim of lower Bass gorge, then bends north. You can easily get turned around in your directions here; you're following above the inner gorge in the direction of the flow of the river—not west, as you might expect, but *north*.

Along this stretch of trail the river and Bass Rapids finally come into view, hidden until now by the low granodiorite walls of the inner gorge. About 200 yards beyond where the trail first curved north away from Bass Canyon, you reach a cairn showing the 200-foot descent route to the beach below. Turn right here and descend the solid black granodiorite, at first via short, tight switchbacks and finally via a steeply descending rock-hop. There are ample cairns built by well-intentioned hikers, but they don't always indicate the best route.

As you approach the beach, you pass the *Ross Wheeler*, a steel boat chained and bolted to the rock. The boat was abandoned here in 1915 by Charles Russell, August Tadje, and a filmmaker by the name of Clements on one of many early, unsuccessful attempts to run the Colorado River through the Grand Canyon.

A brief rock-hop below the boat leads quickly down to the beautiful, small sandy beach at the mouth of Bass Canyon. Fringed with exotic tamarisk and native coyote willow and seep-willow, the beach extends east for about 150 yards. There is ample room for backpackers, but if a river party camps on the site, accommodations will become limited. Fortunately, most float parties prefer the much larger beach on the opposite bank of the river below Bass Rapids. Expect a few float parties to at least stop briefly to inspect the *Ross Wheeler*.

The beach is exceptionally clean and undisturbed, and visitors must do their best to maintain its pristine qualities. The atmosphere of the beach is one of solitude and remoteness. You are far from bustling crowds, busy trails, and out of sight and sound of air tour corridors.

Here the inner gorge is bounded by low walls composed of granodiorite, but not far upriver the walls become progressively higher and are marbled with pink intrusions of granite. Powell Plateau looms overhead to the northwest, and the ranks of ponderosa pines on its rim contrast with the stark cliffs and coarse desert shrubs of the inner Canyon. In addition to Powell Plateau, the view from the beach includes the wooded rim of Masonic Temple in the northwest, Dox Castle to the northeast, and beyond it lofty Guinevere Castle. On the slopes and cliffs above the riparian ribbon at the river's edge are typical hot desert plants such as brittlebush, mormon tea, mesquite, and Engelmann prickly pear.

You can follow the old trail down along the rim of the gorge from the cairned junction with the route to the beach. This trail follows the rim for 0.6 mile, affording fine views of Bass and Shinumo rapids and of the lovely terraced beach on the opposite side of the river, where you will likely see a party of river runners camped with all the accoutrements their rafts can carry. The trail appears to end at an overlook of Shinumo Rapids, but a cairned route continues, steeply descending a rocky chute. This route involves much scrambling, but quickly leads to a sandy, rock- and cactus-studded beach at the head of Shinumo Rapids.

After enjoying your stay, retrace your route to the trailhead.

13 TONTO TRAIL—NEW HANCE TRAIL TO GRANDVIEW POINT

General description:	A rigorous point-to-point See Maps on Pages 82 & 89 backpack of three to four days recommended only for experienced Grand Canyon hikers.
Distance:	17.4 miles.
Difficulty:	Very strenuous.
Average hiking times:	4 to 5 hours from Red Canyon to junction above Hance Creek (see Hikes 2 and 4 for hiking times to and from the Tonto Trail).
Type of trail:	Unmaintained; fair condition.
Trailhead elevation:	7,040 feet.
Low point:	2,560 feet.
High point:	7,420 feet (Grandview Point).
Elevation gain and loss:	+5,240 feet; -4,780 feet.
Water availability:	Seasonal water available in Red Canyon, 5.7 miles from the trailhead; Colorado River, 7.4 miles; Hance Creek, 12.5 miles; Miners Spring, 13.75 miles.
Optimum seasons:	March through June; September through November.
Use Area codes:	BD9, Red Canyon, at-large camping; BE9, Hance Creek, at-large camping; BF5, Horseshoe Mesa, designated campsite.
Management zones:	Primitive; Horseshoe Mesa, Threshold.
Topo maps:	Cape Royal and Grandview Point USGS quads; Trails Illustrated Grand Canyon National Park.

Key points:

0.0   Fire road parking area.
0.6   New Hance trailhead.
1.8   Coronado Butte saddle.
3.5   Top of Redwall descent.
5.7   Red Canyon wash.
7.4   Colorado River.
8.9   Mineral Canyon.
12.5 Hance Creek.
13.25 Junction with trail to Miners Spring and Horseshoe Mesa; turn left.
13.75 Spur trail to Miners Spring.
14.4 Junction with Grandview Trail; turn left.
17.4 Grandview Point.

Finding the trailheads: See directions for Hikes 2 and 3.

The hike: This rigorous trip traces the eastern segment of the Tonto Trail from its beginning at Hance Rapids to Hance Creek in the shadow of Horseshoe Mesa. The segment involves more climbing than any other part of the Tonto and is an exciting and diverse route that follows the Tonto Platform

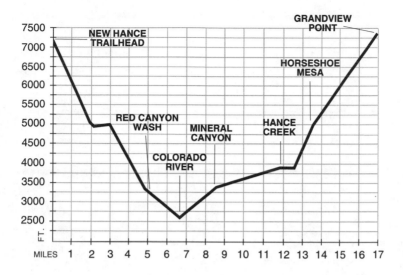

west from its emergence at the upper end of Granite Gorge.

Most hikers will pass their first night at Hance Rapids and continue on to Hance Creek (perennial water, campsites) or Horseshoe Mesa (water from Miners Spring) on the second day. The trail is steep and rocky as it ascends into Mineral Canyon from Hance Rapids. From there the route tops out on the Tonto Platform and maintains a straightforward, easy-to-follow course.

Follow the New Hance Trail (see Hike 2) for 7.4 miles to Hance Rapids on the Colorado River. Plan on spending the night here; rest, rehydrate, and tank up on water for the long, dry haul to Hance Creek 5.1 miles ahead. From the mouth of Red Canyon, follow a sandy path west for several yards to the dunes above Hance Rapids and continue west briefly until you reach a cairn that shows the beginning of the Tonto Trail. The trail rises steadily over dark red slopes of Hakatai shale, following above the course of the river.

Soon you reach a long, boulder-stacked slope of slide debris, then pick your way through from cairn to cairn. Dark walls of Vishnu schist emerge beneath the angular beds of the Grand Canyon Supergroup just below, bounding the beginnings of Granite Gorge. The steadily rising trail swings away from the river after you regain Hakatai slopes, and you soon curve south above the gorge of Mineral Canyon.

The trail contours into the dry wash of Mineral Canyon at 3,360 feet, Bass limestone under foot, beyond which you ascend steeply west, rising through the last exposures of Hakatai shale to contour beneath a broken wall of Tapeats sandstone. After skirting a minor saddle south of Point 3736, a traversing ascent soon leads into a side drainage beneath the towering Redwall cliffs of Ayer Point. Overhangs in the Tapeats sandstone walls of the drainage cast enough shade to warrant a rest stop before tackling the long traverse into Hance Creek canyon.

Hance Creek canyon and the South Rim from the Tonto Trail.

A northbound ascent along the western flanks of the drainage finally leads you out onto the blackbrush-studded Tonto Platform, where the trail swings west. Grand views unfold here, commensurate with the effort required to enjoy them. Below you lies the increasingly deep Granite Gorge, with the distant rumble of Sockdolager Rapids echoing from its somber depths. Asbestos Canyon stretches away to the north, heading in a pair of Redwall-bound amphitheaters. Flanking that canyon are the red-topped buttes of Krishna and Rama shrines, with the Kaibab limestone-capped spire of Vishnu Temple as the centerpiece.

The westbound trail, now comparatively level, leads into a minor draw then out onto the Tapeats sandstone rim of Hance Creek, 900 feet above the floor of its precipitous black-walled gorge. The trail often clings to the very edge of the Tonto Platform as you proceed generally south, heading deeper into the gulf of Hance Creek canyon. Horseshoe Mesa, its rim fringed with gnarled junipers and bounded by 500-foot Redwall cliffs, fills the view to the west.

After curving into innumerable draws, the traverse ends at a brief descent into the wash of Hance Creek, at 3,680 feet, flanked by low walls of Tapeats sandstone. With a trickling flow of perennial water and good campsites on the west side of the wash, Hance Creek is an inviting locale for an overnight stay. Views are limited by the soaring Redwall cliffs that embrace the canyon, separating you from the vastness of the Grand Canyon in a canyon wilderness all to itself. An intermittent, boot-worn path leads down serpentine Hance Creek canyon, and if you have an extra day for the trip it is possible to follow the gorge for about 3.5 miles to the Colorado River at Sockdolager Rapids in the shadowed depths of Granite Gorge.

The Tonto Trail ascends northwest out of Hance Creek's wash, following steep slopes to a brush-clad promontory. The topo map shows the trail to Horseshoe Mesa branching left and ascending the promontory into the draw draining Miners Spring. This trail is faint, however. If you cannot find it, follow the Tonto Trail ahead as it swings out around the promontory and then into the Miners Spring draw, about 0.75 mile from Hance Creek. Just before the Tonto Trail crosses the wash, look for a trail (which may not have a cairn) that branches left, leading up the slopes above the wash. You may need to pick your way through multiple paths to get started, but shortly the trail becomes well-worn and easy to follow as it continues up the draw.

To complete the trip to Horseshoe Mesa and Grandview Point, see Hikes 3 and 4.

14 TONTO TRAIL—GRANDVIEW POINT TO YAKI POINT

General description:	A rigorous point- [See Maps on Pages 89, 105, and 119] to-point backpack of four to five days recommended for experienced Grand Canyon backpackers only.
Distance:	27.8 miles.
Difficulty:	Very strenuous.
Average hiking times:	4 to 5 hours to Tonto Trail in Cottonwood Creek; 10 to 11 hours from Cottonwood Creek to South Kaibab Trail; 4 to 5 hours to South Kaibab trailhead.
Type of trail:	Unmaintained; fair condition.
Trailhead elevation:	7,420 feet.
Low point:	3,560 feet (Cremation Creek).
Elevation gain and loss:	+5,020 feet; -5,040 feet.
Water availability:	Cottonwood Creek, 4.4 miles; Grapevine Springs, 8.9 miles; perennial water 0.5 mile up and down Grapevine Creek from Tonto Trail, 9.9 miles; seasonally available in waterpockets in Grapevine Creek; seasonal springs in Boulder Creek, 15.4 miles, and Lonetree Canyon, 18.4 miles.
Optimum seasons:	March through June; September through November.
Use Area codes:	BF5, Horseshoe Mesa, designated campsite; BG9, Cottonwood Creek, at-large camping; BH9, Grapevine, at-large camping; BJ9, Cremation, at-large camping.
Management zones:	Horseshoe Mesa, Threshold; Cottonwood, Grapevine, and Cremation, Primitive; South Kaibab, Corridor.

Topo maps: Grandview Point, Cape Royal, and Phantom Ranch USGS quads; Trails Illustrated Grand Canyon National Park; Earthwalk Grand Canyon National Park.

Key points:

0.0	Grandview Point.
3.0	Junction with trail to Miners (Page) Spring; continue straight ahead.
3.1	Junction with trail to Cottonwood Creek; turn left.
4.4	Cottonwood Creek spring.
4.9	Junction with Tonto Trail; turn left.
8.9	Grapevine Springs.
9.9	Left (east) fork Grapevine Creek.
15.4	Boulder Creek.
18.4	Lonetree Canyon.
21.3	Left (east) fork Cremation Creek.
23.4	Junction with South Kaibab Trail; turn left.
27.8	South Kaibab trailhead.

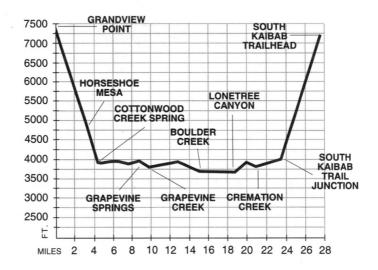

Finding the trailheads: See directions for Hikes 3 and 6.

The hike: This demanding point-to-point backpack, best accomplished over four days, requires careful planning and should be attempted by experienced Grand Canyon hikers only. Long stretches of this scenic, lonely segment of the Tonto Trail are dry most of the year, so, water is your most important consideration on this trip. The last reliable water source on the trail during the dry season is Grapevine Springs, 18.9 miles—and three days—from the South Kaibab trailhead. Since you will likely reach the springs on the second day out and continue beyond in search of a campsite, you must tank up here with enough water to complete the trip—at least 2.5 to 3 gallons per person.

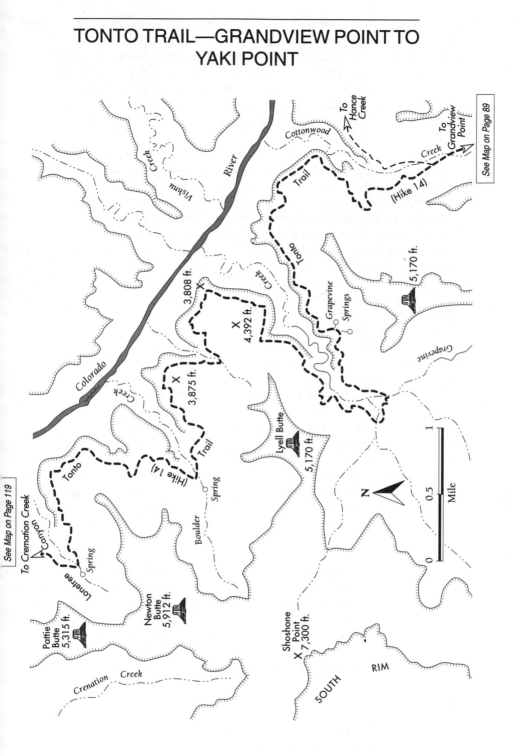

155

From late autumn through early spring, when temperatures cool and evaporation decreases, the springs in Boulder Creek and Lonetree Canyon surface, allowing much greater flexibility in planning your trip. Cremation Creek flows only during flash floods. For a time following significant rainfall, deep waterpockets in Grapevine Creek's east fork and smaller waterpockets in Lonetree Canyon may hold water. Also, perennial water flows 0.5 mile below the Tonto Trail in Grapevine Creek, but it is difficult to reach. Upstream in Grapevine, about 0.5 mile above the Tonto Trail, you will find stagnant water, if not a flowing stream, in the dry season. Be sure to check the latest information on water availability at the Backcountry Reservations Office before beginning this trip. And bring enough sturdy water containers to carry 3 gallons of water per person.

Except for infrequent overflights of commercial jets, this part of the Grand Canyon is quiet, beyond the sight and sound of tour aircraft.

From Grandview Point, follow the Grandview Trail (see Hikes 3 and 4) down to Horseshoe Mesa, turn left at the signed junction and descend Cottonwood Creek to the junction with the Tonto Trail, 4.9 miles and 3,740 feet below the South Rim. Cottonwood Creek is a good choice for your first night's stay. Good campsites are located in the spring draw, 0.5 mile above the Tonto Trail junction and just below the junction in the Tapeats sandstone narrows. Water is usually available at both sites.

This junction marks the beginning of your 18.5-mile trek across the Tonto Platform. Get underway by turning left at the cairned junction and follow the lip of the Tapeats sandstone rim above increasingly deep Cottonwood Creek canyon. Shortly, the trail contours into the northwestern branch of Cottonwood Creek, the first of many such canyon detours on the long journey ahead. The spring shown on the topo map here flows only during winter.

The well-defined, generally smooth trail leads out of the side canyon across the sloping Tonto Platform, passing through the Tonto's typical assemblage of coarse desert shrubs. Before long you will recognize the ubiquitous blackbrush, a round, dark gray shrub with stiff branches and small linear leaves. Also common is mormon tea and prickly pear, hedgehog, and beavertail cacti.

The trail soon leads to the brink of the shadowed confines of Granite Gorge, where you curve around a hilly promontory away from Cottonwood Creek. The roar of the river boils up out of the gorge below, but you glimpse only a slice of the mighty Colorado before bending toward the deep gulf of Grapevine Creek canyon. Its rugged, ribbed black cliffs plunge into the rocky abyss more than 1,000 feet below. Look across Grapevine Creek canyon to the promontory the Tonto Trail traverses on the opposite side, only 0.5 mile away. Yet you will spend the better part of a day getting there—it lies 5.2 miles away via the trail. Grapevine Creek involves the longest contouring detour on the trail, and it is memorable not only for its arduous nature, but for its broad vistas and scenic distractions as well.

The initial segment of the traverse above Grapevine Creek crosses very steep slopes just above the Tapeats sandstone cliff. These slopes are strewn with limestone boulders, so expect progress to be slow. After laboring for 1.25 miles from the point east of Grapevine Creek's canyon, you reach a southeast-trending draw beneath fluted, crimson-shaded Redwall cliffs. Here you find reliable Grapevine Springs, possibly your last source of water on the trail.

The sluggish springs flow in a shallow sheet of water over Tapeats ledges, offering pools just deep enough from which to draw water through the hose of a water filter. Abundant grasses and groves of redbud, willow, and single-leaf ash border this oasis. Coarse shrubs, such as mormon tea, four-wing saltbush, squaw currant, threadleaf snakeweed, and catclaw cling to the parched, broken sandstone ledges just above.

Before reaching the spring, and after continuing the traverse beyond it, you will see a vigorous flow of water in an inaccessible stretch of Grapevine Creek, 300 to 400 feet below. This creek, however, does not flow above, where the Tonto Trail crosses the wash. Unless you have a confirmed report of water in Boulder and/or Lonetree canyons from the Backcountry Reservations Office, you must tank up at Grapevine Springs with enough water to reach Yaki Point.

Beyond the springs, the undulating trail bends in and out of several draws, and the left and right forks of the canyon begin to open up ahead. Due to the Tapeats cliff below, the trail leads farther up the left (east) fork than you might expect.

After reaching the wash in the left fork at 3,550 feet and 1 mile from the springs, you find three excellent campsites set in the slickrock narrows. Several deep waterpockets just downstream hold water long after abundant rainfall. Most hikers opt to continue beyond Grapevine to their second night's camp, thus shortening the possibly waterless gap between themselves and Yaki Point.

A series of switchbacks leads you up and away from the left fork, followed by a traverse into the dry right (west) fork. Drop down into the wash here and follow cairns to the continuation of the trail on the opposite side. The trail ahead follows minor ledges and crosses steep slopes, alternating from the upper layers of the Tapeats sandstone to slopes of Bright Angel shale. The occasionally rocky, generally level trail proceeds northwest high above Grapevine Creek, bending into numerous minor draws along the way. At a point northeast of the great Redwall limestone cliffs that rim Lyell Butte, the trail contours into a shallow bay bounded by green-tinted wall of Bright Angel shale. A striking chimney-like spire of Muav limestone—Point 4392—guards the north wall of the bay.

After a 3-mile, 1.5-to 2-hour trek from Grapevine Creek wash, you round Point 3808, where once again the breadth of the Grand Canyon unfolds before you, inviting you to linger and soak in the panorama. A few fair, exposed campsites among the blackbrush at the point are a good choice for your second night's stay.

Views stretch up and down the dark-walled Granite Gorge, including a

The Tonto Trail affords expansive vistas of the inner Canyon.

view of powerful Grapevine Rapids. The scalloped outline of the South Rim rises far above, and you can discern several prominent features there, including Desert View Watchtower, and Cardenas and Escalante buttes in the east; Sinking Ship and Coronado Butte in the southeast; and Newton Butte in the southwest, with Shoshone and Yaki points for a backdrop.

North of the river the long tributary canyons have carved a dramatic array of buttes and towers, and the views of these features from this point are rivaled by few other inner Canyon viewpoints. From the west to the northeast your view includes Isis Temple; the wooded mesa of Shiva Temple; the blocky butte of Dragon Head; Buddha and Manu temples; Zoroaster and Brahma temples; the twin Coconino spires of Angels Gate; and Wotans Throne, Vishnu Temple, and Newberry Butte.

From Point 3808, the Tonto Trail heads northwest along the rim of the 1,300-foot deep inner gorge. Broken cliffs plunge to the river only a few yards off the trail; brief detours afford the finest river views. Soon you curve southwest into a minor drainage, and you may momentarily lose the trail upon reaching the slickrock of the drainage's right fork. Watch for cairns; they guide you north out of the draw at the same contour. The trail leads you out to another point, this one lacking river views, then backs away from the inner gorge into the Redwall-bound amphitheater of Boulder Creek. Shoshone Point's bold limestone cliffs loom nearly 4,000 feet above the canyon.

At length you reach the aptly named Boulder Creek wash at 3,590 feet, heaped with boulders left behind by ages of rockfall and flash floods, temporarily suspended here on their inexorable journey to the river. Vegetation quickly changes along the margins of the wash. Desert scrub growth gives way to thick stands of single-leaf ash, squaw currant, cliffrose, Apache plume, seep-willow, and catclaw. Don't expect to find the spring in the canyon's left fork flowing during the dry season. Two good campsites on the fringes of the wash here offer another option for your second night on the trail.

Cross the wash, following cairns and relocate the trail on the opposite (northwest) side. More of the same follows as you contour the west rim of Boulder Creek, crossing the catclaw-studded Tonto Platform. Shortly, though, the way becomes indistinct as the trail turns away from the canyon rim toward a broad, low saddle to the north. Cairns help lead the way, but braided sections of trail have been worn by confused hikers. Simply follow the draw north up to the obvious saddle, where the trail once again becomes easy to follow.

Beyond the saddle the trail bends into a side canyon littered with limestone boulders washed down from the Redwall cliffs of the amphitheater above, then you curve back out to the rim of Granite Gorge, where fine river views unfold once more. As you continue northwest along the rim, you glimpse a stretch of Clear Creek, its vigorous waters emerging from its tortuous Vishnu gorge.

About 2 miles from Boulder Creek, the trail swings southwest and you begin an increasingly rocky and brushy traverse into the Redwall amphitheater of Lonetree Canyon, and reach its wash after another mile at 3,640 feet. A few Fremont cottonwoods and tamarisk suggest water here, but you will only find the spring flowing during winter and early spring. A scattering of redbud trees and squaw currant bushes help soften the austere appearance of the canyon. Good campsites on ledges above the east bank of the wash offer the last sheltered sites until Cremation Creek, more than 3 miles ahead. About 30 yards down the wash lies a single waterpocket in the slickrock, offering limited emergency water if recent rains have filled it.

The trail ascends the west bank of the wash for several yards, but exactly where it bends north to begin the traverse is obscure. A few cairns left by hikers may help lead the way, but if cairns are absent, make your way generally north just above the Tapeats sandstone, weaving a way among limestone boulders on the steep, brushy slopes. The following 0.5 mile involves much guesswork and a measure of luck to stay on the faint path. By now you should have a good feel for the Tonto Trail, so use your topo map and trust your judgment to find a good route, if not the trail.

The trail gradually reappears beyond Point 3783, and it then leads northwest, first into a shallow drainage then out to a point at about 3,850 feet from where a fine view of the Colorado River and the broad basin of Cremation Creek opens up. The trail drops east into a minor draw below the point, then follows the draw west down into the open basin of a side drainage. Cross another drainage 0.4 mile farther, then begin the gradual descent into the broad desert basin of Cremation Creek, reaching the dry wash of the east fork at 3,652 feet, 3 miles from Lonetree Canyon.

The canyon derives its name from the practice of ancient inhabitants cremating their dead on the South Rim and spreading their ashes into the canyon's gulf below. The open nature of Cremation Creek affords fine Grand Canyon views. From Shoshone Point to Yaki Point, the great wall of the South Rim rises majestically above the wide basin. Newton and Pattie buttes bound the basin on the east, with Cedar Ridge and O'Neill Butte rising to the west. Douglas-fir can be seen upcanyon, growing at the base of the Coconino sandstone in sheltered recesses within 1 mile of parched flats sparsely clad in blackbrush, catclaw, and Engelmann prickly pear. This abrupt contrast helps illustrate the influence of microclimates on the distribution of plant communities in the inner Canyon.

Views to the north contrast the gentle desert expanse of the Tonto Platform with lofty buttes and points on the North Rim. Recognizable features include Tiyo Point, blocky Buddha Temple, pine-fringed Widforss Point, square-topped Oza Butte, Sumner Butte, Bradley Point, the bold spire of Zoroaster Temple, and Demaray Point.

The trail leads across the wash, passes a good, solitary campsite, then gently ascends back to the Tonto Platform. Soon the canyon's middle fork opens up below, bounded by cliffs of Tapeats sandstone. It is deeper and more confined than the open east fork. The Tonto uncharacteristically, but necessarily, descends steeply, quickly leading into the confines of the wash, where you find two inviting campsites shaded part of the day by the sandstone ledges above. The trail leads you on a steady ascent away from the wash to a low, brushy saddle via an open draw. From the saddle, the west fork of the canyon opens up below, even deeper and more confined than the middle fork. Once again, the trail makes a steep and longer descent of 150 feet into the wash below, where you find another pair of campsites. Hikers are advised to pass their third night in one of the forks of Cremation Creek before tackling the steep grind up to Yaki Point on the fourth hiking day.

Up the trail climbs, beyond the wash, pointing northwest and soon leading you back onto the Tonto Platform, where the grade becomes a gentle incline. The trail begins to skirt a low cliff band of Tapeats sandstone, following the line of the Cremation Fault while heading toward a broad saddle. Beyond the saddle rises Point 3898, crowned by a Park Service radio antenna, an indication of your approach to the "improvements" of the Corridor Use Area.

The trail avoids the saddle by ascending steep slopes to a broad, sloping ridge. Here you bend south and ascend the ridge, gaining 200 feet of elevation. You then follow the westward curve in the trail, resuming a course more typical of the Tonto, bending into three minor draws in rapid succession. The trail ascends above the north slope of the third draw to the 4,000-foot contour where you regain the Tonto Platform, and broad vistas open up once again. A brief stroll west across the platform leads you past the solar-dehydrating toilet building and onto the South Kaibab Trail. Turn left here and follow that view-packed ridgeline trail, ascending 3,200 feet in 4.4 miles to the South Kaibab trailhead (see Hike 6).

15 TONTO TRAIL—HERMITS REST TO BRIGHT ANGEL TRAILHEAD

General description:	A point-to-point backpack of three to five days, following the most popular and well-defined segment of the Tonto Trail.
Distance:	24 miles.
Difficulty:	Strenuous.
Average hiking times:	4 to 5 hours to Hermit/Tonto trail junction; 7 to 9 hours to Indian Garden; 4 hours to Bright Angel trailhead.
Type of trail:	Unmaintained; good condition.
Trailhead elevation:	6,640 feet.
Low point:	2,995 feet at Monument campsite; 2,369 feet at Granite Rapids.
Elevation gain and loss:	+4,810 feet; -4,540 feet.
Water availability:	Hermit Creek, 1.2 miles southwest of Tonto Trail junction at 6.4 miles; Monument Creek, 8.7 miles; Colorado River at Granite Rapids, 9.9 miles; seasonal water at Cedar Spring, 10 miles; Salt Creek, 12.1 miles; Horn Creek, 16.9 miles, is not potable; Indian Garden, 19.4 miles.
Optimum seasons:	March through June; September through November.
Use Area codes:	BM7, Hermit Creek, designated campsite; BL7, Monument Creek, designated campsite; BL8, Granite Rapids, designated campsite; BL6, Cedar Spring, designated campsite; BL5, Salt Creek, designated campsite; BL4, Horn Creek, designated campsite; CIG, Indian Garden, designated campground.
Management zones:	All areas Threshold; Indian Garden, Corridor.
Topo maps:	Grand Canyon and Phantom Ranch USGS quads; Trails Illustrated Grand Canyon National Park; Earthwalk Grand Canyon National Park.

Key points:

- **0.0** Hermits Rest trailhead parking area.
- **6.4** Tonto Trail junction; bear right.
- **8.7** Monument Creek campsite.
- **10.0** Cedar Spring campsite.
- **12.1** Salt Creek campsite.
- **16.9** Horn Creek campsite.
- **18.8** Junction with Plateau Point Trail; stay right.
- **19.4** Indian Garden Campground, junction with Bright Angel Trail; turn right.
- **24.0** Bright Angel trailhead.

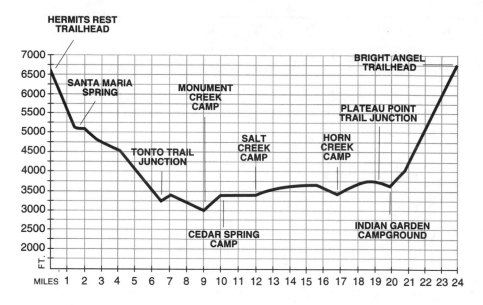

Finding the trailheads: See directions for Hikes 7 and 9.

The hike: This trip, known as the Hermit Loop (not really a loop at all, but a point-to-point trip), traces the most well-worn segment of the Tonto Trail, a segment that is arguably the most spectacular. Much of the trail follows the Tapeats sandstone rim of the inner gorge, offering exciting river views from the points between the six major side canyons it traverses.

Ease of access and dramatic views account for the popularity of this three- to four-day trip. Because of the frequent use, backpackers are required to stay overnight in the five designated campsites en route. Most hikers will pass their first night at either Monument Creek or Granite Rapids. To complete the trip in three days, you should plan on another night as far down the trail as possible, such as Horn Creek or Indian Garden Campground.

You will find reliable water in Hermit Creek, Monument Creek, the Colorado River at Granite Rapids, Horn Creek, and Indian Garden.

The Lost Orphan Mine, perched on the South Rim above Horn Creek, produced rich uranium ore during the 1950s. The development of that mine opened the floodgates for highly radioactive contamination of Horn Creek. Hikers are strongly advised not to drink, cook with, or bathe in Horn Creek's waters. There is emerging evidence that all the springs and creeks in this area, including Hermit Creek, contain levels of radioactivity that exceed EPA standards. When you drink from the waters along this route (piped water at Indian Garden is safe to drink), you do so at your own risk. It is advisable to pack water from sources as far from Horn Creek as possible, such as Granite Rapids or Monument Creek.

From the Hermits Rest trailhead parking area, follow the Hermit Trail (see Hike 9) for 6.4 miles down to the Tonto Trail junction, 3,440 feet below the rim, and turn right. The eastbound Tonto Trail ascends a moderate grade

TONTO TRAIL—HERMITS REST
TO BRIGHT ANGEL TRAILHEAD

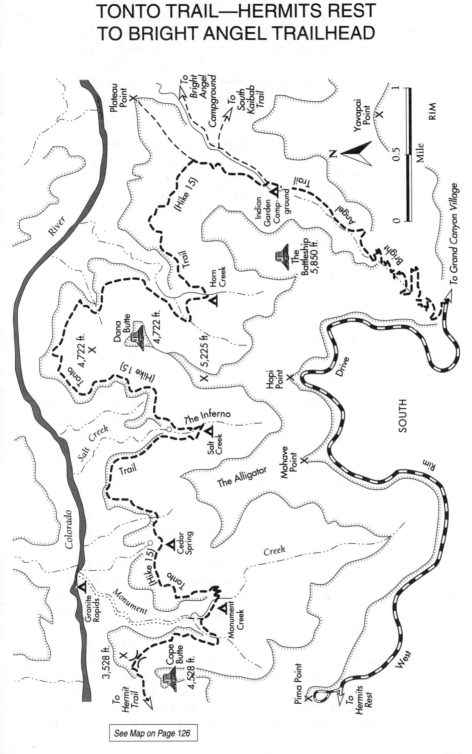

See Map on Page 126

through the green-tinted Bright Angel shale, clad in a shrub cover of blackbrush and mormon tea, to a prominent saddle at 3,280 feet. An ascending traverse follows, staying above the Tapeats sandstone rim of a precipitous side canyon that frames a view of the Colorado River 850 feet below. This traverse soon leads to a second saddle at 3,389 feet, 0.75 mile from the Hermit Trail, where gaping Monument Creek canyon and the towering, sheer cliffs of The Abyss unfold in a breathtaking view.

A gradually descending traverse ensues, leading you ever deeper into Monument Creek canyon via the Tapeats rim. At length you reach the right (west) fork of the canyon. A brief descent leads into the rocky wash below, among fallen sandstone slabs. The trail soon leaves the wash and skirts the base of the cliff band out to a point separating the canyon's forks. A tall spire of Tapeats sandstone perched on a base of Brahma schist rises before you. This is the monument the canyon was named for, and hoodoos such as this are a rare sight in the Grand Canyon.

A spur trail, signed for Granite Rapids, leads into the wash below and follows its gravelly bed downcanyon. The wash is often dry, and only occasional rock-hopping is necessary as you follow the shallow canyon for 1.2 miles among low cliffs, hills, and towers of Vishnu schist to the sandy, rock-strewn beach. There, thundering Granite Rapids is pinched between the Monument Creek debris fan and the opposing Vishnu cliff, forming one of the Grand Canyon's more powerful rapids. The good, sheltered campsites lie among thickets of seep-willow and tamarisk east of the Monument wash.

To continue on the Tonto Trail, follow the trail from the junction as it curves southeast into Monument Creek's left (east) fork and soon you reach mesquite-sheltered Monument campsite at 2,995 feet, a pleasant site set on a bench just above the perennial creek. A toilet lies nearby. Another larger sandstone monolith rises just north of the site, and behind you, the nearly unbroken 2,800-foot walls of The Abyss, sheltering groves of Douglas-fir, soar to the South Rim.

From the campsite, follow the Tonto Trail east via switchbacks. The trail rises 250 feet through the Tapeats sandstone before resuming its characteristic traverse above the canyon. This traverse, however, ascends gradually, rising 300 feet in 0.7 mile to a minor spur ridge, where you curve east around the left arm of The Alligator's mesa. You climb only to descend, though, and after another 0.25 mile, you reach the draw hosting Cedar Spring (seasonal water during winter and early spring) and the small campsite 50 yards below the trail. The camp affords broad Canyon views stretching past the flaming-red, Coconino-capped butte of the Tower of Set to the forested fringe of the North Rim.

From Cedar Spring, you bend into another draw after 0.2 mile, then traverse the rim of the draw's lower gorge on a northeast course, from where you once again gain tantalizing glimpses of the river in an exceptionally narrow stretch of Granite Gorge. This traverse in turn leads out to Point 3461, beyond which begins a memorable traverse upon the very edge of the Tapeats sandstone rim, high above the precipitous gorge of Salt Creek, labeled

The Inferno on the topo map, more likely for the prominent red cliff bands that embrace it, rather than for the stifling heat the canyon gathers during summer.

The trail follows the rim into the dry wash; the small, shadeless Salt Creek campsite lies just above the trail to the south, and the toilet lies beyond. Salt Creek usually has seasonal flowing water about 0.25 mile downstream from the camp. The curving Mojave Wall bounds the great amphitheater at the head of the canyon, stretching from Mojave to Hopi points on the South Rim. Groves of Douglas-fir cling to the foot of the Kaibab and Coconino cliffs in shady recesses in the wall, lying only 1 mile above the arid blackbrush-clad expanse of the Tonto Platform.

The trail traverses north out of Salt Creek, rising gradually above the broken walls of Tapeats sandstone. A long traverse ensues above the tremendous Salt Creek gorge, its shadowed floor lying far below. The Tonto Platform becomes more expansive as you curve in and out of several minor draws en route to Point 3582, 1.5 miles from Salt Creek. Here you swing northeast to the brink of Granite Gorge, where the river comes into view 1,200 feet below.

A steady 200-foot ascent soon leads east away from the rim of the gorge. Shortly you top out on a minor saddle at 3,800 feet, beneath the towering Redwall limestone cliffs bounding Point 4722, an outlier of the Dana Butte massif. The lengthy traverse continues, first with an abrupt 200-foot descent to the rim of a minor side canyon, then followed by a more gentle traverse above the gorge of Horn Creek. The wooded fringe of the South Rim rises to the skyline ahead, beyond Horn Creek's immense twin amphitheaters. Square-edged Dana Butte bounds the western flanks of the canyon, and the Esplanade-capped butte of The Battleship rises to the southeast.

At length you drop into the dry left (west) arm of Horn Creek 4.5 miles from Salt Creek, then curve around Point 3687 and enter the right fork. Here you find a pair of shadeless campsites situated on either side of the creek. Remember, **do not** drink the water from this small stream.

From the campsite, the trail proceeds north then east, high above Horn Creek's increasingly deep gorge, beyond which follows a long traverse of the broad Tonto Platform beneath the Redwall cliffs of The Battleship's ridge. At length you cross a broad saddle, then bend southeast toward Garden Creek canyon. The wide track of the Plateau Point Trail comes into view as you begin a gradual descent south toward the cottonwood-shaded oasis of Indian Garden.

You reach the junction with that heavily used trail 1.9 miles from Horn Creek at 3,700 feet. The 1.4-mile round-trip out to Plateau Point is well worth the detour. The gently rising trail leads to a huge Tapeats sandstone boulder at the point, atop which hikers are treated to an eagle's-eye vantage of Granite Gorge, with the Colorado River coursing through far below, as well as a broad panorama of the Grand Canyon's cliffs, terraces, and buttes.

Once you reach the junction with the Plateau Point Trail, your trail begins to assume a different character. The Tonto Trail becomes a wide, dusty track,

Throughout the course of the Tonto Trail, hikers must traverse innumerable side canyons.

and during the final 0.6 mile to Indian Garden, you'll likely pass a steady stream of hikers and perhaps mule trains, most of them en route to Plateau Point.

After dipping into Garden Creek among the cottonwoods, you quickly ascend to the Bright Angel Trail several yards below Indian Garden Campground and join the throngs of hikers on the 4.6-mile trek back up to the South Rim (see Hike 7).

THE NORTH RIM

OVERVIEW

The North Rim of the Grand Canyon forms an alluring backdrop to vistas from the South Rim. Its fringe of tall conifers holds the promise of a cool refuge from desert heat and solitude in a wilderness setting. The North Rim has an atmosphere of great remoteness and unspoiled grandeur. It is this remoteness that makes it such a special place. Separated from the South Rim by only 10 to 12 miles, there are but two ways to reach the North Rim— by hiking 21 miles across the Grand Canyon or by driving 215 miles around it.

The North Rim lies at the end of a long, dead-end road that traverses the rich conifer forests and grassy parks of the Kaibab Plateau, many miles from the nearest enclaves of civilization. It receives only one-tenth the number of visitors as the South Rim, yet fewer roads and visitor services here concentrate use. Thus places on the North Rim can seem congested at times.

Canyon overlooks on Park roads are not as abundant here as on the South Rim, where it seems every bend in the road presents an incredible vista. Yet as if to compensate for fewer overlooks, North Rim viewpoints afford vistas of the Grand Canyon that are consistently awe-inspiring and overwhelming, even to the most jaded canyoneer. Fringed with forests of pine, fir, spruce, and aspen, North Rim overlooks survey a remarkable landscape of colorful cliffs, bold towers, deep labyrinths, and seemingly barren desert.

Most North Rim trails are as lonely as overlooks are congested. Only one maintained trail descends into the Grand Canyon from the North Rim, and the North Kaibab Trail receives the bulk of use here for good reasons. It is a highly scenic, excellent trail that offers something for everyone, from the visitor out for a stroll to the backpacker taking the plunge into the Grand Canyon.

Three other rim-to-river trails begin on the North Rim, and they are among the most scenic and demanding trails in the Park. North Rim trails are much longer than those on the South Rim, and since the elevations of the North Rim are greater, these trails descend more. While South Rim trails are generally open to the Grand Canyon, some North Rim trails tend to follow long, deep tributary canyons that afford infrequent glimpses of the greater landscape of the Grand Canyon. Hikers are swallowed up in a canyon wilderness that often seems entirely separate from the Grand Canyon.

Numerous trails atop the Kaibab Plateau at the North Rim offer many fine day hiking opportunities. Some of these trails are open to overnight backcountry camping, offering an experience much different from a trip into the inner Canyon. These trails are an excellent choice for summer season backpackers wishing to avoid the overwhelming heat of the inner Canyon, yet still enjoy Canyon views and the incomparable sunrises and sunsets from the comfort of cool conifer forests atop the rim.

NORTH RIM AREA

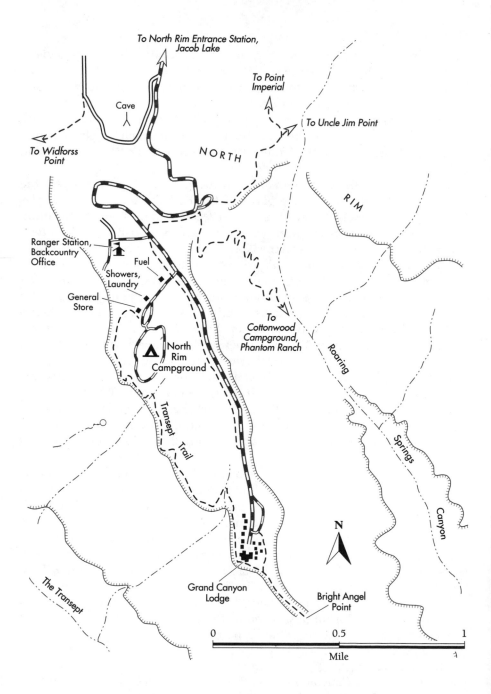

To North Rim Entrance Station,
Jacob Lake

To Point
Imperial

Cave

To Uncle Jim Point

To Widforss
Point

N O R T H

R I M

Ranger Station,
Backcountry
Office

Fuel

Showers,
Laundry

General
Store

To
Cottonwood
Campground,
Phantom Ranch

North
Rim
Campground

Roaring

Transept Trail

Springs

N

Canyon

The Transept

Grand Canyon
Lodge

Bright Angel
Point

0   0.5   1

Mile

General description:	A mostly trailless route in Marble Canyon, for experienced canyoneers, suitable as a three- to four-day backpack.
Distance:	13 miles round-trip.
Difficulty:	Strenuous.
Average hiking times:	5 to 6 hours down to the Colorado River; 7 hours to return to the rim.
Type of trail:	Route; occasional tread with sporadic cairns.
Trailhead elevation:	5,580 feet.
Low point:	2,880 feet.
Elevation loss:	2,700 feet.
Water availability:	Colorado River, 6.5 miles; seasonally available in waterpockets in the Supai rock layer briefly following significant rainfall.
Suggested cache points:	South Canyon wash at the bottom of the descent off the rim.
Optimum seasons:	March through June; September through December.
Use Area code:	AC9, South Canyon, at-large camping.
Management zone:	Primitive.
Topo maps:	Buffalo Ranch, Buffalo Tanks, Tatahatso Point, and North Canyon Point USGS quads; Trails Illustrated: Grand Canyon National Park map (route not shown on map).

Key points:

- **0.0**   South Canyon trailhead.
- **0.9**   South Canyon wash.
- **4.3**   Bedrock Canyon.
- **6.5**   Colorado River.

Best day hike destination: Strong hikers in excellent condition can make the trip to the river and back in one long day. Others will find the hike into the Supai narrows near Bedrock Canyon a rewarding day hike of about 7.5 to 8 miles.

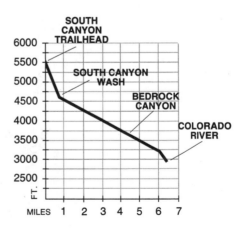

Finding the trailhead: Follow U.S. Highway 89A for 19.5 miles east from Jacob Lake, Arizona, or 35.75 miles west from the junction with US 89, to a southbound dirt road prominently signed for House Rock Buffalo Ranch. Be sure to have a full tank of gas and ample water before venturing down this remote desert road.

This dirt road (Road 8910) is wide but invariably rocky and rough with

SOUTH CANYON

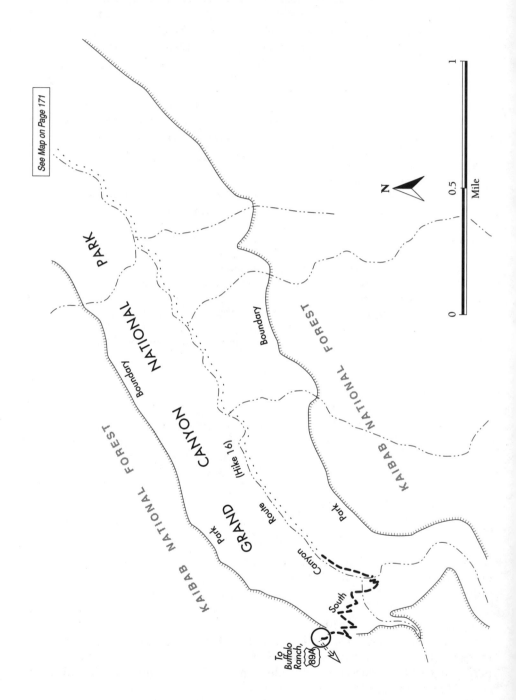

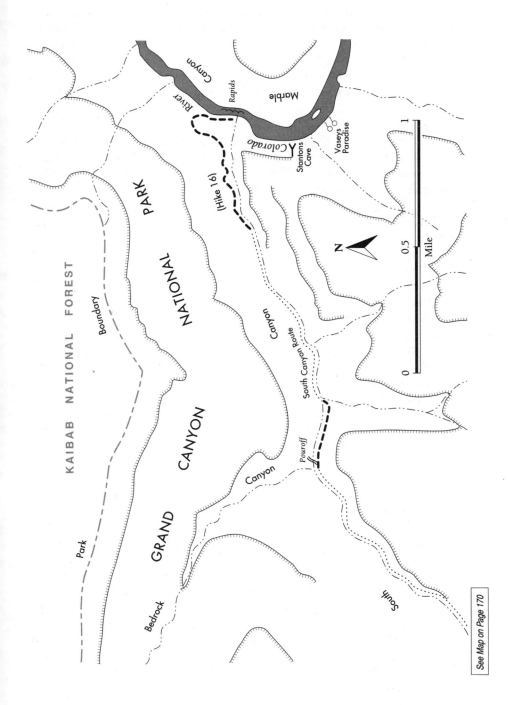

KAIBAB NATIONAL FOREST

Park

Boundary

PARK

NATIONAL

(Hike 16)

CANYON

GRAND

Bedrock

Canyon

Canyon

South Canyon Route

Pouroff

South

Colorado

River

Canyon

Marble

Rapids

Stantons
Cave

Vaseys
Paradise

N

0   0.5   1
Mile

See Map on Page 170

washboards. As you proceed south on 8910 across the Marble Platform, ignore several spur roads along the way.

After 18.9 miles, turn left onto Forest Road 632, signed for Buffalo Ranch and South Canyon Trail. (Note: The Kaibab National Forest map shows FR 632 as FR 3510). Follow this narrow dirt road for 1.9 miles to a junction adjacent to the buildings of the Buffalo Ranch. A sign points to South Canyon Trail. Turn right here and follow the narrow dirt track for 1.2 miles to a wire gate (close the gate behind you) and thence another 250 rough and rocky yards to the road's end at the rim above South Canyon, 22.1 miles from the highway.

Hikers arriving late in the day can camp at the trailhead (within the Kaibab National Forest) or almost anywhere along the course of Road 8910 on lands administered by the BLM or Kaibab National Forest. Consult the Kaibab National Forest Map to determine land ownership in this area.

The hike: This challenging, mostly trailless route, suitable for experienced canyoneers only, follows Marble Canyon's longest tributary gorge to the Colorado River. Marble Canyon, though part of the Park, is much different than the Grand Canyon. Marble Canyon is a narrow incision in the relatively flat expanse of the Marble Platform, averaging only 1 mile wide from rim to rim. At the confluence of South Canyon and the Colorado River, Marble Canyon is "only" 2,500 feet deep.

South Canyon and other tributaries on the western side of Marble Canyon trends northeast, incised along the regional dip of the sedimentary rock layers. Most canyons are short, narrow gorges and are youthful in appearance. Canyon walls rise abruptly from the canyon floors in an unbroken wall of cliffs and ledges. Erosion has yet to isolate buttes, mesas, and ridges from the canyon's walls, as in the Grand Canyon. The simple profile of South Canyon is more reminiscent of a southern Utah canyon rather than the typical Grand Canyon tributary.

This trip is a rewarding backpack of three or more days, offering an entirely different kind of Grand Canyon experience. The route is accessible even during winter, but the roads to the trailhead may become briefly impassable due to snow or wet conditions. Although much of the route follows South Canyon's wash, without the benefit of a trail, the route is straightforward. Cairns help guide hikers around pouroffs, and most of these bypass routes have been worn into traceable paths.

Yet South Canyon offers more than simply an exciting off-trail route to the Colorado River. South Canyon has been used as a route to the river for thousands of years, and you will be following in the footsteps of ancient cultures and nineteenth-century explorers. Anasazi ruins dating back to A.D. 1050 or A.D. 1150 are found just above the river near the mouth of South Canyon. Vaseys Paradise, an oasis of vigorous springs, lies less than 0.5 mile below South Canyon on the right side of the river. John Wesley Powell named the springs during his epic expedition of the Colorado River in 1869.

South Canyon cuts a deep and narrow gorge into Marble Platform.

Stantons Cave, about 100 feet above the river between South Canyon and Vaseys Paradise, is another interesting highlight of the area. Robert Brewster Stanton, the chief engineer of an ill-fated railroad surveying expedition through the Grand Canyon in 1889, abandoned the river at South Canyon. His expedition members cached their remaining supplies in the Redwall cave (returning the following year to retrieve them) and left the river via a route up South Canyon. Deeper inside the cave, and overlooked by the Stanton Expedition in its haste to leave the Canyon, was a cache of split-twig animal figurines, presumably left behind as spiritual offerings by people of the Desert Culture 4,000 years ago.

The beach at the South Canyon/Colorado River confluence offers good riverside camping, but is frequently used as the first night's camp of commercial river trips, which often carry thirty or more people. To avoid such an invasion of your camp, take this hike before May or after September, off-season for river running.

It is advisable to cache water in South Canyon for the hike out, perhaps at the foot of the descent off the rim. There are fair campsites just above the wash there, and some hikers use them on a two-day hike out to the rim.

The far-ranging views from the trailhead are enjoyed only briefly, for South Canyon will quickly swallow you into its cliff-bound confines. The Vermilion Cliffs bound the north end of the Marble Platform, and the invisible Colorado River begins its journey through Marble Canyon between that barrier wall and the craggy Echo Peaks far to the northeast. Even more distant is southern Utah's Kaiparowits Plateau, bounded by the White Cliffs of Navajo sandstone. The long sweep of the Echo Cliffs rise on the eastern horizon. The summit dome of Navajo Mountain reaches above the crest of those cliffs, 60 miles distant.

The lofty tableland of the Kaibab Plateau dominates the view to the west. The rock that caps the plateau—the Kaibab limestone—is the same rock present at the rim of South Canyon. The East Kaibab Monocline has warped this rock more than 3,000 feet above the surface of the Marble Platform.

To the south, the Marble Platform ends at Boundary Ridge and Saddle Mountain. The deep notch that gave the mountain its name frames a memorable view of Mount Hayden's stony spire.

The trail is well-defined as it leaves the road's end on a southbound course, quickly descending to a Park Service information sign, then dropping moderately via Kaibab ledges to a fenceline. You will have to crawl under this fence, then proceed southwest via a stair-step series of ledges to the rim of South Canyon. Here a fine view of South Canyon opens up, framing the sheer walls of Marble Canyon far below.

From the rim the trail turns abruptly left, and you descend steeply through a narrow crack in the Kaibab limestone, just wide enough to afford passage with a pack. The trail emerges from the crack onto the steep, boulder-strewn, red-and gray-banded slopes of the Toroweap formation. Here you begin a plunging, knee-pummeling descent, aided by only a few switchbacks. There is a well-developed cryptobiotic soil crust on these slopes, so try to stay on the trail.

After descending 800 feet in 0.6 mile, the grade abates and the trail traverses upcanyon through boulder fields, passing above a red- and white-streaked slickrock chute. Beyond the chute, a series of steeply descending switchbacks leads 200 feet down through a break in the Coconino sandstone cliff into the dry wash of South Canyon. The red slopes of Hermit shale flank the canyon here, and as you proceed down the wide, boulder-studded wash, you'll find segments of trail avoiding the rockiest stretches. Much of the route ahead involves considerable rock-hopping and winding your way among the boulders in the wash.

After following the wash northeast for about 2 miles, the salmon-tinted slickrock of the Supai Group begins to flank the wash. Now the wash becomes narrow and winding and is entrenched in an increasingly deep inner gorge. Two 20-foot pouroffs, typical of the resistant layers of the Supai, are bypassed on the right via cairned routes, en route to the confluence with gaping Bedrock Canyon, a precipitous gorge that opens up to the northwest.

Within moments of passing the mouth of Bedrock Canyon you reach a formidable pouroff blocking the wash. A cairned route on the right (south) leads you along a red rock ledge for about 0.2 mile to a south-trending side canyon. Descend the rocky slope here and return to South Canyon's wash. The canyon becomes increasingly confined below Bedrock Canyon, but there are few significant obstacles until you reach the Redwall limestone.

Soon after the wash begins cutting into the Redwall, about 1.4 miles and 1 hour beyond Bedrock Canyon, cairns indicate a trail that ascends out of the wash via the left bank. Follow this trail as it traverses the upper layers of the Redwall, heading eastward above the wash. You will bend into three minor draws and boulder-hop your way through a slide of Supai boulders. When you reach a point above the mouth of South Canyon, spectacular Marble Canyon and the Colorado River open up before you. The rich hanging gardens of Vaseys Paradise decorate the canyon walls a short distance downriver.

The trail then turns northeast, following the rim of the Redwall upriver for about 300 yards to a shallow draw choked with angular Supai boulders. Cairns then lead you on a steeply descending course down toward the river along the flanks of the slide. Midway down the 300-foot descent, you may need to lower your pack to proceed over a 15-foot dropoff. The route follows ledges below that obstacle, leading south (downriver). Within several yards you quickly descend rocky slopes, dotted with clumps of mormon tea, to the rock-strewn beach below, at 2,870 feet.

After enjoying this fine area, return the way you came.

General description:	A rigorous rim-to-river backpack of four to five days, for experienced Grand Canyon backpackers only, tracing one of the most difficult trails in the Park.
Distance:	27.8 miles round-trip.
Difficulty:	Very strenuous.
Average hiking times:	1 to 1.5 hours to Saddle Mountain saddle; 3 to 4 hours to Tilted Mesa; 3 hours to Nankoweap Creek; 1.5 hours to the river; expect 12 to 14 hours to return to the rim.
Type of trail:	Unmaintained; generally poor condition.
Trailhead elevation:	8,840 feet.
Low point:	2,800 feet.
Elevation gain and loss:	+400 feet; -6,400 feet.
Water availability:	Nankoweap Creek, 10.6 miles; Colorado River, 13.9 miles.
Suggested cache points:	Marion Point ridge; Tilted Mesa ridge.
Optimum seasons:	May through June; September through mid-October.
Use Area code:	AE9, Nankoweap, at-large camping.
Management zone:	Primitive.
Topo maps:	Point Imperial and Nankoweap Mesa USGS quads (trail not shown on quads); Trails Illustrated Grand Canyon National Park.

Key points:

0.0 Saddle Mountain trailhead.
2.7 Saddle Mountain saddle, junction of northbound Forest Service Trail 57 and Park Service Nankoweap Trail; bear right onto Nankoweap Trail.
4.6 Marion Point ridge.
6.8 Tilted Mesa ridge.
10.6 Nankoweap Creek.
13.9 Colorado River.

Best day hike destinations: The 5.4-mile round-trip to Saddle Mountain saddle offers the rewards of glorious Marble Canyon vistas from the cool forests of Boundary Ridge. Strong hikers will enjoy the 9.2-mile round-trip to Marion Point ridge, which affords unforgettable views into the broad basin of Nankoweap Creek and the forest-fringed rim above.

Finding the trailhead: Follow Arizona Highway 67, the Kaibab Plateau-North Rim Parkway, south from Jacob Lake (31 miles south of Fredonia, Arizona, and 55.2 miles west of the U.S. Highway 89/89A junction) for 26.5 miles to a signed T junction with westbound Forest Road 22 and an eastbound Forest Road signed "Viewpoints." This junction is located in the meadows of DeMotte Park, 0.9 mile south of Kaibab Lodge and immediately south of the signed pothole of Deer Lake.

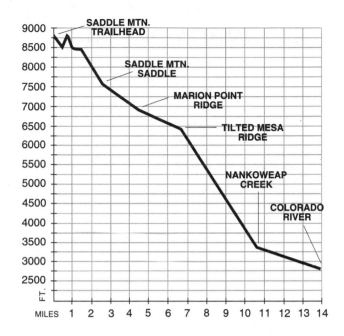

Turn left (east) here and follow the pavement for 250 yards to the beginning of the gravel road, Forest Road 611. This wide washboard road steadily ascends through the forest for 1.2 miles to a junction with Forest Road 610, signed for Saddle Mountain, your destination. Bear right at the junction and, after 100 yards, bear right again and follow the undulating course of FR 610 first south then east.

This good, wide, gravel road passes through rich subalpine forests with an abundance of aspen, providing a memorable display of golden foliage during late September. The road to Marble View (affording a panorama of Marble Canyon) branches left (north) 8 miles from the highway. Continue straight ahead on FR 610; the road becomes narrow and winding for the remaining 5.5 miles to the Saddle Mountain trailhead parking area, 13.5 miles from the highway.

Hikers arriving late in the day will find camping areas at the trailhead and in numerous places along the course of FR 610 in the Kaibab National Forest.

The hike: The spectacular Nankoweap Trail is perhaps the most difficult and demanding in the Grand Canyon. This trip requires previous Grand Canyon hiking experience, route-finding ability, good judgment, and ample planning. The trail, with the greatest elevation loss from rim-to-river in the Canyon, is ill-defined in places, involves much scrambling over and around boulders, and often has a very narrow tread with considerable exposure along the edge of plunging cliffs.

The trail begins in the cool Canadian Zone forests of the Kaibab Plateau, then descends Boundary Ridge to Saddle Mountain saddle. A seemingly

NANKOWEAP TRAIL

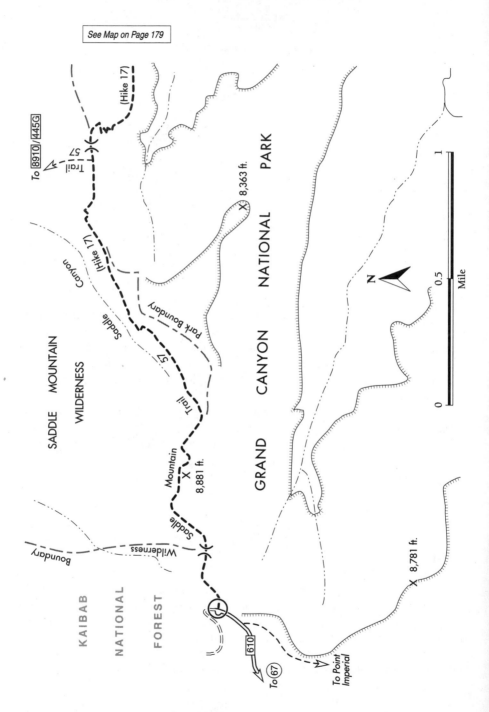

See Map on Page 179

178

See Map on Page 180

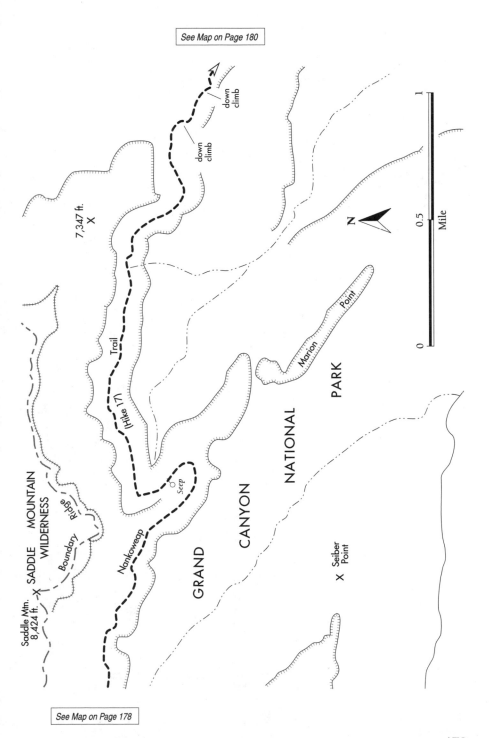

down climb

down climb

7,347 ft.
X

Trail

(Hike 17)

N

Marion Point

PARK

NATIONAL

CANYON

GRAND

Seep

Nankoweap

SADDLE MOUNTAIN WILDERNESS

Ridge

Boundary

Saddle Mtn.
8,424 ft.
X

X Seiber
Point

0   0.5   1
Mile

See Map on Page 178

179

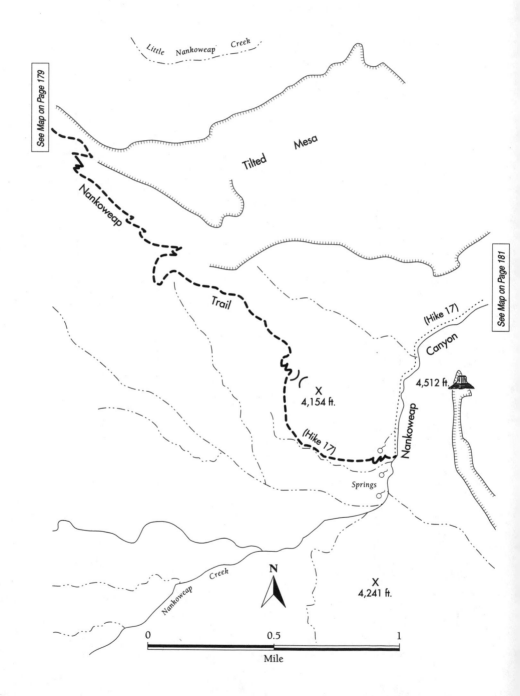

Little Nankoweap Creek

See Map on Page 179

Tilted Mesa

Nankoweap

Trail

See Map on Page 181

(Hike 17)

Canyon

4,512 ft.

X
4,154 ft.

Nankoweap

(Hike 17)

Springs

Nankoweap Creek

N

X
4,241 ft.

0   0.5   1

Mile

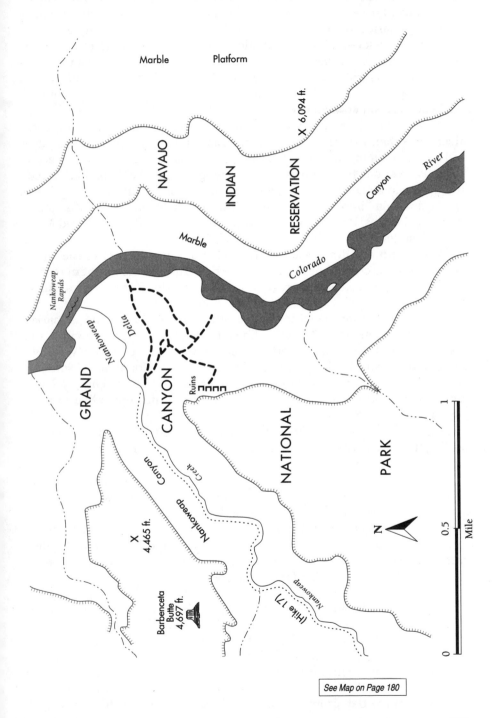

Marble   Platform

NAVAJO

INDIAN

RESERVATION

X 6,094 ft.

Canyon   River

Marble

Colorado

Nankoweap Rapids

Nankoweap

Delta

GRAND

CANYON

Ruins

NATIONAL

PARK

Creek

X
4,465 ft.

Nankoweap Canyon

Barbenceta
Butte
4,697 ft.

(Hike 17)   Nankoweap

N

0.5   1

0   Mile

See Map on Page 180

181

endless Supai traverse follows, then the trail plummets abruptly into the broad basin of Nankoweap Creek. A lengthy boulder-hop down that wash leads you to the Colorado River in the Lower Sonoran Zone of Marble Canyon.

Dramatic, far-ranging vistas, varied landscapes and fascinating geology, Anasazi granaries, the broad Nankoweap Delta—the Grand Canyon's largest tributary delta—and a long, challenging trail all combine to make this one of the most rewarding trips in the Grand Canyon. Plan at least four days to complete this trip; five or six days would be ideal to get the most out of the journey. There is no reliable water for the first 10.6 miles between the trailhead and Nankoweap Creek.

The 8- to 9-hour hike down to Nankoweap Creek is a long haul; some hikers pass their first night on either the Marion Point or Tilted Mesa ridges and continue on to Nankoweap Creek or the Colorado River on the second day. A layover day there allows ample time to explore the delta. Rather than attempting to make the grueling hike out in one long, exhausting day, break up the hike out into two days, spending the night on one of the above-mentioned ridges. Be sure to cache water near Marion Point or Tilted Mesa; 1 to 1.5 gallons per person should be sufficient.

There is but one drawback to this wild and remote corner of the Grand Canyon. Tour aircraft in the Zuni Point Corridor fly over the northern reaches of Nankoweap in an endless procession from shortly after sunrise to sunset each day.

The trail begins at the eastern edge of the parking area, and is marked "Saddle Mountain Trail 57." From the start you enjoy expansive views that reach northeast across the broad Marble Platform to the distant Vermilion Cliffs and beyond to the White Cliffs and Navajo Mountain in southern Utah. Views also reach southeast into the broad gulf of Nankoweap basin, where scores of towering buttes jut skyward from the depths like so many jagged teeth.

The trail descends steeply at times upon burned over slopes now supporting thickets of aspen. You reach the first saddle among groves of Gambel oak and New Mexican locust on Boundary Ridge at 8,500 feet and after 0.3 mile, where you enter the Saddle Mountain Wilderness. From there the trail ascends steeply to the summit ridge of Peak 8881, from where trailside aspens frame distant views of the folded strata of the East Kaibab Monocline, the Echo Peaks and the barrier of the Echo Cliffs, and distant plateaus in southern Utah. In the southeast your view stretches beyond the deep gash of Marble Canyon to the Palisades of the Desert and south across the Coconino Plateau to the San Francisco Peaks.

The descent of the peak's east slopes is moderate, and soon you drop into groves of white fir, Rocky Mountain maple, New Mexican locust, and aspen. Beyond the eastern foot of the peak you amble across a broad flat dotted with clumps of manzanita and an open, parklike forest of ponderosa pine. The trailbed here is rocky with sparkling slabs of Coconino sandstone. The trail leads out to the north rim of the flat, where you will find a junction with a faint path that branches right. Ignore that path and descend steeply northeast off the flat, dropping through the Coconino sandstone in a shady forest of ponderosa pine and white fir above the head of Saddle Canyon.

This rough, steep, and sometimes brushy stretch of trail eventually leads you to the first in a series of low saddles beneath the towering cliffs of Saddle Mountain. An undulating course follows across the red slopes of the Hermit shale and onto the ledges of the Esplanade sandstone. After passing a national forest sign pointing to the Nankoweap Trail, you meander down to a traverse of south-facing slopes. Here the Canyon's influence is reflected by the woodland of pinyon and juniper, while just over the ridge the north-facing slopes support a cool forest of pine and fir.

Soon you mount another saddle and reach a junction where you find a Park Service information sign. Trail 57 branches left here, northbound for 3 miles to another trailhead (accessible for much of the winter) on Forest Road 8910/445G, at the southern end of the House Rock Buffalo Ranch Road, about 9 miles south of the South Canyon trailhead (see Hike 16).

The Nankoweap Trail officially begins here, and you briefly wind down its course to the last and lowest saddle, clothed in a woodland of pinyon and Gambel oak. The rocky trail then abruptly descends south-facing slopes through the cliff band of the Esplanade sandstone, aided by a few constructed switchbacks. Some scrambling is necessary along this descent. Below the cliff, the trail begins a generally descending traverse of steep, red Supai slopes, a traverse you will follow just beneath the Esplanade sandstone cliff for the next 3 to 4 hours.

Not far below the cliff you cross a seep that flows across the trail, momentarily making the tread quite slippery. The traverse proceeds high above the north branch of Nankoweap Creek, where scrub live oak, littleleaf mountain mahogany, and manzanita deck the trail, necessitating some bushwhacking along the way. The trail ahead undulates between cliff bands and requires frequent scrambling over and around boulders and minor rockslides. The way is mostly well-defined, and where it is obscure, cairns lead the way.

At length you round the Marion Point ridge; a few scenic campsites lie just below the trail, with a backdrop of interesting sandstone hoodoos. Although a well-worn path drops down to the campsites several yards below, the Nankoweap Trail turns north at the ridge and is not readily apparent. Plunge into a Gambel oak thicket and make your way north on the poor trail, bushwhacking through the stiff branches of various shrubs and netleaf hackberry trees, and detouring over and around slabs and boulders, heading into the bay that opens up to the north.

A seep is located 175 yards north of the campsites, where water drips slowly and spreads down the Esplanade sandstone cliff. There is not enough flow here to fill a bottle, only enough to wet your lips.

A very deep and narrow Redwall limestone gorge lies directly below the narrow ledge the trail follows, making this an exciting stretch. After reaching the head of the bay, the trail swings east once again. The trail ahead, all the way to Tilted Mesa ridge, is ill-defined, with few cairns to guide the way. The tread is exceptionally narrow, with much scrambling and considerable effort is required at times to maintain purchase on the steep, rubbly slopes.

The dry bed of Little Nankoweap Creek and the Desert Facade come into view from Tilted Mesa ridge on the Nankoweap Trail.

This stretch does afford fine vistas from the array of splintered buttes jutting above the gulf of Nankoweap basin to the forest-fringed North Rim, and beyond the cliffs of the Desert Facade to the vast, brush-studded Marble Platform.

At length the trail rounds a point opposite Marion Point above a deep side canyon, from where you can see the sloping platform of Tilted Mesa lying ahead, and you enjoy a feeling of relief that the endless Supai traverse will soon end. Beyond the point the trail angles downhill more steadily, and soon you reach the red-rock ridge leading down to Tilted Mesa at 6,360 feet. A small campsite lies alongside the trail here, the first of several more on this scenic ridge. Whether you pass your first night on this ridge or stop to cache water, you'll enjoy the broad panorama that unfolds before you. After nearly 7 miles of demanding, dry hiking, the visible green ribbon of riparian growth along Nankoweap Creek still lies far below and a few hours away.

Little Nankoweap Creek canyon opens up to the east just enough to reveal a short stretch of the Colorado River. The Desert Facade rises from the depths of Marble Canyon to the rim of the Marble Platform in an unbroken, 3,000-foot wall of gray, red, and tan rocks, from the Muav limestone below to the Kaibab limestone on the rim. The broad tableland of the Marble Platform stretches away to the east, studded with red, flat-topped hills composed of younger Moenkopi formation rocks long ago removed by erosion from much of Grand Canyon National Park. The long line of the Echo Cliffs bounds the platform in the eastern distance, with the wooded rim of the Kaibito Plateau rising above.

Tilted Mesa, composed of Redwall limestone, clearly shows the eastward dip of the rock layers here on the flanks of the East Kaibab Monocline. The Redwall limestone of Tilted Mesa lies 2,500 feet higher than the same formation on the cliffs of the Desert Facade.

The eastern rim of the Kaibab Plateau, fringed with tall conifers, rises to the western skyline. The forks of Nankoweap Creek reach far back toward the plateau, each separated colorful rocky ridges and lofty buttes. The most striking of those buttes, perhaps the most spectacular erosional outlier in the Grand Canyon, is the slender, 400 foot Coconino sandstone spire of Mount Hayden, rising to 8,362 feet.

The Butte Fault Zone, marking the boundary of the horizontal rock layers to the east and the upsloping rocks of the East Kaibab Monocline to the west, is plainly visible stretching to the south along the flanks of Nankoweap Mesa and Kwagunt and Chuar buttes. In this mile-wide fault zone, the varied rock layers of the Pre-Cambrian Grand Canyon Supergroup have been upthrusted, folded, and in places overturned, in curious juxtaposition to much younger rock layers. The Butte Fault Zone displays such excellent exposures of Supergroup rocks that the USGS, under the direction of John Wesley Powell, conducted surveys of these rocks here in 1882 and 1883. Although the USGS has been credited with constructing the Nankoweap Trail, it is unclear if the trail used today follows the same route.

From the west side of the ridge, cairns mark the descent of a sandstone ledge, which in turn quickly leads to a 12-foot downclimb, accomplished with the aid of a juniper snag. Care must be taken here not to allow the snag to catch your pack and throw you off balance. You climb down the pair of ledges to the resumption of the trail, then descend steeply for several yards to a broad flat on the ridge, where you find several fine campsites among the gnarled pinyons and junipers.

The trail follows the narrow ridge below the camping area to another low cliff, which you also downclimb this time with the aid of a live pinyon. Beyond this obstacle you continue down the ridge toward Tilted Mesa, passing one final small campsite before dropping southeast off the ridge. The very steep descent ahead, dropping 2,400 feet in 3.5 miles, was reconstructed by Park Service trail crews in 1996. The trailbed has been stabilized in several spots and the route is now well-defined and easy to follow.

A series of well-constructed switchbacks, some of them exceedingly steep, lead off the ridge and across a very steep slope of slide debris that masks the underlying Redwall limestone. A descending, southeastbound traverse follows the switchbacks, leading down to the colorful cliff bands and slopes of the Bright Angel shale. Upon this formation the trail swings back to the west, via short switchbacks, then descends very steeply along the western flanks of a plunging draw. Rock steps in the trailbed afford good footing here. At the foot of the abrupt 200-foot descent, just above a splintered red pinnacle (a slumped block of Redwall limestone) and a jumble of yellow hoodoos, the trail resumes its traversing course, first northeast then southeast. The trail ahead is very narrow as it follows the high angle shale slopes down to a gentle ridge studded with blackbrush and mormon tea.

This respite is short-lived, however, as you soon drop off the ridge and descend steeply east of its crest among fault-shattered blocks of Tapeats sandstone. As you descend a few minor switchbacks, you begin to cross soft gray slopes of weathered Cardenas lavas studded with clumps of scrub live oak. You cross over the ridge just above a wide, gray saddle, then you descend a moderate rocky grade into the draw below. The grade finally abates where you emerge from the draw onto a broad terrace amid a sea of blackbrush, prickly pear, and yucca. Fine views reach westward from the terrace up the forks on Nankoweap Creek to the conifer-fringed east rim of the Kaibab Plateau, rising a mile overhead.

The trail ahead crosses a minor wash several times as you head southeast to the rim of the terrace. From there, a few switchbacks quickly lead you down to the boulder-littered wash alongside the cool waters of Nankoweap Creek at 3,440 feet. Short, spreading cottonwoods here cast minimal but welcome shade. Nearby thickets of giant common reed grass and vines of canyon wild grape mark the location of seeps and springs that augment the flow of Nankoweap Creek's clear waters. An excellent campsite, about 100 yards downstream, above the left bank, is shaded by cottonwoods for much of the day. Other, smaller sites are located downcanyon within the next few hundred yards, on the bench above the wash among groves of mesquite.

From your vantage deep in Nankoweap Canyon, what appeared to be insignificant cliffs and buttes from above now resemble great rockbound peaks, peaks that jut skyward some 2,000 to 3,000 feet and more. The horizontal strata of Nankoweap Mesa rises boldly above the canyon to the southeast, but just to the west of the mesa's sheer cliffs, the Butte Fault Zone has dramatically altered the landscape.

Vegetation here is an interesting admixture of species from various environments in the Grand Canyon. Riparian vegetation in the wash includes Fremont cottonwood, willow, seep-willow, tamarisk, canyon wild grape, and giant reed. Mesquite, prickly pear, yucca, and mormon tea, plants of the Lower Sonoran Zone's desert scrub, inhabit the dry, rocky slopes above the wash. Shrubs common to the pinyon-juniper woodland have also established a foothold here, including cliffrose, New Mexican locust, sagebrush, and rabbitbrush. The setting of Nankoweap Creek is at once both spectacular and diverse.

The route down Nankoweap Canyon to the Colorado River is trailless; it is simply a matter of following the path of least resistance. As you follow the wash downcanyon, you must cross the small creek time and again—usually a jump or rock-hop will suffice. As you enter the confines of the canyon, you pass eastward beyond the warped strata of the East Kaibab Monocline/ Butte Fault Zone. The rock layers here are much lower in elevation than the same rock layers you traversed en route to the creek. Here the canyon is cut into the Muav limestone and Bright Angel shale, with the higher cliffs of Redwall limestone confining the canyon both north and south.

A number of seeps and springs add their moisture to the creek along the way, and you may notice many rainbow trout fingerlings in pools as you cross the creek repeatedly. After rock-hopping and picking your way down the canyon for about 3 miles, which takes most hikers about 1.5 hours, the canyon opens up into the broad Nankoweap Delta. The soaring cliffs of the Desert Facade appear ahead, and you finally can see the river and hear the muffled roar of Nankoweap Rapids, amplified by the confining walls of Marble Canyon.

Notice where the Muav limestone cliff on the canyon's south side bends from the east to the south. An outcrop of green and purple Bright Angel shale is on the opposite side (north) of the wash. At this point leave the boulder-heaped wash and begin looking for a trail on the south slopes just above it. Once you locate the trail, follow it east for several yards to a fork. One branch continues east to the river via the southern margins of the wash and the other fork climbs briefly to a broad ridge. The ridge is unusual in that Tapeats sandstone blocks are strewn along its crest, and there are no outcrops of Tapeats remaining in this part of the Canyon and for another 7 river miles downstream.

Atop the ridge you will find a maze of rock-lined trails. Stick to the established trails as you explore this area to avoid crushing the cryptobiotic soil crust and creating multiple pathways. One branch of the trail heads east for several yards to an overlook of Nankoweap Delta, then loops back to the main trail. If you continue south, you soon come to another junction on the rim of the ridge. The right-hand fork steeply ascends 500 feet in 0.4 mile to several Anasazi granaries, perched on the ledge of an alcove in the Muav limestone cliff. Tread lightly near the granaries; Park Service archaeologists have yet to stabilize them. The left, southbound fork of the trail leads down to numerous excellent campsites situated in groves of mesquite about 200 yards from the river, just above a noisy riffle.

It is possible to follow the riverbank downcanyon for at least 0.75 mile, where you can establish a more private campsite, a preferable alternative to sharing the beach with a river party. Other sites can be found out on the delta near the wash, but these sites are mostly unshaded. Sites in mesquite groves along the beach north of Nankoweap Creek offer more shade.

The delta supports a common assemblage of Lower Sonoran Zone shrubs, including four-wing saltbush, mormon tea, brittlebush, catclaw, mesquite, and prickly pear cactus. Willow, seep-willow, and tamarisk hug the banks of the river in a green ribbon of riparian foliage that contrasts with the stark, towering cliffs of Marble Canyon.

Here the canyon walls soar abruptly to the east and west, rising more than 3,000 feet in a lateral distance of only 0.5 mile. The rims of the Marble Platform to the east and Nankoweap Mesa to the west, both barely exceeding 6,000 feet in elevation, are capped by the Kaibab limestone, the same rock layer that caps the rim of the Kaibab Plateau at 8,800 feet.

After enjoying this magnificent canyon, retrace your route to the trailhead.

Broad Nankoweap Creek basin and the folded rocks of the Butte Fault are displayed in raw grandeur from Tilted Mesa ridge on the Nankoweap Trail.

18   KEN PATRICK TRAIL

General description:	A half-day, round-trip day hike along the east rim of the Kaibab Plateau.
Distance:	6 miles round-trip.
Difficulty:	Moderately easy.
Average hiking time:	3 to 4 hours round-trip.
Type of trail:	Unmaintained; good condition.
Trailhead elevation:	8,819 feet.
Low point:	8,450 feet.
Elevation gain and loss:	+360 feet; -730 feet.
Water availability:	No water available.
Optimum season:	Mid-May through mid-October.
Topo maps:	Point Imperial USGS quad (trail not shown on map); Trails Illustrated Grand Canyon National Park.

Key points:

   0.0   Point Imperial parking area.
   3.0   Cape Royal Road.

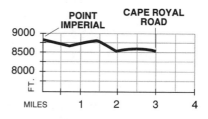

Finding the trailhead: From Jacob Lake, Arizona, follow Arizona Highway 67 south for 31.2 miles to the North Rim entrance station, and proceed into the Park for another 9.5 miles to the junction with the Cape Royal/Point Imperial Road; turn left.

Follow the narrow, winding pavement for 5.4 miles to a Y junction and bear left toward Point Imperial. You will reach the Point Imperial parking area after another 2.7 miles.

The Ken Patrick Trail crosses the Cape Royal Rd. 1 mile from the Y junction. Hikers can shuttle a car or arrange for a pickup at a turnout 0.1 mile before (to the west) the trail crosses the road.

The hike: The Ken Patrick Trail stretches 10 miles across the Kaibab Plateau from Point Imperial to the North Kaibab trailhead, surveying cool Canadian Zone forests throughout its length. Only the 3-mile segment between Point Imperial and the Cape Royal Road follows the plateau rim.

This segment of the trail maintains mostly gentle grades as it traverses the east rim of the Kaibab Plateau, alternating from cool, shady conifer forests to openings that afford panoramic vistas into Nankoweap Creek canyon and beyond. This trip is an excellent choice for a summer day hike when searing heat envelops the inner Canyon. The trail is also a good warmup for hikers planning a trip on the Nankoweap Trail, for it offers an aerial perspective of that trail.

The trail begins at the west end of the Point Imperial parking area, the

KEN PATRICK TRAIL

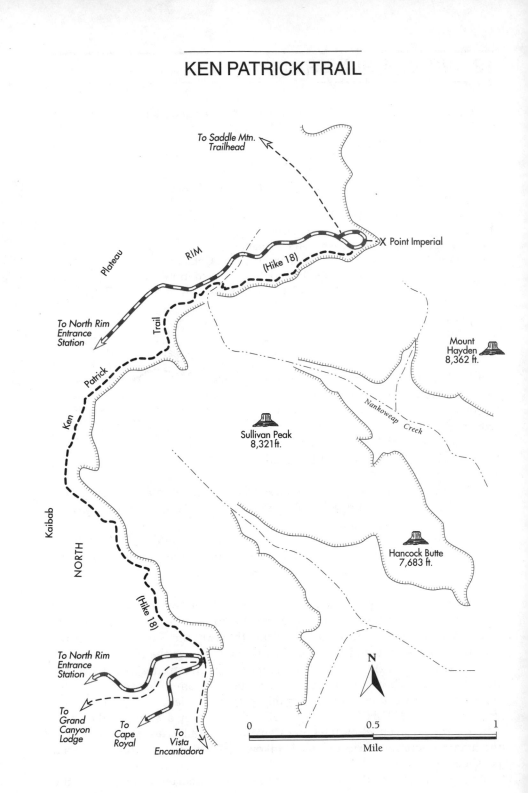

To Saddle Mtn.
Trailhead

Plateau

RIM

(Hike 18)

X Point Imperial

To North Rim
Entrance
Station

Ken

Patrick

Trail

Mount
Hayden
8,362 ft.

Nankoweap Creek

Sullivan Peak
8,321 ft.

Kaibab

NORTH

Hancock Butte
7,683 ft.

(Hike 18)

To North Rim
Entrance
Station

To
Grand
Canyon
Lodge

To
Cape
Royal

To
Vista
Encantadora

N

0   0.5   1

Mile

highest point reached by road in Grand Canyon National Park. A series of rock stairs leads you to the trail below, which begins a winding southwest course along the rim.

Views from the beginning are dramatic, stretching past the slender Coconino sandstone spire of Mount Hayden into the broad basin of Nankoweap Creek. Distant features in your view include Marble Canyon, the tortuous gorge of the Little Colorado River, Marble Platform, and the Painted Desert, stretching east to distant mesas that fade away into the desert's heat haze. Even the San Francisco Peaks near Flagstaff are visible on the far southern horizon. Your view also reaches south along the east rim of the Kaibab Plateau, where dense forest stretches far below onto slopes of the Toroweap formation and Hermit shale. An abundance of Rocky Mountain maple on those slopes enliven the somber forest with their crimson foliage in early autumn.

The trail, only occasionally rocky, undulates along the rim for 0.4 mile, passing through a forest of ponderosa pine, Douglas-fir, white fir, and aspen. Gambel oak, manzanita, and New Mexican locust crowd sunny openings near the rim.

After 0.4 mile, the trail abruptly descends 120 feet, via moderately steep switchbacks, into the shady confines of a narrow draw just below the Point Imperial Road. After you reach the fir- and aspen-shaded floor of the draw, descend briefly through thorny thickets of locust, then begin a steady,

Mount Hayden lies below the Kaibab Plateau and the Ken Patrick Trail.

moderate ascent away from the road through the cool pine and fir forest to the next high point on the rim.

The pleasant trail ahead undulates generally southward, rising gently over minor hills and dropping slightly into saddles and shallow draws, staying a short distance west of the rim. En route you capture glimpses into Nankoweap Creek basin and the splintered buttes that punctuate its depths. Views to the northeast begin to open up as you proceed southward along the rim, reaching to Boundary Ridge, the Marble Platform, the Echo Cliffs, and distant Navajo Mountain, a broad dome guarding invisible Glen Canyon in southern Utah.

As you gaze southward along the east rim of the plateau, you may notice various features that set this area apart from much of the rest of the Grand Canyon. The Kaibab limestone, which typically forms a broken cliff, has been subdued by erosion here into a steep slope, densely covered with conifer and aspen forest that extends unbroken down to the Coconino sandstone. These east-facing slopes below you receive sunlight only during the morning and early afternoon hours, creating a microclimate that mimics conditions found on the plateau above. You will see tall conifers extending down to the Supai layer, and isolated groves even reach down to the base of the Redwall limestone. In most places throughout the Grand Canyon, the Redwall separates the pinyon-juniper woodland above from desert scrub communities below.

After 2.5 miles, the trail curves east to the last point affording views into Nankoweap basin, where a green ribbon of Fremont cottonwoods shades the canyon's perennial stream, more than 5,000 feet below. From that point, you quickly descend to a saddle, then rise and fall in roller-coaster fashion over two forest-covered hills, finally reaching the rock stairway leading up to the Cape Royal Road at 8,480 feet after 3 miles. A rim trail, seldom used, continues south for another 3 miles to the parking area at Vista Encantadora (Vista Encantada on some maps). The Ken Patrick Trail, once nearly impassable due to blowdowns, has been brushed and cut out, mainly by volunteer trail crews, and now the trail is easy to follow through the forest for another 7 miles to the North Kaibab trailhead.

If you have not managed to arrange a car shuttle to the one-vehicle turnout 250 yards west of the curve where the trail crosses the road, you will enjoy retracing your view-filled route back to Point Imperial.

19   CAPE FINAL

General description:	A short but rewarding plateau-top day hike or overnighter on the North Rim.
Distance:	4 miles round-trip.
Difficulty:	Easy.
Average hiking time:	2 to 2.5 hours round-trip.
Type of trail:	Rehabilitated dirt road; good condition.
Trailhead elevation:	7,847 feet.
High point:	8,000 feet.
Elevation gain:	150 feet.
Water availability:	No water available.
Optimum season:	Mid-May through mid-October.
Use Area code:	NA9, Walhalla Plateau, at-large camping.
Management zone:	Primitive.
Topo maps:	Walhalla Plateau USGS quad; Trails Illustrated Grand Canyon National Park.

Key points:

0.0   Cape Final trailhead.
2.0   End of trail, west of Cape Final.

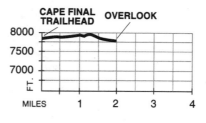

Finding the trailhead: Follow driving directions for Hike 18 to the Y junction with the Cape Royal Road, and bear right toward Cape Royal. You pass the crossing of the Ken Patrick Trail after 1 mile and the Vista Encantadora overlook after 4.6 miles. The small, easy-to-miss Cape Final trailhead lies on the left (east) side of the road 11.8 miles from the Y junction with the Point Imperial Road and 2.5 miles north of the road's end at Cape Royal.

The hike: This trail offers the greatest rewards for the smallest investment of time and effort of any of the North Rim's plateau-top trails. The route follows a gently rising, long-closed road through parklike forests of ponderosa pine to a panoramic viewpoint on the east rim of the Kaibab Plateau, affording an unusual perspective of the Grand Canyon from high above Unkar Creek canyon.

This trip can be taken as a leisurely day hike or as an overnighter and is particularly attractive when summer heat grips the inner Canyon. The entire route affords excellent camping areas on the needle-carpeted ponderosa forest floor and other sites can be found among the pinyons closer to the rim. Few places in the Park offer a finer setting for a Grand Canyon sunrise over the Painted Desert.

From the trailhead, follow the signed Cape Final Trail east into the open forest of ponderosa pine. The trail rises gently to moderately to the crest of an 8,000-foot ridge after 0.75 mile, then follows an undulating course for

CAPE FINAL

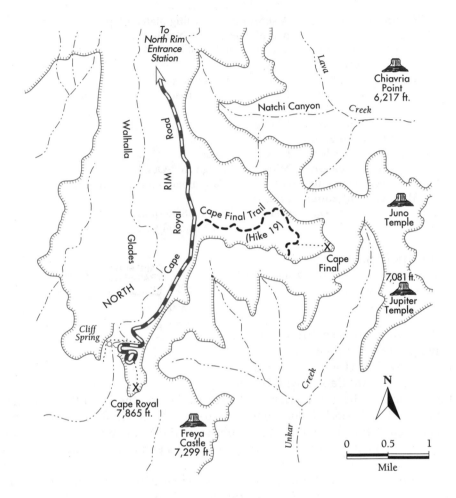

another 0.5 mile through the peaceful forest to a clearing at the rim of the plateau, where a dramatic view suddenly unfolds.

The depths of Chuar Valley spread out far below. Its broad lower reaches, where hills and gentle slopes are composed of soft Galeros formation rocks (part of the Pre-Cambrian Grand Canyon Supergroup), contrast with the angular profile of the soaring cliffs above. Lava Creek, Chuar's western tributary, is bounded by a striking array of colorful buttes, including the square-edged crag of 7,914-foot Siegfried Pyre and red Supai-capped Gunther Castle. The deep serpentine gorge of the Little Colorado River opens up beyond Marble Platform in the southeast, slicing through the platform into the distance.

From the Cape Final Trail, the blocky tower of Siegfried Pyre rises to the skyline above Lava Creek, a Chuar Creek tributary.

From the overlook, sometimes used as a campsite, the trail bends south, then west, where pinyons begin to supplant the ponderosa pines. The pinyons, along with Gambel oak, sagebrush, cliffrose, and curl-leaf mountain mahogany, signal your approach to the rim, where an increase in available sunlight, thin soils, high evaporation, and hot, dry updrafts from the Canyon below create an environment inhospitable to ponderosa pine.

Soon the trail, more apparently an old road, curves back to the south, where it ends. A foot path winds a short distance through the pinyon from there to the south rim of Cape Final, where a panoramic Grand Canyon vista unfolds. Far below lies Unkar Creek, with the bold pyramid of Vishnu Temple as a backdrop, winding through its cliff-bound canyon to broad Unkar Delta at the Colorado River. There the river silently flows through a comparatively wide valley, where long slopes of soft, red Dox sandstone spread out on both sides of the river.

Unkar Delta is notable not only for its size—some 300 acres—but also for the number of Anasazi dwelling sites discovered there by archaeologists. At least ninety-four sites, many with large rooms and some featuring kivas, suggest Anasazi occupation of Unkar Delta until the late twelfth century.

The vista encompasses a broad sweep of Grand Canyon landscapes. In the southeast your view reaches well into the shadowed gorge of the Little Colorado River and to the towering walls of the Palisades of the Desert, with the rolling hills of the Painted Desert stretching far into the distance beyond. Far to the south rises Grand Canyon's South Rim, incised by a multitude of steep, short canyons plunging into the Colorado River's gorge.

Beyond the South Rim, the wooded expanse of the Coconino Plateau reaches out to the San Francisco volcanic field, punctuated by its namesake peaks, and other lofty cones such as Kendrick Peak and Bill Williams Mountain.

The actual point of Cape Final lies about 0.3 mile east of the overlook, and since it projects well into the void of the Canyon, it affords an all-encompassing view of lower Marble Canyon and the eastern Grand Canyon. You can reach Cape Final by a bushwhack route from the overlook, but perhaps the best way to reach it is to backtrack along the trail to the point where it first bends back to the north, about 200 yards beyond the margins of the pinyon woodland.

There, a faint path branches southeast from the main trail (the junction may be marked with a cairn), and you can follow this path for about 150 yards through the ponderosa forest. Once this path begins to fade out, you can see Cape Final's Kaibab limestone promontory up ahead. Simply weave a way through the pinyons, Gambel oaks, and curl-leaf for another 0.2 mile or so to the point.

After enjoying this brief, but rewarding hike, retrace your steps to the trailhead.

General description:	A short but fascinating walk below the rim of Walhalla Plateau.
Distance:	2 miles round-trip.
Difficulty:	Easy.
Average hiking time:	0.5 to 1 hour round-trip.
Type of trail:	Unmaintained; good condition.
Trailhead elevation:	7,750 feet.
Low point:	7,500 feet.
Elevation loss:	150 to 200 feet.
Water availability:	Cliff Spring requires treatment; bring your own water instead.
Optimum season:	Mid-May through mid-October.
Topo maps:	Walhalla Plateau USGS quad; Trails Illustrated Grand Canyon National Park.

Key points:
- 0.0   Cliff Spring trailhead.
- 0.5   Cliff Spring.
- 1.0   End of trail.

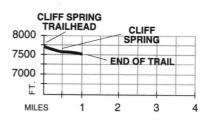

Finding the trailhead: Follow driving directions for Hike 19 to the Cape Final trailhead and continue south on the Cape Royal Road for another 1.9 miles to the signed Cliff Spring trailhead, on the left (east) side of the road at Angels Window overlook. The trailhead lies 0.6 mile north of the road's end at Cape Royal and 13.7 miles south of the Point Imperial Road junction.

The hike: This trail is a fine, albeit brief, introduction to the plateau and rim environments of the Grand Canyon's North Rim. Distant views, a well-preserved Anasazi granary, and a dripping spring hidden in an alcove beneath the rim offer a rewarding diversion for North Rim visitors budgeting their time and energy.

This brief stroll gets underway at the Angels Window overlook, which affords a fine view of that interesting natural opening in the Kaibab limestone on the east rim of Cape Royal. Carefully cross the busy roadway and follow the wide gravel trail west down a shallow draw through the open forest of ponderosa pine. After only 100 yards, you reach the ruins of a well-preserved Anasazi granary, hidden beneath a large Kaibab limestone boulder. The Kayenta Anasazi that inhabited the Grand Canyon from A.D. 900 to A.D. 1150, were limited in numbers by the scant availability of water and arable land. Generally living in small bands, these people farmed in the canyons and atop the plateaus of the North Rim and stored their corn, beans,

CLIFF SPRING TRAIL

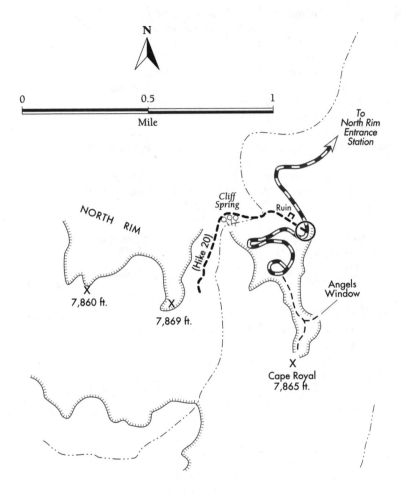

N

0   0.5   1
Mile

To
North Rim
Entrance
Station

NORTH RIM

*Cliff
Spring*

Ruin

(Hike 20)

Angels
Window

X
7,860 ft.

X
7,869 ft.

X
Cape Royal
7,865 ft.

and squash in granaries such as this one alongside the trail.

Stroll down the draw beyond the ruin, descending a moderate grade into a larger draw joining on your right (north). Here, Douglas-fir joins the forest of ponderosa pine, and groves of Gambel oak mass their ranks on the slopes above. You soon cross the dry, rocky wash on the floor of the draw beneath the spreading branches of boxelder, then follow a red ledge of Toroweap formation rocks west. Walls of Kaibab limestone begin to overhang the ledge as you contour above the increasingly deep and rugged draw.

Seeps soon begin to emerge from the base of the Kaibab cliff, nurturing small clumps of mosses. Within moments you reach a deeper alcove where Cliff Spring emerges. Much like Dripping Spring on the South Rim (see Hike 10), numerous seeps converge here and drip steadily into shallow, mossy pools. Fine views, framed by scattered pines and Douglas-fir, stretch southeast down the precipitous Clear Creek tributary below, past the erosion-isolated mesa of Wotans Throne, to Kendrick Mountain and the San Francisco Peaks, nearly 60 miles distant.

The trail continues on beyond the spring for 0.5 mile, offering a sampling of the nature of inner Canyon trails. That trail is rough and rocky, and undulates over and around obstacles including boulders and trees. This trail follows the Toroweap ledge past another dripping spring, then bends south and begins to descend along the western flanks of the plummeting canyon below. Here you may notice a change in the environment, for pinyon, agave, Utah serviceberry, mormon tea, and roundleaf buffaloberry have supplanted the conifer forest, due to the thin soils, southern exposure, and hot, dry updrafts from the Canyon far below.

The peninsula of Cape Royal rises boldly beyond the precipitous canyon to the southeast, bounded by cliffs of Kaibab limestone and the buff-toned Coconino sandstone, its cross-bedding preserving the great dunes of a vast desert that covered the region 270 million years ago. Vishnu Temple's pyramidal spire juts skyward above Grand Canyon's vast gulf, beyond the narrow isthmus separating Cape Royal from Wotans Throne.

The trail ends in a shady slickrock alcove surrounded by red Toroweap formation rocks. Don't attempt to follow the slickrock ledge around the point ahead—sheer cliffs plunge 1,000 feet below. Be content with the view from the trail's end, then backtrack to the trailhead.

General description:	A plateau-top day hike or backpack on the Grand Canyon's North Rim.
Distance:	9.8 miles round-trip.
Difficulty:	Moderate.
Average hiking time:	4 to 5 hours round-trip.
Type of trail:	Unmaintained; good condition.
Trailhead elevation:	8,080 feet.
High point:	8,250 feet.
Elevation gain and loss:	+450 feet; -650 feet.
Water availability:	None available.
Optimum season:	Mid-May through mid-October.
Use Area code:	NF9, Widforss, at-large camping.
Management zone:	Threshold.
Topo maps:	Bright Angel Point USGS quad; Trails Illustrated Grand Canyon National Park ; Earthwalk Grand Canyon National Park or Bright Angel Trail.

Key points:
- **0.0**   Widforss trailhead.
- **2.1**   Post 14, end of self-guiding segment of trail.
- **4.8**   Picnic table.
- **4.9**   Widforss Point overlook.

Finding the trailhead: Follow driving directions for Hike 18 to the Cape Royal/Point Imperial road junction and continue straight ahead; the sign points to visitor services. You will reach a sign showing the turnoff to Widforss Point after another 0.25 mile. Turn right here onto a good gravel road and skirt the margins of Harvey Meadow for another 0.6 mile to the signed trailhead on the left (west) side of the road.

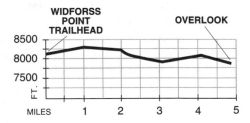

The hike: The Widforss Trail is arguably the finest plateau-top trail in the Park. The route hugs the rim of The Transept, an abysmal tributary of Bright Angel Creek, as it passes splendid Grand Canyon viewpoints between shady stands of conifer and aspen. The mildly undulating trail is well-defined and easy to follow throughout its length to the North Rim high above Haunted Canyon, where a panoramic vista of the Grand Canyon unfolds.

This trip is popular with both day hikers and summer backpackers who wisely choose to observe the ovenlike inner Canyon from the cool heights of

WIDFORSS TRAIL

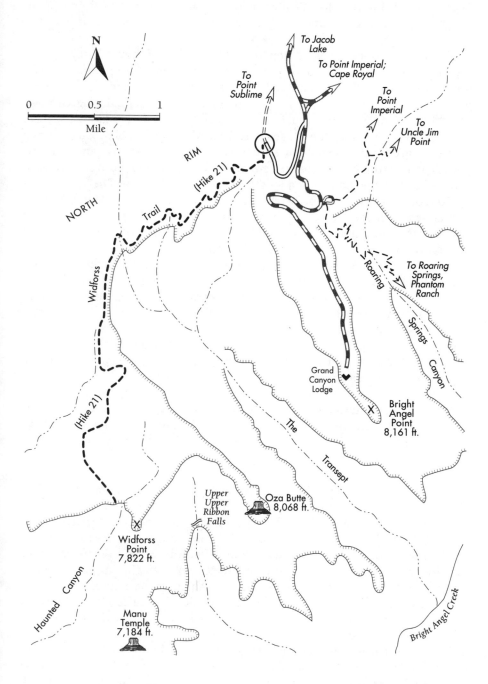

To Jacob Lake

To Point Imperial; Cape Royal

To Point Sublime

To Point Imperial

To Uncle Jim Point

N

0   0.5   1
Mile

NORTH RIM Trail (Hike 21)

Widforss

(Hike 21)

Roaring

To Roaring Springs, Phantom Ranch

Springs Canyon

Grand Canyon Lodge

Bright Angel Point 8,161 ft.

The Transept

Upper Upper Ribbon Falls

Oza Butte 8,068 ft.

Widforss Point 7,822 ft.

Haunted Canyon

Manu Temple 7,184 ft.

Bright Angel Creek

the rim. No water is available en route; be sure to pack an ample supply.

The trail and a point on the North Rim were named in honor of the artist Gunnar M. Widforss, the "Painter of the National Parks." Widforss spent much time in the 1920s and 1930s creating vivid watercolor images of the Grand Canyon, his favorite national park.

Fourteen numbered posts along the first 2.1 miles of the trail are keyed to a pamphlet available from a dispenser at the trailhead (the pamphlet inaccurately estimates the distance at 2.5 miles). Pick one up before heading out on the trail; it will enhance your enjoyment and understanding through insight into some of the natural features and processes found along the trail.

The trail begins along the fringes of Harvey Meadow, heading south among scattered groves of Engelmann spruce, white fir, ponderosa pine, and aspen. A pair of rocky switchbacks soon lead up and over exposures of Kaibab limestone to the beginning of a lengthy traverse high above The Transept, a 4,000-foot-deep tributary of Bright Angel Canyon. Francois Matthes, a topographer with the USGS, declared in the early 1900s that The Transept was far grander than Yosemite Valley. Although you may not agree, The Transept is an impressive defile nonetheless.

The trail bends in and out of seven minor draws just north of the rim during the first 2.2 miles. At first you proceed above the headwaters draw of The Transept, where you can see a dense forest of spire-topped spruce and fir, reminiscent of a subalpine forest in the Rocky Mountains, on the north-facing slopes above it. Soon, that draw begins to plummet away into the gaping abyss of The Transept, as the trail proceeds west along the rim through a forest of ponderosa pine, white fir, and aspen. Engelmann spruce joins the forest only in the shadiest draws.

Typical of most rim trails, the route often stays away from the rim, so rather than a continuum of Grand Canyon vistas, you enjoy occasional tree-framed views from the points separating the draws en route. Long-range views extend down The Transept into the depths of Bright Angel Creek, bounded on the southeast by the towering buttes of Brahma and Zoroaster temples, and far beyond to the Coconino Plateau, its wooded expanse punctuated by Red Mountain, Kendrick Peak, the San Francisco Peaks, and Bill Williams Mountain.

The trend of the trail favors descending into the draws and rising gently beyond them. After passing Post 14 in 2.1 miles, a more noticeable descent of 100 feet leads you into the seventh and final draw. You regain much of that lost elevation on the way out, where the trail begins trending southward. Beyond that draw you enjoy an ever-changing panorama as you closely follow the west rim of The Transept for 0.5 mile. Thereafter, the trail heads gently down a shallow draw for another 0.5 mile, a pleasant, shady walk affording views of only the surrounding forest.

You exit the draw curving east and gently ascend another draw nearly to the rim, where the trail turns abruptly away to the southwest, ascending a moderately steep grade onto a forest-crowned ridge situated well to the west of the rim of The Transept. As you continue generally south along this ridge, ponderosa pines eventually begin to dominate the forest, crowding out fir and aspen. Soon after, the pines grow smaller in stature—a sure sign you are approaching the Canyon rim. After reaching a picnic table and campsite, you descend for several yards to an extraordinary overlook of the Grand Canyon, at 7,920 feet, affording perhaps the finest view from the North Rim.

The "rim effect" is well-pronounced here. Below the picnic table, the ponderosa forest rapidly thins, and you descend among thorny New Mexican locust to the overlook, where a few remaining pines share space with pinyon, juniper, cliffrose, Gambel oak, and silktassel.

Although Widforss Point is actually the Kaibab limestone pinnacle beyond the draw to the southeast, most hikers are content to enjoy the incomparable view from the trail's end. If you're not a Grand Canyon veteran, you may need to use your topo map to help identify some of the many landmarks visible from the point.

Since the overlook is higher in elevation (7,900 feet) than the South Rim, you look down onto the Coconino Plateau and across its wooded expanse to the lofty cones of the San Francisco volcanic field. The South Rim stretches from the southeast near Desert View to the southwest at Yuma Point high above Hermit Creek and the Boucher Trail. Sun reflecting from cars' windshields helps you locate popular South Rim viewpoints, such as Yaki, Yavapai, and Mather points. The town of Tusayan and the El Tovar/Bright Angel Lodge complex are also visible, yet these enclaves of civilization seem insignificant in the wild vastness of canyon and plateau.

To the southeast, prominent North Rim features include the wooded mesa of Wotans Throne, the twin buttes of Angels Gate, and Brahma and Zoroaster temples, which together frame a more distant view of Horseshoe Mesa beneath the South Rim. Below your vantage rises the Coconino sandstone-capped cone of Manu Temple and Esplanade-crowned Clement Powell Butte. A notch in that butte reveals a view of the distant South Kaibab Trail and The Tipoff. West of Clement Powell Butte lies the crag of Buddha Temple and beyond it, Isis Temple, which together guard the red rock defile of Haunted Canyon far below.

After absorbing the tremendous vista, retrace your steps.

General description:	A plateau-top half-day hike or overnighter on the North Rim of the Grand Canyon.
Distance:	3.9 miles round-trip.
Difficulty:	Moderately easy.
Average hiking time:	2 to 3 hours round-trip.
Type of trail:	Unmaintained; good condition.
Trailhead elevation:	8,250 feet.
High point:	8,450 feet.
Elevation gain and loss:	600 feet.
Water availability:	None available.
Optimum season:	Mid-May through mid-October.
Use Area code:	NA9, Walhalla Plateau, at-large camping.
Management zone:	Primitive.
Topo maps:	Bright Angel Point USGS quad; Trails Illustrated Grand Canyon National Park; Earthwalk Grand Canyon National Park or Bright Angel Trail.

Key points:
- **0.0** North Kaibab trailhead.
- **0.4** Junction with Ken Patrick Trail; bear right.
- **0.9** Junction with loop trail; bear left.
- **2.0** Uncle Jim Point overlook.
- **3.0** Return to junction with loop trail; bear left.
- **3.9** North Kaibab trailhead.

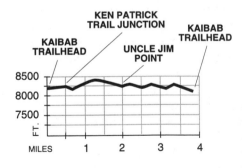

Finding the trailhead: Follow driving directions for Hike 23.

The hike: Much like the longer Widforss Trail, the mildly undulating Uncle Jim Trail traverses cool Kaibab Plateau forests en route to a splendid Grand Canyon viewpoint. From the trail's end hikers gain an excellent overview of Roaring Springs Canyon and can visually trace the route of the North Kaibab Trail as it winds its way from the North Rim to the Redwall limestone.

The trail, waterless throughout its length, is rougher and rockier than other North Rim trails due to occasional mule traffic. Overnight camping is allowed on this route (with a Backcountry Use Permit, of course), making it a good choice for a short backpack when intense summer heat grips the inner Canyon. Most hikers can complete this semi-loop hike in about 2 hours, but 3 hours allows for a more leisurely pace.

UNCLE JIM TRAIL

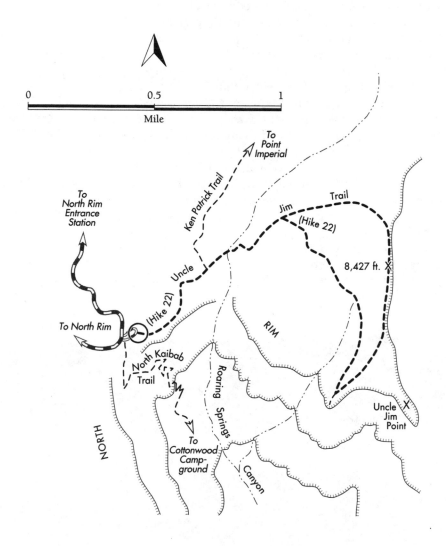

0   0.5   1

Mile

To
Point
Imperial

To
North Rim
Entrance
Station

Ken Patrick Trail

Jim   Trail

(Hike 22)

Uncle

8,427 ft. X

(Hike 22)

To North Rim

RIM

North Kaibab

Trail

Roaring

Springs

Uncle
Jim
Point

NORTH

To
Cottonwood
Camp-
ground

Canyon

The trail was named in honor of James T. "Uncle Jim" Owens. Formerly a game warden in Yellowstone National Park, Owens was hired in 1906 by the Forest Service to serve as game warden in the Grand Canyon Game Reserve on the Kaibab Plateau. He lived part time in the cave near the Widforss trailhead on the north edge of Harvey Meadow. Game management of the time called for the elimination of "undesirable," predatory species in favor of "harmless" wildlife, such as deer. By 1918, Uncle Jim claimed to have killed 532 mountain lions, and the tragic result was explosive growth of the Kaibab deer population, reaching an estimated 100,000 deer by 1924.

The population was far greater than their limited range on the Kaibab Plateau could sustain, and thousands died of starvation during the hard winter of 1924-1925. The result was a recognition that predators are more efficient "game managers," and today mountain lions thrive on the Kaibab Plateau.

Uncle Jim Owens did leave a lasting legacy in the Grand Canyon region. In 1906, he and others brought bison to the Kaibab Plateau. This herd was the progenitor of the herd that now occupies the House Rock Valley, and occasionally some of the approximately 125 bison range up into the meadows of the plateau.

The Uncle Jim and Ken Patrick trails begin as a single path from the east edge of the North Kaibab trailhead parking lot adjacent to the mule corral. At first you follow the North Rim east through a forest of ponderosa pine and aspen, their ranks open enough to afford fine views into the rugged

The switchbacks of the North Kaibab Trail come into view from the end of the Uncle Jim Trail.

depths of Roaring Springs Canyon, and beyond to the South Rim and the distant San Francisco Peaks.

Soon you contour away from the rim, entering heavy forest dominated by white fir. Shortly the previously level trail dips into a minor draw, then gradually ascends to a signed junction, at 8,300 feet, beneath a grove of stout, towering pines. Bear right here onto the Uncle Jim Trail. The tread becomes quite gravelly ahead as you descend a moderate grade northeast through mixed conifer forest into the shady confines of a draw—the head-waters draw of Roaring Springs Canyon.

As you ascend a moderate grade out of the draw, Engelmann spruce makes a brief appearance among the pine, fir, and aspen, on the sheltered north-west-facing slopes. After ascending a few minor switchbacks, you then rise to an unsigned junction at 8,350 feet, where you are faced with the only decision you must make on this trip. This junction marks the beginning of a loop trail to Uncle Jim Point; both legs of the loop are about 1 mile long, but since the left leg leads to Canyon views sooner, most hikers will bear left at the junction.

That leg of the loop continues ascending gently through the peaceful forest, and after 0.3 mile you gain the top of a broad ridge at your high point of 8,450 feet, then begin a long curve toward the south. Soon the trail skirts the east rim of the ridge, where views open up into the cliff-bound depths of upper Bright Angel Canyon and beyond it to the flat, forested expanse of Walhalla Plateau. These features soon fade from view as you duck back into

The Uncle Jim Trail provides fine views from the North Rim of Roaring Springs Canyon; Deva, Brahma, and Zoroaster temples; and of the South Rim.

the forest and head southwest away from the rim. After 1.1 miles from the loop trail junction, you meet the west leg of the loop joining from the north. Continue straight ahead, past a dilapidated mule hitch rail, and follow the path down over slabs of Kaibab limestone out to the overlook, just below the rim at 8,300 feet.

Here the "rim effect" is well-pronounced, as pinyon, juniper, cliffrose, and Utah serviceberry from the inner Canyon share space with Gambel oak, ponderosa pine, and white fir, trees of the Kaibab Plateau high country.

Your view, somewhat obstructed by the small trees and shrubs that are massed at the point, reaches far below into the abyss of Roaring Springs Canyon, past its confluence with Bright Angel Canyon, to a high ridge capped by bold towers: Deva Temple, Hattan Butte, and Brahma and Zoroaster temples. The long-range view stretches 12 miles across the Grand Canyon to the South Rim and beyond. You'll see across the thickly wooded expanse of the Coconino Plateau, punctuated by the summits of Red Butte near the town of Tusayan, 9,256-foot Bill Williams Mountain, 10,418-foot Kendrick Peak, and the lofty San Francisco Peaks, crowned by 12,633-foot Humphreys Peak, the highest point in Arizona.

The well-defined switchbacks of the North Kaibab Trail can be seen leading through the cliffs into Roaring Springs Canyon, and you can visually trace that trail through the Redwall and into the canyon far below.

To return to the trailhead, backtrack for several yards to the junction and bear left onto the west leg of the loop. This pleasant but viewless trail mildly undulates through a forest of white fir, ponderosa pine, and aspen for 1 mile to the junction with the other leg of the loop. Bear left there and retrace your steps for 0.9 mile to the trailhead.

General description:	A rim-to-river backpack of four or more days, frequently used as part of a rim-to-rim trip.
Distance:	28 miles round-trip.
Difficulty:	Strenuous.
Average hiking times:	4 to 5 hours down to Cottonwood Campground; 4 hours both ways to Bright Angel Campground; 6 to 7 hours to return to rim from Cottonwood Campground.
Type of trail:	Maintained; excellent condition.
Trailhead elevation:	8,250 feet.
Low point:	2,480 feet (Bright Angel Campground).
Elevation loss:	5,770 feet.
Water availability:	Piped drinking water is available May through October at Supai Tunnel, 1.8 miles, and Cottonwood Campground, 6.9 miles; all year at Bright Angel Campground, 14 miles; Bright Angel Creek provides a perennial water supply along much of the trail, but must be treated before drinking.
Suggested cache points:	Caching water along this trail is not necessary.
Optimum season:	Mid-May through mid-October.
Use Area codes:	CCG, Cottonwood, designated campground; CBG, Bright Angel, designated campground.
Management zone:	Corridor.
Topo maps:	Bright Angel Point and Phantom Ranch USGS quads; Trails Illustrated Grand Canyon National Park; Earthwalk Bright Angel Trail or Grand Canyon National Park.

Key points:

0.0	North Kaibab trailhead.
1.8	Supai Tunnel.
4.7	Junction with Roaring Springs Trail; bear right.
6.9	Cottonwood Campground.
8.0	Junction with Ribbon Falls Trail; bear left.
13.3	Junction with Clear Creek Trail; stay right.
13.8	Phantom Ranch.
14.0	Bridge spanning Bright Angel Creek at entrance to Bright Angel Campground.

Best day hike destinations: The 3.6-mile round-trip to Supai Tunnel offers memorable inner Canyon views and a fine introduction to Grand Canyon hiking. Strong hikers frequently take the 10-mile round-trip to Roaring Springs, which is far enough below the rim (3,300 feet) for hikers to gain the *feel* of Grand Canyon hiking and to appreciate its great dimensions.

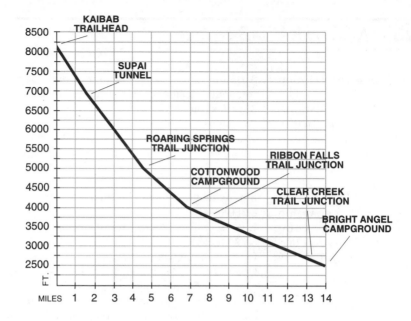

Finding the trailhead: From Jacob Lake, Arizona, follow Arizona Highway 67 south for 31.2 miles to the North Rim entrance station, then continue south into the Park. The Park highway ahead winds through lovely meadows and forests of pine, fir, spruce, and aspen. You pass the Cape Royal/Point Imperial road junction after 9.5 miles and continue straight ahead for another 0.9 mile, where a prominent sign indicates the Kaibab Trail parking lot on the left (east) side of the road.

This parking lot fills to capacity nearly every day by late morning. If it is full when you arrive, you must drive to the public parking areas near Grand Canyon Lodge, then either walk the mule trail that parallels the Park road for 1.5 miles to the trailhead or ride the shuttle bus (inquire at the Grand Canyon Lodge transportation desk for shuttle schedules).

The hike: The North Kaibab Trail is the North Rim's only maintained trail, lying within the frequently patrolled Corridor Zone of the Park. Unlike many of the Grand Canyon's trails that follow the path of least resistance in search of breaks in the cliff bands, this straightforward trail forges its way through the Canyon's obstructions.

More hikers pound this trail than any other on the North Rim, and for ample reasons. The tread is wide, only occasionally rocky, and it descends moderately, rarely steeply. The way offers a classic sampling of all the life zones present in the Grand Canyon, and the landscapes it traverses and the views it affords are dramatic. Not only is the trail popular for rim-to-river and rim-to-rim backpack trips, day hikers use the trail to reach a variety of scenic destinations: the top of the Coconino sandstone cliffs, Supai Tunnel, and Roaring Springs.

NORTH KAIBAB TRAIL

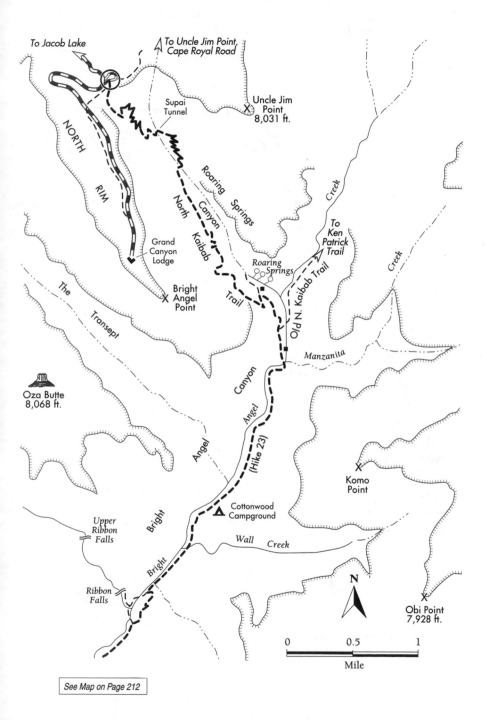

To Jacob Lake

To Uncle Jim Point,
Cape Royal Road

Supai
Tunnel

Uncle Jim
Point
8,031 ft.

NORTH RIM

Roaring Springs Canyon

North Kaibab Trail

Creek

To
Ken
Patrick
Trail

Grand
Canyon
Lodge

Roaring
Springs

Creek

Bright
Angel
Point

Old N. Kaibab Trail

The Transept

Manzanita

Oza Butte
8,068 ft.

Bright Angel Canyon

Komo
Point

(Hike 23)

Upper
Ribbon
Falls

Cottonwood
Campground

Bright

Wall   Creek

Bright

N

Ribbon
Falls

Obi Point
7,928 ft.

0   0.5   1

Mile

See Map on Page 212

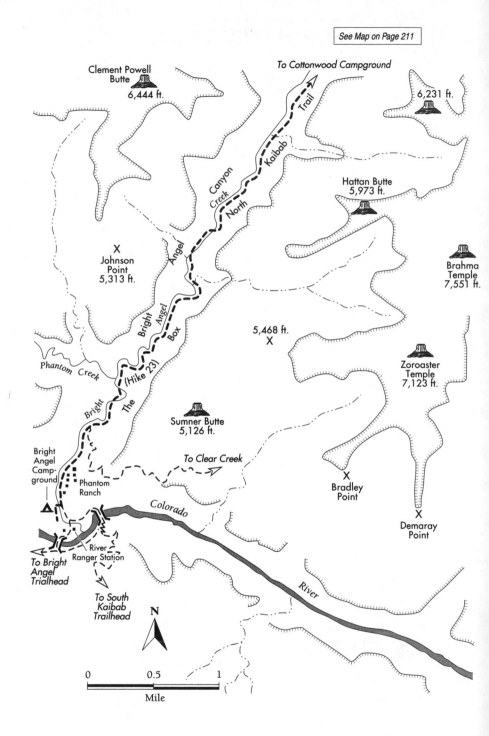

See Map on Page 211

Clement Powell
Butte
6,444 ft.

To Cottonwood Campground

6,231 ft.

Hattan Butte
5,973 ft.

North Kaibab Trail

Canyon Creek

X
Johnson
Point
5,313 ft.

Bright Angel

Angel Box

Brahma
Temple
7,551 ft.

5,468 ft.
X

Zoroaster
Temple
7,123 ft.

Phantom Creek

(Hike 23)

Bright   The

Sumner Butte
5,126 ft.

Bright
Angel
Camp-
ground

Phantom
Ranch

To Clear Creek

X
Bradley
Point

X
Demaray
Point

Colorado

River

River
Ranger Station

To Bright
Angel
Trailhead

To South
Kaibab
Trailhead

N

0   0.5   1

Mile

Backpackers on the trail are restricted to staying in developed campgrounds and usually pass their first night at Cottonwood Campground (6.9 miles and 4,200 feet below the rim), and their second night at Bright Angel Campground. Hiking out to the South Rim from the latter campground is much shorter and less strenuous than backtracking to the North Rim, and the rim-to-rim hike is a popular and rewarding way to see the Grand Canyon. A commercial rim-to-rim shuttle service, which requires advance reservations and a substantial fee, is available (see "Planning Your Trip").

First-time Grand Canyon hikers taking the rim-to-rim trip should consider spending a third night on the trail at Indian Garden Campground, rather than making the long, strenuous hike out to the South Rim in one day.

The trail begins behind the information sign at the rim, below the entrance to the trailhead parking lot. You descend steadily at once, passing through a cool forest of white fir, Douglas-fir, ponderosa pine, and aspen. The initial descent through the Kaibab limestone passes unnoticed, since erosion has subdued the Kaibab's typical cliff into a slope cloaked behind dense vegetation.

Switchbacks soon lead you deeper into the void of Roaring Springs Canyon, and the grade abates briefly atop the sheer, desert-varnished cliffs of Coconino sandstone. Gnarled pines and firs clinging to the slickrock rim of the cliffs are reminiscent of a scene from Yosemite.

Conifers persist as you follow switchbacks through the break in the Coconino. A wide variety of shrubs dress these slopes and the red slopes of Hermit shale below. En route the trail forges a way through thickets of Rocky Mountain maple, Gambel oak, mallow ninebark, elderberry, thorny New Mexican locust, wildrose, and silktassel. An occasional juniper begins to infiltrate the ranks of Douglas-fir and white fir that dominate the forest on the shady slopes.

After 1.8 miles, at 6,840 feet, you reach a water faucet offering seasonal water and toilets in a confined, rocky draw. Then you plunge through the Esplanade sandstone via the short Supai Tunnel. Rather than traverse the Supai rock layer as do most Grand Canyon trails, the North Kaibab Trail descends the Supai more directly, via switchbacks, where the grade becomes moderately steep. As you descend, you will notice that the inner Canyon desert begins to exert its influence on the sun-drenched slopes and ledges of red rocks. Utah serviceberry, cliffrose, Apache plume, and shrubs of the pinyon-juniper woodland begin to appear on trailside slopes, plus the small trees of redbud, hophornbeam, and boxelder.

The hot, shadeless descent leads to the top of the Redwall limestone, where a sturdy bridge spans the rocky gorge of Roaring Springs Canyon. Beyond the bridge the trail ascends briefly upon brushy slopes, then begins a lengthy, generally descending traverse through the Redwall. Unlike most Grand Canyon trails that use a natural break in the Redwall cliff to descend, this trail was carved into the cliff, making this Redwall descent more gradual and thus less strenuous.

The traverse is spectacular, following the wall of cliffs that plunge from the trail's edge into the increasingly deep nadir of Roaring Springs Canyon. The undulating trail eventually descends via several switchbacks to a rocky notch just below the Redwall spire of The Needle. This notch lies on the western upthrust side of the Roaring Springs Fault.

More switchbacks ensue below the notch, leading into a shady, spring-dampened grotto, beyond which the traverse resumes. Soon the green oasis below Roaring Springs comes into view on the canyon floor below. As you approach a point opposite the springs, you first spy three vigorous springs spouting from the Muav limestone cliff, but they certainly aren't roaring. Shortly, though, a much larger spring appears, its waters falling down the canyon wall in a pretty, terraced cascade. Roaring Springs supplies water to both Canyon rims, and the pumphouse that serves the North Rim is visible in the canyon far below.

Soon the trail descends more steeply, over slopes of Bright Angel shale cloaked in a dense woodland of pinyon and juniper, and after a single switchback you meet the signed spur trail to Roaring Springs at 5,040 feet. That trail descends 100 feet in about 0.3 mile to a cottonwood-shaded picnic area.

Bear right at the junction and begin a moderately descending, occasionally steep, traverse of the shale slopes, now only sparsely clad by gnarled pinyons, junipers, scrub live oak, and manzanita. Views begin to open up to the east from this stretch into upper Bright Angel Canyon, flanked by brushy slopes, towering cliffs, and the forest-fringed North Rim. After meandering across the shale slopes, you begin to enter the Tapeats sandstone narrows as you approach the roiling waters of Bright Angel Creek, a sizable, vigorous stream. As you proceed down into the Tapeats-rimmed gorge, you pass above the pumphouse operator's residence and reach a seasonal water faucet just beyond it.

Within another hundred yards you bridge Bright Angel Creek at the mouth of Manzanita Canyon, then proceed downstream several yards above the winding course of boisterous, willow-bordered Bright Angel Creek. The desert continues to exert its influence as you descend, and plants of the Lower Sonoran Zone, including datura, yucca, mormon tea, and Engelmann prickly pear, mix into the thickets of scrub live oak that mass along the trailside slopes.

Not far below the bridge you emerge from the Tapeats sandstone onto red and gray slopes of Dox sandstone, the upper layer of the Grand Canyon Supergroup. The final stretch to Cottonwood Campground reveals good views down the long trough of Bright Angel Canyon to the South Rim and the head of the Bright Angel Trail.

After walking 1.4 miles from the bridge, a trailside sign proclaims the entrance to Cottonwood Campground, at 4,040 feet, opposite the mouth of The Transept's exceedingly deep gorge. The campground lies in an open setting in a broad part of the canyon, embraced by colorful cliffs, with the music of the ebullient creek nearby. Soaring cliffs, ranging from the Tapeats sandstone to the Kaibab limestone, bound Bright Angel Canyon and The Transept, framing views of the conifer-fringed North Rim more than 4,000 feet above. Bright Angel Point juts into the canyon almost overhead to the

Cottonwood Campground, deep in Bright Angel Canyon, is a fine place to pass your first night on the North Kaibab Trail.

north, and Komo Point looms above to the east.

Spreading clumps of scrub live oak offer a modicum of shade and afford reasonable privacy between campsites. A variety of desert shrubs, cacti, and bunchgrasses dress the slopes above the sites. Drinking water (May through October) and toilets are provided, and each site features a picnic table, pack poles, and ammo cans for food storage. At the lower end of the campground is a seasonally staffed ranger station, situated in the only shady grove of Fremont cottonwoods in the campground.

After the trail leaves the campground, it follows an undulating course, at times edging close to the creek but more often contouring along the slopes above. Here desert shrubs achieve dominance on trailside slopes, and they include yucca, catclaw, mormon tea, various cacti, Apache plume, plus rabbitbrush, a shrub common to the plateaus. Excellent views stretch down-canyon to the South Rim and above to Oza Butte on the northwest skyline.

About 0.5 mile below the campground you cross a sill composed of intrusive diabase, then drop down to a rock-hop crossing of perennial Wall Creek. Beyond, the trail proceeds through open flats, now on a tread of dark red Shinumo quartzite. About 1.2 miles below the campground, the signed trail to Ribbon Falls continues straight ahead, while the main trail branches left, ascending the steep, 100-foot hill ahead.

Few hikers forgo the spur trail to Ribbon Falls, which bridges the creek several yards ahead, then contours into a shallow amphitheater bounded by dark red cliffs of Shinumo quartzite, reaching the falls after 0.3 mile. Ribbon Falls plunges about 100 feet over the resistant ledge of a diabase sill and lands on a moss-draped travertine cone. Water-loving hanging gardens vegetation thrives here, including maidenhair fern, golden columbine, and scarlet monkeyflower. The cool spray of the falls nurtures this delicate vegetation, and is irresistible to hikers on a hot day.

Back at the junction, follow the switchbacks of the North Kaibab Trail, rising steeply over the hill, then descend just as steeply down the other side to the edge of the creekbed below. After about 0.3 mile, another signed trail branches west to Ribbon Falls. This trail, however, requires a difficult crossing of Bright Angel Creek via slippery boulders and is best avoided.

The trail continues down the broad, spectacular canyon, staying atop a shrub-dotted bench above the creek. Up ahead, the creek dives into an inner gorge known as The Box. As you approach The Box, you slosh through the mud of one seep and shortly thereafter encounter a more vigorous spring that flows down the trailbed. Bordered by thickets of willow, saw grass, and horsetails, there is no avoiding this wet stretch. Partly submerged slabs help you avoid wet feet, and soon you emerge from the quagmire back onto dry tread.

Walls of gray-green Bass limestone begin to enclose the canyon as you enter The Box. Soon the canyon becomes a narrow, twisting hallway, hemmed in by the dark, convoluted cliffs of Rama schist that amplify the music of the rushing stream. The walls grow higher as you twist and turn through the meanders of The Box. Four bridges en route facilitate passage across the creek. When this trail was in its infancy prior to reconstruction by the Park Service in the 1920s, more than forty stream crossings were required in The Box.

About 300 yards upstream from the slot at the mouth of Phantom Creek, you may notice an exotic palm tree growing on the west bank of Bright Angel Creek. Unlike the tall palms of the California desert, this tree is a low mound of fronds only about 10 feet tall.

After 3.7 miles and about 1.5 hours of hiking through the shadowed confines of The Box, the canyon begins to open up; clumps of gray brittlebush and thickets of arrow weed begin to fringe the trail. Once again, South Rim views unfold, reaching up to Yavapai Point, now looming very close rather than the distant, almost unattainable goal it appeared to be from the Cottonwood Campground environs.

Soon you pass the Clear Creek Trail branching left (see Hike 8). Cottonwoods and mesquite soon appear as you approach the Phantom Ranch complex. The trail skirts the snack bar building, then becomes quite rocky and dusty as it passes Phantom Ranger Station, and soon reaches the bridge at the entrance to Bright Angel Campground. From Bright Angel Campground, either backtrack to the North Rim or see Hikes 6 and 7 to reach the South Rim.

---

24 NORTH BASS TRAIL

General description:	A rigorous rim-to-river backpack of four or more days, tracing one of the North Rim's most difficult trails, for experienced Grand Canyon hikers only.
Distance:	27 miles round-trip.
Difficulty:	Very strenuous.
Average hiking times:	2 to 3 hours to the top of the Redwall descent; 4 to 5 hours to Shinumo Creek/White Creek confluence; 2 hours to the Colorado River. The return to the rim will nearly double your hiking time.
Type of trail:	Unmaintained; poor condition.
Trailhead elevation:	7,520 feet.
Low point:	2,200 feet.
Elevation gain and loss:	+300 feet; -5,620 feet.
Water availability:	Muav Saddle spring, 1.3 miles; available intermittently in upper White Creek; perennial in Tapeats narrows of White Creek and Shinumo Creek; Colorado River.
Suggested cache points:	Muav Saddle or at the top or bottom of the Redwall descent.
Optimum season:	Late May or early June through mid-October.
Use Area code:	AS9, North Bass, at-large camping.
Management zone:	Primitive.
Topo maps:	King Arthur Castle and Havasupai Point USGS quads; Trails Illustrated Grand Canyon National Park.

Also See Map on Page 143

Key points:

- **0.0** Swamp Point trailhead.
- **1.0** Trail junction at Muav Saddle; turn left.
- **1.2** Junction with trail to spring; bear right.
- **4.5** Top of Redwall descent.
- **5.3** Muav Canyon wash (White Creek).
- **10.3** Shinumo Creek.
- **12.0** Shinumo (Bass) Camp.
- **13.5** Colorado River.

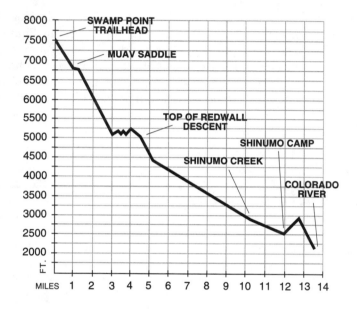

Best day hike destinations: The 2-mile round-trip to historic Muav Saddle cabin offers a unique destination for a short day hike. Many hikers, however, continue on to Powell Plateau (see Hike 25). The rugged, brushy, and obscure North Bass Trail is demanding. The 9-mile round-trip to the top of the Redwall is a good destination for seasoned hikers, where they will enjoy fine views into lower Muav Canyon and Shinumo Amphitheater.

Finding the trailhead: From Jacob Lake, Arizona, follow Arizona Highway 67 south for 26.5 miles to the prominently signed junction with Forest Road 22 (also signed for Dry Park 10) and turn right (west). This junction lies 0.9 mile south of Kaibab Lodge and immediately south of tiny Deer Lake.

This good gravel road, with washboards, ascends steadily through spruce, fir, and aspen forest for 2.1 miles to the signed junction with Forest Road 270, where you turn left (south). Follow this occasionally rough and rocky road south for 2.3 miles, avoiding two unsigned right-forking roads en route, to a junction where a sign points west to Fire Point 12. Turn right here onto

NORTH BASS TRAIL

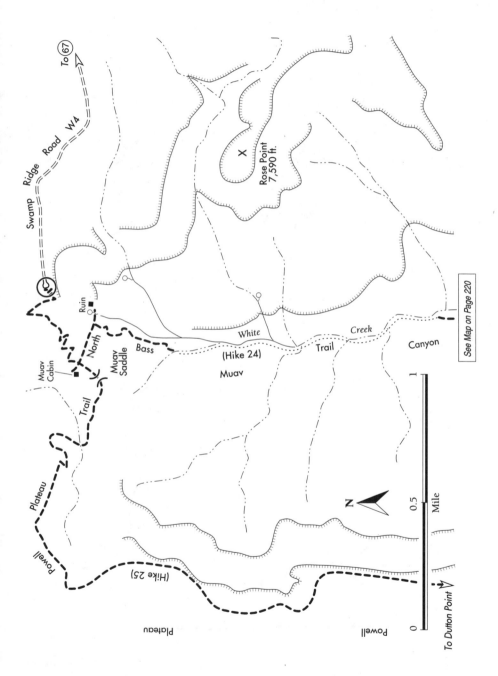

To 67

Swamp Ridge Road W4

Rose Point
7,590 ft.
X

See Map on Page 220

Ruin

North

Bass

White

Creek

Trail

Canyon

Muav Cabin

Muav Saddle

Muav

(Hike 24)

Trail

Plateau

Powell

(Hike 25)

Plateau

Powell

N

0.5   Mile   1   0

To Dutton Point

See Map on Page 219

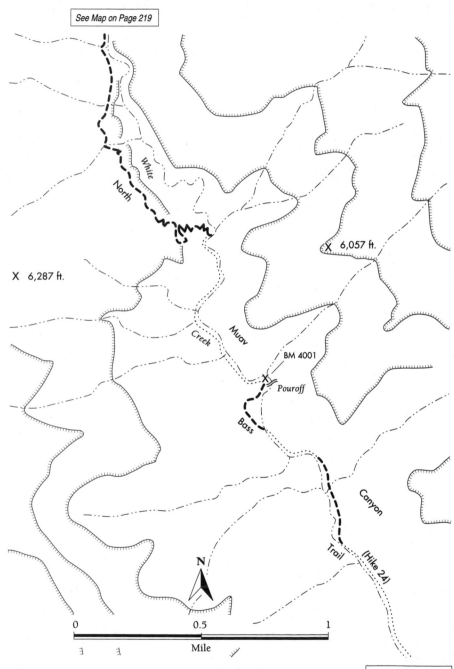

X 6,287 ft.

White

North

X 6,057 ft.

Creek

Muav

BM 4001

Pouroff

Bass

Canyon

Trail

(Hike 24)

N

0   0.5   1

Mile

See Map on Page 221

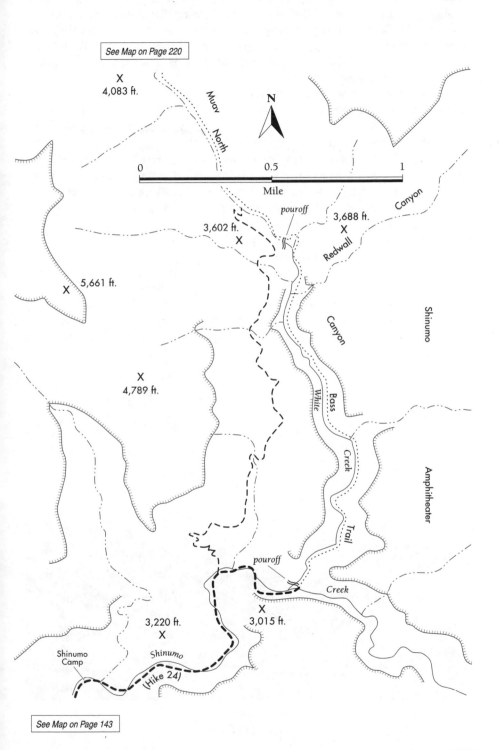

See Map on Page 220

X
4,083 ft.

Muav North

N

0   0.5   1

Mile

pouroff

3,688 ft.
X

Redwall Canyon

3,602 ft.
X

5,661 ft.
X

Shinumo

Canyon

White

Bass

4,789 ft.
X

Creek

Amphitheater

Trail

pouroff

Creek

3,220 ft.
X

X
3,015 ft.

Shinumo
Camp

Shinumo

(Hike 24)

See Map on Page 143

Forest Road 223, also rough and rocky in places, and proceed 5.8 miles to left-branching Forest Road 268, signed for Swamp Point, your destination.

Follow FR 268 south, again rough and rocky in places, for 0.3 mile, then turn left onto FR 268B, a good but narrow gravel road. Follow FR 268B for 1.2 miles to the Park boundary, where the road is designated W4, and its condition quickly deteriorates.

Rocks and roots, potholes, and farther on, high centers make the use of a high-clearance vehicle advisable. After driving 0.2 mile from the Park boundary, avoid an unsigned road that branches left to Kanabownits Spring, and bear right, proceeding generally west through the pristine forest of pine, fir, and aspen. You pass an inviting camping/parking area 7.8 miles from the Park boundary, after which the road becomes extremely rough and rocky for the final 0.1 mile to the Swamp Point trailhead, 19.6 miles from AZ 67.

Hikers arriving late in the day can camp wherever they wish along the access roads within the Kaibab National Forest. You can camp at the Swamp Point trailhead after obtaining a permit from the Backcountry Reservations Office (Use Area NJ9, Swamp Ridge).

(Note: The final segment of the road to Swamp Point, within Park boundaries, is blocked each winter by fallen trees. Park Service fire crews may not clear the road until mid-June or later each year. Be prepared to spend an extra day or two walking if you find the road blocked by fallen trees. Remember that Park Service regulations prohibit driving off established roadways.)

Muav Canyon and Shinumo Amphitheater.

The hike: The North Bass Trail, actually more a route than a trail, is one of the most difficult and demanding trails in the Grand Canyon. Erosion and dense brush thickets have reclaimed much of the trail and only segments of discernible tread remain. In between, hikers follow a sporadically cairned route.

This trail, an old Indian route once known as the Shinumo Trail (shinumo is a Paiute word referring to the ancient cliff-dwelling inhabitants of the Canyon), was later improved by a prospector known only as White, who may have lived for a time near Muav Saddle spring. William Wallace Bass, who constructed the South Bass Trail in the 1880s, rebuilt the so-called White Trail to the North Rim by 1900. Using a cable crossing at the Colorado River, Bass guided tourists from the South Rim to the North Rim via his trail, some on sightseeing trips, others on hunting trips.

Only seasoned hikers with a yearning for adventure should attempt this route, allowing at least four to five days to complete the trip. The way involves considerable, often inventive, route-finding, boulder-hopping, scrambling, bushwhacking, and, at times, a good deal of exposure to plunging cliffs. Don't become discouraged by the first third of the trail to the top of the Redwall; that segment is the hardest part of the trail. The remainder of the trail, though it involves much boulder-hopping and detours around obstacles, is much easier—for experienced hikers—than the rim-to-Redwall segment.

Much of the scenery en route is quite different from any other area in the Grand Canyon. Erosion along the Muav Fault, which separates Powell Plateau from the North Rim, has softened the abrupt edges of the rim and upper Muav Canyon, which has a broad, V-shaped profile. Soils in the canyon are well-developed, and a dense brush cover forms a perpetually green veneer that masks the broken, rocky slopes. Once you reach lower Muav Canyon and Shinumo Creek, however, the classic Grand Canyon landscape of splintered buttes and soaring, colorful cliffs dominates the scene.

Depending upon your experience and determination, hiking times along this route may vary widely. A very long day is required to reach Shinumo Creek, but to make the trip less strenuous, consider passing your first night in Muav Canyon between the bottom of the Redwall and the head of the Tapeats narrows, where intermittent water flows. Continue on to Shinumo on the second day.

Water is usually available below the Redwall and in the Tapeats narrows. Shinumo Creek is a vigorous perennial stream. It is advisable to cache water near the top of the Redwall for the hike out. Many hikers on this trail spend two days hiking out, camping in one of several sites atop the Redwall.

Hikers are advised to wear long pants for the first third of the trail for protection from stiff brush and cactus. Be sure your gear is securely lashed to your pack while thrashing through dense thickets of brush.

From the road's end at Swamp Point, follow a series of switchbacks on a moderately descending grade via the steep slopes west of the point. Views from the beginning are excellent, stretching northwest across the wooded red rock platform of the Esplanade into broad Tapeats Amphitheater. The slopes below the point were charred in a 1989 fire, and now, among the blackened snags of pinyon and juniper, the slopes have been reclaimed by thickets of Gambel oak, silktassel, and Utah serviceberry.

As the rocky switchbacks lead you closer to Muav Saddle, you exchange views of Tapeats Amphitheater for views down the deep, brushy trough of Muav Canyon to an array of colorful buttes and the distant South Rim. Muav Cabin comes into view, nestled in a shady grove of ponderosa pines, as you approach the saddle. After 1 mile you reach an unmarked junction in the deep notch of Muav Saddle in a thicket of Gambel oak at 6,711 feet. Trails lead straight ahead to Powell Plateau (see Hike 25), right to Muav Cabin, and left to Muav Canyon.

Muav Cabin, built as a patrol cabin by the Park Service in 1925, lies several yards north of the saddle via a well-worn path. President Theodore Roosevelt camped near the site while hunting mountain lions in 1903, hence the cabin is sometimes called Teddy's Cabin. The structure, with two rooms and cots, is in remarkably good condition. Backpackers may stay overnight here if they wish.

By the time you have reached the saddle, you may notice that you have descended through the Kaibab, Toroweap, and Coconino rock layers, though erosion along the Muav Fault has subdued the usual cliffs into broad slopes. Bear left at the junction and follow the poor, rocky trail, traversing southeast below a cliff band of Coconino sandstone. Thickets of manzanita and scrub live oak require occasional bushwhacking and give you a hint of what lies ahead. As you follow the Coconino/Hermit shale contact zone, you pass several alcoves where seeping springs nurture hanging gardens and a scattering of water birch, a rare tree along Grand Canyon trails.

About 250 yards from the saddle, you reach a prominently cairned junction. A poor trail leads 100 yards east to a trickling perennial spring. Several yards east of the spring are the ruins of a stone chimney, perhaps the remains of prospector White's cabin.

Bear right at the cairn and begin the extremely steep plunge into Muav Canyon, descending 1,000 feet in less than 1 mile. This unforgiving stretch of "trail," filled with loose chunks of Coconino sandstone, requires constant attention and extreme caution. Midway down the descent, you reach slopes of red Hermit shale, where the trail is often barely one footprint wide. Considerable effort is required to maintain purchase on these steep, slippery slopes.

At length you reach a drainage and follow it briefly to a pouroff in the Esplanade sandstone—the first of innumerable pouroffs that lie ahead. The trail exits the drainage on the right and continues descending through thickets of scrub live oak and manzanita. After reaching the floor of a second drainage, the trail disappears. Simply follow the wash downstream; it is the only clear path through the brush. Within minutes you reach the dry, red bed of White Creek, which courses through Muav Canyon, and continue south downcanyon, scrambling and rock-hopping over the Esplanade boulders and slickrock on the canyon floor.

Soon another narrow wash joins White Creek on the left, draining the springs below Swamp Point and adding its waters to the floor of the wash. Follow the small stream down to a pouroff, and bypass it via an exposed, cliff-hanging path on the right. The wash descends through the Supai rock layer, and its banks support willows and a scattering of small Fremont cottonwoods. Above the banks of the wash, the stiff branches of scrub live oak, Gambel oak, silktassel, pale hoptree, and New Mexican locust weave together to form an impenetrable thicket that covers the slopes and rocky shelves above.

Eventually the small stream sinks into the thirsty gravels of the wash, and your route ahead alternates from smooth gravel to boulder-choked stretches, where many detours are required to navigate over and around the smooth, water-polished boulders. After about 2 miles from Muav Saddle, you reach the top of the gray Redwall limestone at the head of a narrow gorge. Watch for a cairn here that shows the beginning of the trail that bypasses on the right.

This trail quickly ascends above the Redwall, then levels out and meanders through manzanita-blanketed pinyon-juniper woodland. Soon you pass a pair of campsites, then dip into a minor side canyon draining the western flanks of Powell Plateau, which rises above to the west. You ascend out of this drainage back into the woodland, pass another campsite, then begin a very steep, rocky descent into a second drainage. The roller coaster route

Muav Cabin, built by the Park Service in 1925, is an interesting highlight of the hike to Muav Saddle.

continues as you ascend an exceedingly steep and rocky grade to the ridge above, where you find a few more poor campsites.

The trail improves on the ridge, and you follow an undulating course past a final campsite and then drop into a third drainage. Cairns lead you down the wash briefly, after which the trail leaves its brushy confines on a southeasterly course. A descending traverse through the upper reaches of the Redwall follows, leading past a few shallow caves en route to a limestone point jutting out into the abyss of Muav Canyon. Take a well-earned break here and enjoy the view before tackling the steep descent ahead.

You can gaze down the long trough of Muav Canyon, stretching from its Redwall-bound confines below you, down across the Tonto Platform into the Tapeats sandstone narrows below. Beyond the narrows, the canyons and towering buttes of Shinumo Amphitheater unfold in a classic Grand Canyon scene. On the eastern skyline above are the pine-fringed points of Rainbow Plateau. At last, with desert flats, sandstone narrows, and castellated buttes so close, you finally feel as if you are in the Grand Canyon.

A prominent break in the Redwall cliff lies just below; here the break is a steep slope filled with jagged limestone boulders. The rocky and brushy, but otherwise well-defined, trail descends this slope via moderately steep switchbacks. At the foot of the 600-foot descent you regain the gravelly, rock-strewn wash of White Creek and follow it downcanyon. The canyon route ahead, initially confined by towering Redwall cliffs, requires considerable rock-hopping and bypass routes around pouroffs. Occasional cottonwoods arch their branches over the wash as you wind down through the Muav limestone narrows. There will likely be intermittently flowing water for the remaining distance to the Tapeats narrows.

As the canyon begins to open up into the broad slopes of Bright Angel shale, you reach a cairned trail that bypasses a major pouroff on the right, at Benchmark 4001. This trail leads you out onto the blackbrush and juniper-studded Tonto Platform. Views finally open up enough from the bypass route to reveal butte-bounded Shinumo Amphitheater in all of its majesty. Holy Grail Temple (Bass Tomb) rises to the east, and Dox Castle and Evans Butte rise beyond in the south.

After about 0.3 mile you return to the wash and follow it southeast as it cuts a shallow course through the Tonto Platform for 1.5 miles to a cairned junction. Here the North Bass Trail leaves the wash, bound for Shinumo Creek in 2.5 miles. This old trail, obscure in places, is seldom used, however, as most hikers opt to follow the wash through the exciting narrows ahead—one of the longest and deepest narrows found along a trail in the Grand Canyon. Much like the Tonto Trail of the South Rim, this old trail follows a shadeless, waterless course in and out of drainages and up and over minor divides, eventually descending 450 feet via a steep draw to Shinumo Creek.

Stay in the wash at the junction and proceed toward the head of the Tapeats narrows. After 0.25 mile, you reach a narrow slot that harbors a pouroff. Cairns here lead to the left of this obstacle and soon lead you north away from White Creek into a side canyon. Follow this drainage downstream to the south for several yards back to the floor of White Creek. A brief downclimb is encountered en route; most hikers find it necessary to lower their packs here. Once you reach White Creek, you can look back into the narrow slot above, where a chockstone is suspended between the tight canyon walls.

You will find perennial waters in these narrows, and when combined with the abundant boulders here, your progress will be slow and arduous as you encounter numerous obstacles. Redwall Canyon enters from the left (east) about 0.2 mile below the bypass, where another chockstone hangs suspended between the narrow canyon walls. The route is shaded much of the day, even during summer, making it a tolerable route in the midday heat. But few escape routes are available should the wash flash-flood; avoid the route if thunderstorms threaten.

Not far below Redwall Canyon, the dark, convoluted walls of Brahma schist crop out to flank the wash and, farther on, the Rama schist appears. Except to the trained geologist, however, these dark members of the Vishnu Complex appear much the same. Along this stretch the canyon becomes somewhat less confined, and spreading cottonwoods reach upward toward the narrow sliver of sky. The route follows low shelves above the wash at times, and as you approach the confluence with Shinumo Creek, a dark, coarse-grained outcrop of granodiorite appears. Soon after you reach a cairned bypass that avoids a pouroff on the left (east). Follow remnants of constructed trail for the remaining several yards to Shinumo Creek at 2,750 feet, a wide, vigorous stream fringed by cottonwoods, willows, and seep-willow.

Most hikers give in to exhaustion here, as the well-worn campsites at the confluence attest. Moreover, the trail ahead requires fording the creek seven times en route to Shinumo (Bass) Camp and is easier accomplished on a day hike. More fine campsites, however, some shaded by tall cottonwoods, will be found downstream. Keep in mind that no camping is allowed at the Colorado River at the mouth of Shinumo Creek.

During spring, especially following a heavy snow year on the North Rim, the creek may be impossible to ford. Use caution; the current is strong and the creekbed is filled with smooth, moss-covered rocks. There is a route that bypasses the many fords, following the south side of the creek over ledges and cliff bands of Shinumo quartzite. It is an arduous route, however, and it involves much scrambling and climbing over and around the low cliffs. If the water level in the creek is low, particularly in autumn, it is far easier to ford the creek.

Whichever route you follow, expect another hour or more of travel to reach the site of Shinumo Camp, about 1.7 miles below the White/Shinumo confluence. Across the creek from the camp, thickets of arrow weed have invaded the terrace where W.W. Bass's orchard and garden once thrived. The only evidence that remains are the depressions of irrigation ditches Bass carved into the alluvium.

To reach the Colorado River, continue downcanyon on the trail for about 300 yards beyond the site of the camp, where you will find a well-worn trail (popular with river parties) heading south, uphill. This trail steeply ascends out of the serpentine confines of Shinumo Creek to a broad saddle at 2,917 feet, where a memorable view of the river and Bass Rapids unfolds. The trail descends just as steeply south of the saddle, dropping down to the Colorado River at 2,200 feet, 1.4 miles from Shinumo Creek. Here you will find a superb riverside campsite. If you choose to camp here expect to share it; the site is a very popular stopover for river parties.

This broad sandy site, broken by black granodiorite terraces, is fringed with groves of tamarisk that cast ample shade during midday. If a river party has occupied the site, other sites are available in a small draw several yards west, just above a quiet bay in the river on sandy shelves among the tamarisk thickets. Other sites might be established on rocky shelves above the river several hundred yards upriver.

After enjoying this remote canyon, retrace your route to the trailhead.

25   POWELL PLATEAU

General description:	A rewarding plateau-top day hike or backpack to a remote North Rim plateau. See Map on Page 219
Distance:	5 to 12 miles or more round-trip.
Difficulty:	Moderate.
Average hiking times:	30 minutes to Muav Saddle; 1 hour to the rim of Powell Plateau.
Type of trail:	Unmaintained; fair to good to rim of plateau.
Trailhead elevation:	7,520 feet.
Low point:	6,711 feet.
High point:	7,600 feet.
Elevation gain and loss:	-820 feet; +900 feet.
Water availability:	Muav Saddle spring, 0.2 mile east of Muav Saddle.
Suggested cache point:	Muav Saddle.
Optimum season:	Late May or early June through mid-October.
Use Area code:	AT9, Powell Plateau, at-large camping.
Management zone:	Primitive.
Topo maps:	King Arthur Castle and Powell Plateau USGS quad; Trails Illustrated: Grand Canyon National Park map.

Key points:
- **0.0**   Swamp Point trailhead.
- **1.0**   Muav Saddle trail junction; continue straight ahead.
- **2.5**   Rim of Powell Plateau.

Finding the trailhead: Follow directions for Hike 24.

The hike: Powell Plateau, an 8-square-mile, pine-forested tableland detached from the North Rim, has been the destination of travelers for centuries. From A.D. 1050 to A.D. 1150, several hundred Anasazi occupied more than eighty sites atop the plateau. John Wesley Powell visited the plateau on September 26, 1870, prior to his second Colorado River expedition. In 1873, Powell revisited the plateau with landscape artist Thomas Moran. Moran combined the view from Powell Plateau with that from the top of the Redwall limestone in Muav Canyon in his famous painting *Grand Chasm of the Colorado*, which hung for a time in the Senate Wing of the U.S. Capitol.

In 1903, President Theodore Roosevelt hunted mountain lions on Powell Plateau. Uncle Jim Owens, master Kaibab Plateau lion hunter, guided Western novelist Zane Grey to the plateau in 1908, where they captured several of the big cats for Eastern zoos.

The Park Service, following construction of Muav Cabin in 1925, built the trail to Powell Plateau the next year. The trail is still fairly easy to follow to the rim of the plateau, and the hike is becoming increasingly popular, both as a day hike and overnight trip. A rich, parklike forest of ponderosa pine forms a mantle on the plateau and vistas from its rim are outstanding. Fine camping places abound, ranging from rim sites to those nestled in groves of Gambel oak or out in the open, needle-carpeted forest floor.

Hikers who pack enough water can easily wander around the plateau for days, visiting various rim overlooks and exploring hidden draws. Most backpackers, however, stay only one night. Three days would be the ideal amount of time to spend wandering here, and the rewards easily justify the long drive to the trailhead and the effort required to pack in two to three gallons of water.

The Fossil Canyon Corridor brings occasional tour aircraft from the South Rim to the North Rim via Tapeats Amphitheater and Fire Point about 1.5 miles north of Swamp Point. Air traffic in this corridor is infrequent and not likely to significantly disrupt your solitude on the plateau.

From Swamp Point, one of the finest viewpoints on the North Rim, Powell Plateau fills your view from west to southwest. The broad red slickrock terrace of the Esplanade stretches away to the northwest. Beyond the Esplanade, you see the charred knob of Monument Point, Bridgers Knoll, and, in the distance, Fishtail Mesa and the Kanab Plateau. On the far northwest horizon rise the Vermilion Cliffs and southwest Utah's Pine Valley Mountains near St. George. On the western horizon, beyond the cinder cone-studded plateaus, rise the highlands of the Beaver Dam Mountains in the southwest corner of Utah and the Virgin Mountains straddling the Arizona/Nevada border.

The Powell Plateau Trail is clearly visible as it rises via switchbacks up brushy slopes to the plateau rim. From Swamp Point, follow the North Bass Trail (see Hike 24) for 1 mile and 800 feet down to Muav Saddle, a steady descent that passes in 20 to 30 minutes. From the unsigned junction at Muav Saddle continue straight ahead, heading southwest, and descend gently through stands of Gambel oak to a slightly lower saddle. From there you begin a moderately ascending traverse, soon passing above an isolated grove of fire-blackened ponderosa pines.

Since the 1989 fire that swept these slopes, the trail ahead has become overgrown with Gambel oak and New Mexican locust. For 0.2 mile the trail is a tunnel through the brush. You bushwhack your way into a draw 300 feet above the saddle, then begin a gently rising, northbound traverse. During autumn, the brushy slopes of the plateau will be ablaze with the crimson of Rocky Mountain maple, the orange-gold of the oaks, and the yellow of the locust.

Views from this traverse are excellent, stretching northwest past the colorful, rocky depths of Tapeats Amphitheater to many of the distant features observed from Swamp Point. Once the traverse ends, you ascend a series of short, brushy switchbacks to gain a gentle, west-trending ridge. The trail follows the ridge on a moderate grade into the ponderosa pine forest, passes a small green shed housing a Park Service firefighters' cache, and shortly thereafter you mount the rolling plateau, where the trail curves first southwest then south.

The trail ahead becomes increasingly faint on the needle-carpeted forest floor, and you proceed through a beautiful parklike forest harboring many towering, massive old trees. Clumps of young pines and a scattering of Gambel oak and New Mexican locust occasionally interrupt the airy, open nature of the forest.

Powell Plateau is a pristine place, never grazed or logged as other parts of Grand Canyon's rims. The 1989 fire that burned here was mostly a beneficial ground fire, recycling nutrients and clearing the forest floor of debris and encroaching groves of young pines and brush, and seldom "crowning," or burning standing trees. Park Service fire managers have designated the plateau as a "let burn" area, where lightning-caused fires are closely monitored and allowed to run their course, seldom burning more than a few acres.

As the trail leads south along the east rim of the plateau, occasional blowdowns require minor detours. Trees along the way are intermittently blazed with metal diamond-shaped markers and old tin can lids. But the blazes are unreliable. It seems they are most frequent where the trail is well-defined and there are few, if any, blazes along obscure stretches. But you really don't need a trail to hike here, simply follow the east rim, undulating over its gently rolling surface.

Memorable views open up from points on the rim, and short detours to the cliff edge beyond the pine forest reveal broad panoramas that reach across the brushy trough of Muav Canyon to Swamp, Rose, and Emerald points and beyond to the gently rolling, forest-clad landscape of the Kaibab Plateau. Muav Canyon frames a tremendous view of Shinumo Amphitheater, where the shadowed Tapeats sandstone narrows of White Creek slice through the Tonto Platform and the buttes of Holy Grail Temple and Dox Castle jut skyward from the Amphitheater's depths.

Point Sublime on the North Rim rises above Shinumo Amphitheater on the southeast skyline, and beyond the mile-deep nadir of the Grand Canyon is the South Rim and the distant alpine summits of the San Francisco Peaks.

From Dutton Point, you can enjoy what Powell declared to be the finest view in the Grand Canyon. The trail, however, is not traceable to that southeasternmost point of the plateau. To get there, use your topo map and follow the east rim of the plateau, perhaps following faint traces of the trail. Eventually you dip into the southwest-trending draw of Dutton Canyon, about 2 miles from the point where you first reached the plateau. Cross the draw and continue south, following the rim for another 1.4 miles to the point, dipping into two saddles en route.

The pines and oaks part and give way to Kaibab limestone on the 7,555-foot point, where unobstructed views into the Grand Canyon unfold.

Other points on the plateau, particularly those on the west rim beyond Blacktail Valley, afford unforgettable views into Middle Granite Gorge below Great Thumb Mesa.

After enjoying this remote plateau, backtrack to the trailhead.

Camping in the ponderosa forest on Powell Plateau.

26 THUNDER RIVER AND TAPEATS CREEK VIA THE BILL HALL TRAIL

General description:	A rigorous but very rewarding rim-to-river backpack of four or more days, for experienced Grand Canyon hikers only.
Distance:	25.4 miles round-trip.
Difficulty:	Very strenuous.
Average hiking times:	3 to 4 hours to the rim of Surprise Valley; 3 hours to Upper Tapeats campsite; 2 hours to the Colorado River. Expect to nearly double hiking times on your return to the rim.
Type of trail:	Unmaintained; fair to good condition.
Trailhead elevation:	7,050 feet.
Low point:	2,000 feet.
Elevation gain and loss:	+800 feet; -5,850 feet.
Water availability:	Thunder Spring, 9.5 miles; Thunder River, Tapeats Creek, and the Colorado River. Briefly following significant rainfall, water may be available in slickrock waterpockets on the Esplanade.
Suggested cache points:	On the Esplanade; Surprise Valley.
Optimum season:	Mid-May through mid-October.
Use Area codes:	AY9, Esplanade, at-large camping; AM9, Surprise Valley, at-large camping; AW7, Upper Tapeats; AW8, Lower Tapeats, designated campsites.
Management zones:	Upper and Lower Tapeats, Threshold; other areas, Primitive.
Topo maps:	Tapeats Amphitheater and Powell Plateau USGS quads; Trails Illustrated Grand Canyon National Park.

Key points:
- **0.0** Bill Hall trailhead.
- **0.8** Monument Point.
- **3.4** Junction with Thunder River Trail; turn left.
- **6.4** Rim of Surprise Valley.
- **7.7** First junction with Deer Creek Trail; bear left.
- **8.1** Second junction with Deer Creek Trail; bear left again.
- **8.9** Rim of Thunder River canyon.
- **9.5** Spur trail to Thunder Spring; stay right.
- **10.3** Tapeats Creek.
- **10.4** Upper Tapeats campsite.
- **12.7** Lower Tapeats campsite, Colorado River.

Best day hike destinations: The easy 1.6-mile round-trip to Monument Point affords far-ranging vistas of the remote central Grand Canyon. Strong hikers will enjoy the 12.8-mile round-trip to the rim of the Esplanade above Surprise Valley, where views of the Colorado River unfold.

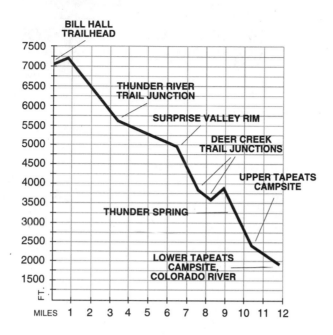

Finding the trailhead: Although the driving distance to the Bill Hall trailhead is longer than any other in the Grand Canyon, the gravel roads are in very good condition, and the 1.5-hour trip from the highway is an enjoyable scenic drive through the rich forests of the Kaibab Plateau.

From Jacob Lake, Arizona, follow Arizona Highway 67 south for 26.5 miles to the junction with Forest Road 22 (also signed for Dry Park 10) and turn right (west). This junction lies 0.9 mile south of Kaibab Lodge and immediately south of tiny Deer Lake.

All junctions ahead are well-signed, and you stay on FR 22 (sometimes signed as Forest Road 422) for 17.6 miles, then turn left onto Forest Road 425, signed for Thunder River Trail 13. After another 7.7 miles, avoid right-branching Forest Road 233 signed for "Wilderness Trails" (that road leads to trailheads on the fringes of the Kanab Creek Wilderness).

After another 0.6 mile, also avoid right-branching Forest Road 232, signed for Thunder River Trail 5. That road leads to the Indian Hollow trailhead. Stay left at that junction, remaining on FR 425, signed for Crazy Jug Point 4. Continue straight ahead for another 1.7 miles (10 miles from FR 22), where FR 425 branches left and becomes a poor, unmaintained road at a junction adjacent to the Big Saddle Cabin and corrals. Bear right here, staying on the good gravel road, now Forest Road 292. Bear right again after 0.25 mile; follow signs pointing to Crazy Jug Point.

Soon you reach a four-way junction atop the North Rim, 1.5 miles from FR 425. Follow the middle fork, FR 292A, a smooth but narrow dirt road, for the remaining 1.7 miles to the spacious trailhead parking area at the road's end, 30.8 miles from the highway.

THUNDER RIVER AND TAPEATS CREEK, VIA THE BILL HALL TRAIL

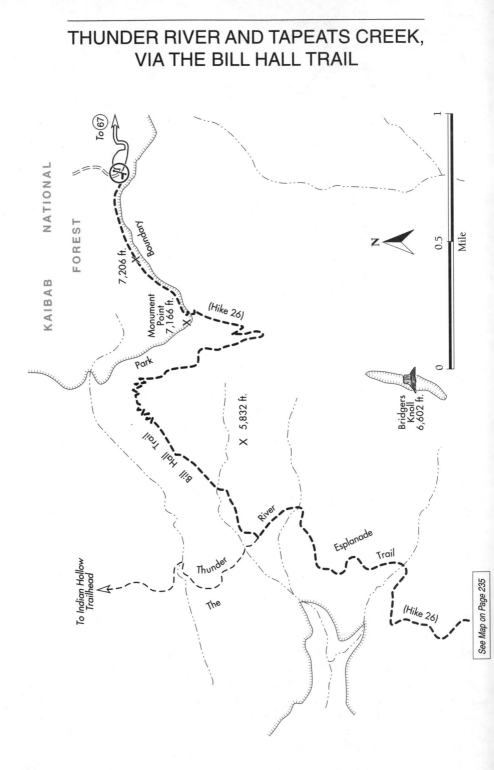

To 67

KAIBAB NATIONAL FOREST

7,206 ft.

Boundary

Monument Point
7,166 ft.

(Hike 26)

Park

X 5,832 ft.

Bill Hall Trail

Bridgers Knoll
6,602 ft.

River

Esplanade

Trail

To Indian Hollow Trailhead

Thunder

The

(Hike 26)

N

0   0.5   1
Mile

See Map on Page 235

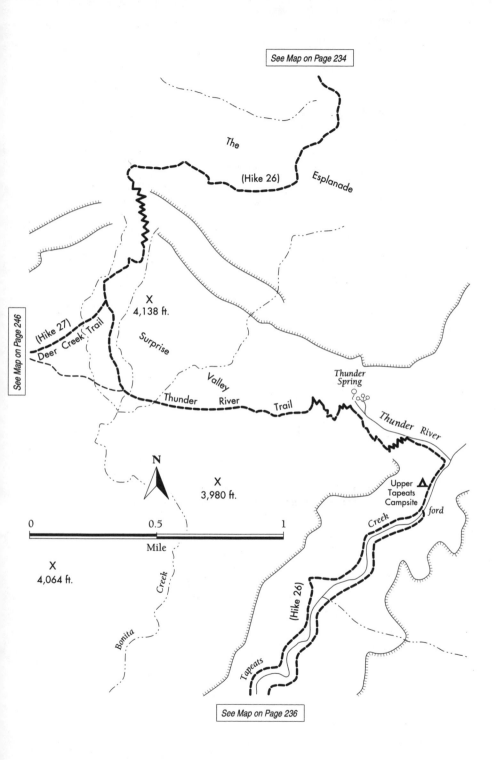

See Map on Page 234

The

(Hike 26)

Esplanade

See Map on Page 246

(Hike 27)

Deer Creek Trail

X
4,138 ft.

Surprise

Valley

Thunder River Trail

Thunder
Spring

Thunder River

N

X
3,980 ft.

Upper
Tapeats
Campsite

Creek

ford

0   0.5   1

Mile

X
4,064 ft.

Bonita

Creek

(Hike 26)

Tapeats

See Map on Page 236

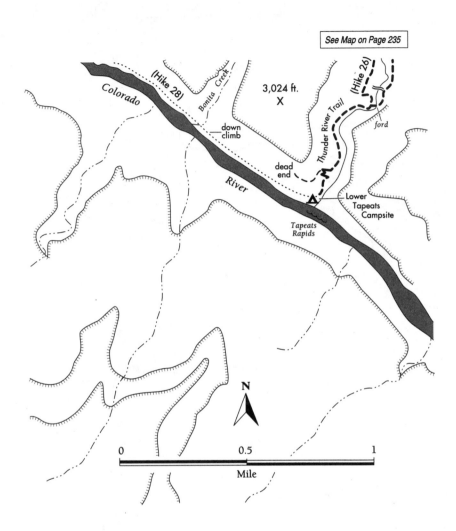

See Map on Page 235

Colorado

(Hike 28)

Bonita Creek

3,024 ft.
X

Thunder River Trail

(Hike 26)

ford

down
climb

dead
end

River

Lower
Tapeats
Campsite

Tapeats
Rapids

N

0   0.5   1
Mile

All roads en route, and the trailhead, lie within the boundaries of the Kaibab National Forest. Hikers arriving late in the day can camp wherever they wish along the route to the trailhead.

The hike: This memorable trail offers a combination of the finest scenery in the Grand Canyon, long-range vistas, the broad slickrock terrace of the Esplanade, turbulent streams, waterfalls, lush riparian oases, exciting narrows, and excellent campsites. Thunder Spring is unquestionably the highlight of the trip. Perhaps the most memorable and incongruous sight in the Grand Canyon, Thunder Spring is a virtual river that surges out of a limestone cave, surrounded by cliff-bound desert. Below the spring, Thunder River's powerful waters and verdant riparian ribbon accompany hikers for the remaining distance to Tapeats Creek and its scenic campsites.

In the 10.4 miles to Upper Tapeats campsite, the trail makes three significant descents. The first two are separated by lengthy segments of gentle grades, unlike many South Rim trails that descend from rim to river steadily and abruptly. Most backpackers make the trip down to Tapeats Creek in one long day, averaging about 7 hours of hiking. Those who get a late start can choose among the many fine, but dry, camping areas on the Esplanade. The hike out is best accomplished over 2 days, using an Esplanade campsite en route back to the rim. Hikers are advised to cache water on the Esplanade for the hike out; at least 2 quarts per person for those hiking through to the rim, and one to 1.5 gallons per person for those who intend to camp there.

Although the hike is often taken as a round trip, some seasoned backpackers combine this trip with the Tapeats to Deer Creek Route (see Hike 28) and the Deer Creek Trail (see Hike 27), forming the most memorable and rewarding loop via a trail in the Grand Canyon.

The trailhead lies several yards back from the North Rim on the fringes of a burn that consumed thousands of acres of forest and woodland on the western reaches of the Kaibab Plateau in the spring of 1996.

From the trailhead, pass through a gate in an old fenceline, avoid a right-branching forest road, and follow the trail to the left, indicated by Park Service signs. The trail leads within moments down to a saddle on the rim, where the trail forks. The right branch is the main trail and the left branch leads a short distance to a point offering a fine view of Tapeats Amphitheater. On the point is a plaque placed in memory of Ward "Bill" Hall, after whom the trail was named.

Beyond this detour, the Bill Hall Trail begins a moderate ascent of the hill ahead, passing through a charred woodland of pinyon and juniper. After topping the hill at 7,206 feet, the trail angles briefly downhill, then gently ascends the rim to turn south just east of Monument Point. Fine vistas from this point on the trail extend northwest across the vast tableland of the Kanab Plateau to the distant Vermilion Cliffs. Views into the Grand Canyon open up below to the south. The slickrock expanse of Tapeats Amphitheater spreads out far below, surrounded by Muav Saddle, Powell Plateau, Steamboat Mountain, and Bridgers Knoll. Great Thumb Mesa looms boldly on the

South Rim, separated from your vantage by the 6-mile-wide void of the Grand Canyon.

Here the trail drops abruptly off the rim in broken ledges of Kaibab limestone. The initial part of the descent is extremely steep and rocky, requiring some scrambling and boulder-hopping. The footing is poor, and the exposure to steep cliffs makes this a trail for experienced hikers only. Beyond the first Kaibab cliff band, a very steep descent of the south ridge of Monument Point ensues. You drop to a fire-charred saddle, then follow switchbacks down to Point 6520, just above the rocky notch of Bridgers Knoll saddle.

There the narrow trail curves northwest and begins an undulating 0.5-mile traverse beneath Monument Point. Gnarled pinyons and junipers dot the slopes, sharing space with sagebrush, mormon tea, and buffaloberry. One of the more memorable views of the Grand Canyon opens up from this part of the trail. Your view stretches far away to the southwest down the trough of the central Grand Canyon. Sheer cliffs of Redwall limestone embrace the deep inner gorge. These cliffs are flanked on both sides by the extensive red platform of the Esplanade. The forested hills of Mounts Logan and Trumbull define the western horizon. These broad views will remain with you for many miles to come.

At length you reach a break in the Toroweap limestone cliffs below and begin descending. The inviting slickrock expanse of the Esplanade, with its blackbrush flats and pinyon-juniper woodlands, spreads out below. After one switchback, you reach a bulging limestone outcrop that you must care-

Broad views of Surprise Valley, the Colorado River, Powell Plateau, and Great Thumb Mesa unfold from the rim of the Esplanade on the Thunder River Trail.

fully downclimb. Some hikers may feel more comfortable lowering their packs here with a stretch of rope. Another minor downclimb soon follows, after which a series of steep switchbacks takes you down a wooded debris cone that obscures the Coconino sandstone.

After the angle of the slope moderates, you follow a steep, straightforward course down the sagebrush and blackbrush-clad slopes, enter a minor draw, then briefly ascend out of the draw to meet the cairn-marked Thunder River Trail on the Esplanade at 5,420 feet.

Bear left at the junction and proceed southeast. The 3-mile stretch ahead is delightful, reminiscent of Utah's canyon country. Much of the trail across the Esplanade is nearly level, vistas are panoramic, and the tread ranges from slickrock to firm sand. Abundant cairns show the way across the slickrock platform. The trail contours around the head of three Deer Creek tributary canyons, while passing through scattered woodlands of pinyon and juniper. A variety of typical Upper Sonoran Zone shrubs crowd together in pockets where soil has collected, including scrub live oak, blackbrush, Utah serviceberry, Fremont barberry, manzanita, Gregg ceanothus, littleleaf mountain mahogany, yucca, agave and broom snakeweed.

If recent rains have fallen, some of the innumerable waterpockets on the slickrock terrace may be filled, and you can augment your water supply. The waterpockets here are shallow, though, and evaporate quickly.

At length you approach the south rim of the Esplanade, then curve west, and begin descending in earnest just north of the rim. After following a draw brushy with scrub live oak, you reach the rim of Surprise Valley at 4,900 feet at the head of the second major descent on the trail. A pause here rewards you with fine views across the scrubby expanse of Surprise Valley to Cogswell Butte and the soaring cliffs abutting Great Thumb Mesa in the south. A stretch of the Colorado River, upstream from Tapeats Creek, is visible to the southeast, coursing through Middle Granite Gorge 3,000 feet below. Looming far above the river is the pine-clad tableland of Powell Plateau.

Surprise Valley appears to be an isolated segment of the Tonto Platform, which is absent this far west in the Canyon. The valley was formed, however, along the trailing edge of a huge slump block of Supai and Redwall rocks that slipped southward toward the inner gorge. Towering blocks of Redwall limestone are suspended well to the south of the main valley walls, and Supai boulders are strewn across the valley and up the opposite slope toward Cogswell Butte.

The steep and rocky, but well-constructed trail takes advantage of the slump to descend through the Supai and what remains of the Redwall. You descend via moderately steep switchbacks to a rocky saddle below one of the great slump blocks, then traverse steadily downhill above a draw, and you soon thereafter reach the cairned junction with the Deer Creek Trail (see Hike 27) at 3,800 feet.

Bear left at the junction and descend a moderate grade through Surprise Valley's sun-baked hills, which gather tremendous heat during summer.

Thunder River surges out of a limestone cave and plummets in a memorable veil of whitewater.

Blackbrush, catclaw, yucca, mormon tea, and a variety of cacti and bunch-grasses clothe the shadeless slopes of the broad valley. Views stretch up-ward to the massive walls of Great Thumb Mesa to the south and reach back to the cool pine forests blanketing the hilly points of the North Rim.

About 200 feet and 0.4 mile below the last junction, you reach another junction with a spur leading west to the Deer Creek Trail. Bear left again, drop into the headwaters wash of Bonita Creek, then begin a moderate, winding ascent through hilly terrain to a broad saddle at 3,850 feet, flanked by large Supai boulders. From here you can hear Thunder Spring, and a minor detour a few yards east to a nest of boulders reveals your first view of the spring.

The third, and steepest, rockiest descent follows, initially dropping down the broken rib of a Redwall slump block and into the Thunder River drain-age. Thunder Spring, a large stream surging out of the twin portals of Thun-der Cave in the Muav limestone cliff to the north, is in constant view as you slowly descend the rugged trail. The roar from the spring's veil of whitewater intensifies your thirst on the time consuming descent.

About 600 vertical feet below the Surprise Valley rim, you reach the junc-tion with a spur trail on a small platform opposite Thunder Spring. Few hikers can resist the 150 yard detour; though the spur trail rises steeply at times, it quickly leads to the foot of the 120-foot waterfall. There is no finer oasis in the Grand Canyon. Here you can rest on slabs beneath the falls in a cool refreshing spray. Tall cottonwoods cast ample shade, willow thickets and a profusion of scarlet monkeyflowers in season hug the banks of the infant Thunder River. Mosses and maidenhair ferns cling to the cliffs along-side the terraced waterfall. Many smaller springs below Thunder Cave con-tribute their waters to Thunder River. This river, only about 0.5 mile in length, is a mad torrent rushing headlong down its narrow, steep canyon in an unending series of low waterfalls and foaming cascades. Remember that no camping is allowed in the Thunder River drainage.

The exceedingly steep descent continues down the canyon beyond the spur trail, shortly passing through an outlying grove of cottonwoods, from where you enjoy a fine view back to the springs and falls. The trail crosses outcrops of Muav limestone and then emerges onto the green slopes of the Bright Angel shale. Soon you reach a boulder field studded with barrel cac-tus and Tapeats sandstone blocks. After weaving your way through the boul-der field, the trail leads to the banks of Thunder River in the cool spray of a low waterfall. Soaring cliffs and wooded mesas in the background contrast with the river's ebullient waters and shady riparian ribbon.

The relentlessly steep descent is more pleasant now as you follow the creekside beneath a canopy of cottonwood and redbud trees. Thickets of thorny mesquite soon signal your approach to Tapeats Creek, and within minutes you reach the banks of that large stream, below the Thunder River confluence, and turn south, heading downcanyon. Ignore the cairned trail on the opposite bank and follow the west banks of the creek for 0.1 mile through a jungle of willow and arrow weed to Upper Tapeats campsite at

2,440 feet.

Here you will find about three small-party campsites and a larger group site. A solar dehydrating toilet is provided. Due to the north-south orientation of Tapeats Creek canyon, the camp enjoys considerable shade in the morning and afternoon hours. Voluminous Tapeats Creek rumbles by next to the camp, and the stark desert environment loosens its grip along the banks of the stream.

Willows and cottonwoods thrive at the creekside, casting a modicum of shade over some of the campsites. Scarlet monkeyflowers grace the banks with delicate blossoms that nod in the breeze. Arrow weed and seep-willow, being slightly less moisture-dependant than the willows and cottonwoods, grow vigorously several yards back from the brawling torrent. Only a short distance beyond, the riparian growth gives way to true desert, where mormon tea, brittlebush, mesquite, Engelmann prickly pear, and barrel cactus are widely scattered across boulder-littered slopes and rocky shelves.

Cliffs of 1-billion-year-old Shinumo quartzite embrace the camp, above which rises progressively younger rocks: the Tapeats sandstone, Bright Angel shale, Muav and Redwall limestones, and the red rocks of the Supai Group, towering skyward more than 3,000 vertical feet to the east and north. While in lower Thunder River canyon en route to Tapeats Creek, you may have noticed a particularly obvious angular unconformity, where the steeply dipping Shinumo quartzite is overlain by horizontal beds of Tapeats sandstone. There the Shinumo was once an island in a Cambrian sea, and sandy sediments that would become the Tapeats were deposited along its flanks. Later, the island and the Tapeats sands were buried by Bright Angel muds in a marine environment.

Upper Tapeats campsite makes a fine base camp for day hiking forays into upper Tapeats Creek canyon, to the Colorado River, or to Deer Creek. Most backpackers taking the Tapeats Creek/Deer Creek loop will want to pass their first night here; trying to hike through to the river and Lower Tapeats campsite in one long day is simply too exhausting for most hikers.

To reach the Colorado River, follow the well-worn trail downcanyon from the camp, along the west banks of the creek. Sometimes choked with boulders, other times requiring a bushwhack through thickets of willow and arrow-weed, the trail alternates from the riparian ribbon to the hot, dry slopes above. About 15 minutes and about 0.3 mile from the camp, the red Hakatai shale forms outcrops several yards past a campsite lying beyond the confines of the designated camping area; a site that hikers should avoid using.

Here, where the trail begins to ascend, another trail forks left, leading quickly down to a ford of Tapeats Creek, knee-deep during low stream flows, 20 feet wide, and deceptively swift, with a slippery, rocky bed. Beyond the ford is a trail that follows the east bank downstream. Although the Park Service recommends using that trail, it is accessible only when the creek is low, and the route requires a second ford farther downstream, and occasional scrambling and two short downclimbs en route.

The trail that follows the west bank is equally as rough, but it avoids the potentially hazardous fords. From the junction with the trail to the ford, this trail begins with a steep ascent onto red Hakatai shale slopes, then quickly descends into a gully. Be sure to turn left and *descend* this gully; there may be a cairn showing the turn in the trail. The descent begins on the right-hand side of a large boulder. You must lower your pack and downclimb two ledges to proceed.

Beyond that obstacle, you contour along the very narrow trail, soon reaching a more resistant layer of the Hakatai shale. Look for fossil mudcracks and ripple marks on the red slabs alongside the trail, recording a shallow marine environment that prevailed here about 1 billion years ago. Soon you reach another gully and descend it back down to the bench above the creek. The trail shortly veers away from the creek, however, and ascends above a cliff band before dropping into a boulder field beneath a prominent bay in the Tapeats cliff above. Once again you descend, via switchbacks, to the creekside bench among scattered mesquite, and a cactus garden of Engelmann prickly pear.

The rugged trail continues its abruptly undulating course, generally staying on slopes well above the creek until finally descending switchbacks to a point just above a low but surging waterfall, where the creek plunges over a ledge of Bass limestone. Quite soon thereafter you descend back to the creekside and are joined by the trail crossing back from the east bank at 2,120 feet, 1.6 miles and about 1 hour and 15 minutes from Upper Tapeats camp. Hikers on the east-bank trail must be sure to cross the creek just below the falls. Do not continue following game trails downcanyon above the narrows; you'll get rimrocked high above the Colorado River.

The trail ahead follows the curving stream into the head of the narrows cut into the gray-green Bass limestone. Soon you leave the streambank via a ledge and traverse high above the ever-deepening, narrow gorge. This is an exciting stretch of trail, and you can hear the thundering creek, but it is shielded from view by the near-vertical, 200-foot canyon walls below, walls composed of black, Pre-Cambrian diabase.

At length the mouth of Tapeats Creek and the rocky beach along the Colorado River come into view. Shortly thereafter, about 2.1 miles from Upper Tapeats camp, you reach a junction at the head of a plunging gully. One trail leads straight ahead, continuing the traverse. That high trail is marked with cairns and has led many hikers astray. It dead-ends high above Bonita Creek and 400 feet above the river. **Be sure not to follow that trail!**

Instead, turn left onto the trail that descends the gully via steep, rocky switchbacks, dropping 250 feet in about 0.2 mile to the mouth of Tapeats Creek and the Colorado River at 2,000 feet. Here you find Lower Tapeats campsite, but the camping area is not well defined. Several possible campsites can be established on the beach sand among scattered boulders. Willows and seep-willows border the creek, but there is no shade at the camping area nor is there a toilet. Tapeats Creek is your fresh water source. Excellent riverside camping areas can be found farther west (see Hike 28 for route description) along the beach, but your permit must specify Use Area AM9, which lies immediately to the west of the mouth of Tapeats Creek.

Views from Lower Tapeats, deep in Middle Granite Gorge, reach eastward to forest-fringed Powell Plateau and south to the abrupt cliffs that soar 4,500 feet from the river to the rim of Great Thumb Mesa.

To return to the rim via Deer Creek is longer but less arduous than retracing your steps, however, it should only be attempted by experienced Grand Canyon hikers (see Hikes 27 and 28).

27 DEER CREEK AND THE COLORADO RIVER VIA THE BILL HALL TRAIL

General description:	A rigorous rim-to-river backpack of four or more days, for experienced Grand Canyon hikers only.
Distance:	21.6 miles round-trip.
Difficulty:	Very strenuous.
Average hiking times:	(See hiking times for Hike 26 to the rim of Surprise Valley). 2.5 to 3 hours from Surprise Valley to Deer Creek; 30 to 45 minutes to reach the Colorado River. Expect to nearly double hiking times on the return to the rim.
Type of trail:	Unmaintained; fair to good condition.
Trailhead elevation:	7,050 feet.
Low point:	1,936 feet.
Elevation gain and loss:	+300 feet; -5,400 feet.
Water availability:	Deer Spring, 9.5 miles; Deer Creek; Colorado River. Briefly following significant rainfall, water may be available from slickrock waterpockets on the Esplanade.
Suggested cache points:	On the Esplanade; Surprise Valley.
Optimum season:	Mid-May through mid-October.
Use Area codes:	AY9, Esplanade, at-large camping; AM9, Surprise Valley, at-large camping; AX9, Deer Creek, at-large camping.
Management zones:	All areas, Primitive.
Topo maps:	Tapeats Amphitheater and Fishtail Mesa USGS quads; Trails Illustrated Grand Canyon National Park.

Key points:

- **0.0** Bill Hall trailhead.
- **0.8** Monument Point.
- **3.4** Junction with Thunder River Trail; turn left.
- **6.4** Rim of Surprise Valley.
- **7.7** Junction with Deer Creek Trail; bear right.
- **9.5** Deer Spring.
- **9.8** Deer Creek.
- **10.3** Head of Deer Creek narrows.
- **10.8** Deer Creek Falls, Colorado River.

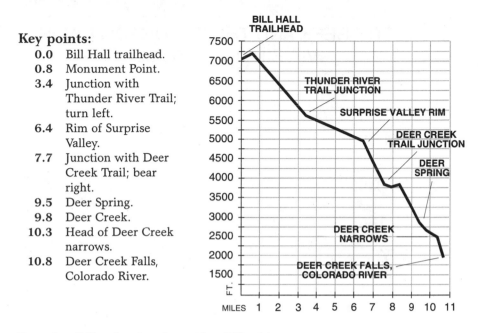

Best day hike destinations: See Hike 26.

Finding the trailhead: Follow directions for Hike 26.

The hike: After following the Bill Hall and Thunder River trails (see Hike 26), this trip leads west out of the desert expanse of Surprise Valley to the broad canyon and perennial waters of Deer Creek. Much like Thunder Spring, Deer Spring, though smaller, surges from the limestone cliffs alongside the trail, offering its waters to the thirsty cottonwoods and thickets of giant reed grass that form a ribbon of greenery on the canyon floor.

Fine campsites await backpackers in the canyon from below the spring to the head of the narrows, below which camping is not allowed. (Note: Eventually, the Park Service plans to establish one or two designated campsites and install a toilet at Deer Creek. Check with the Backcountry Reservations Office for current information.)

The Tapeats sandstone narrows of Deer Creek are among the most exciting narrows traversed by a trail in the Grand Canyon. The trail leads through that shadowed stone hallway to the Colorado River, where Deer Creek Falls emerges from the narrows in a memorable, thundering ribbon of whitewater.

From the trailhead, follow Hike 26 for 7.7 miles to Surprise Valley and the cairned junction with the Deer Creek Trail and turn right. The trail undulates through a shrub cover of blackbrush, mormon tea, and yucca, heading southwest through the shadeless expanse of the valley. After 0.4 mile, your trail is joined from the left by the spur trail coming from the Thunder River Trail. Soon after, you top out on a long saddle at 3,750 feet. Fine views stretch eastward across the hilly reaches of Surprise Valley to

DEER CREEK AND THE COLORADO RIVER, VIA BILL HALL TRAIL

See Map on Page 235

See Map on Page 236

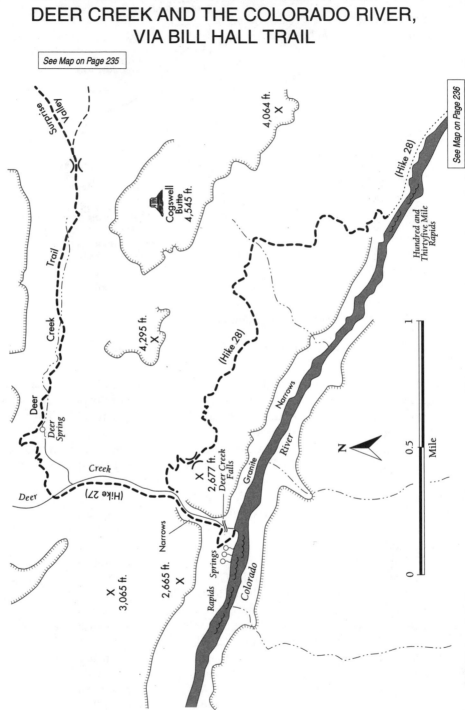

Surprise Valley

Trail

Creek

Deer

Deer Spring

Creek

Deer

(Hike 27)

4,295 ft. X

2,677 ft. X
Deer Creek Falls

Cogswell Butte 4,545 ft.

4,064 ft. X

(Hike 28)

(Hike 28)

Hundred and Thirtyfive Mile Rapids

Narrows

River

Granite

X 3,065 ft.

2,665 ft. X
Narrows

Rapids

Springs

Colorado

N

0.5   1

0   Mile

246

the Redwall limestone cliffs bounding Tapeats Terrace and to 7,410-foot Steamboat Mountain rising beyond.

The trail ahead descends moderately for 1.3 miles, traversing the length of a starkly beautiful little valley, bounded on the north by sheer Redwall limestone cliffs and on the south by the broken walls of Cogswell Butte. The rolling contours of the valley are studded with angular Redwall boulders, coarse shrubs, and barrel and hedgehog cactus. The scene is more reminiscent of a lonely canyon in a Great Basin mountain range, rather than the Grand Canyon.

At length the trail begins a moderately steep descent as the valley becomes increasingly narrow, and soon you reach the brink of the Muav limestone cliff and traverse out of the wash on the very edge of the cliff, directly above now-audible Deer Spring. Views of Deer Creek open up from this stretch, but the cliff-edge nature of the trail demands that you pause to enjoy them. Lower Deer Creek is a small, mile-long valley, its verdant floor rich with thickets of giant reed grass and decorated by stately cottonwoods. Tall Redwall limestone cliffs confine its upper reaches, and downstream the creek disappears into the dark labyrinth of the Tapeats sandstone narrows.

The traverse ends on the steep slopes of a rock slide, and the trail descends the slide on an extremely steep grade. Near the bottom of the grade, you meet a spur trail at 2,680 feet that leads 100 yards east to Deer Spring. Issuing from a small cave in the Muav limestone cliff, Deer Spring emerges

Good views reach into the shadowed gorge of Granite Narrows from the Deer Creek Trail.

as a 20-foot waterfall. Its waters nurture a grove of redbud trees that offer shady refuge to hikers on a hot day.

Beyond the spring you negotiate a series of short, steep switchbacks. Rock steps help you descend the steepest pitches. The grade moderates as you enter groves of mesquite, and finally you are funneled down an avenue through thickets of giant reed grass to the banks of Deer Creek, which you must ford. During low water flows, you may be able to rock-hop the 6-foot-wide creek. During spring, or after heavy rains, a ford is necessary. The creek, with a modest current and cobble bottom, is only shin-deep during low flows.

After crossing the creek, you follow above its west banks for 0.5 mile to the head of the narrows. The Deer Creek valley gradually broadens as you proceed, with boulder-covered slopes rising above the trail and a mesquite-dotted bench spreading out east of the creek. The trail undulates over and around boulders, and at times you must plunge through thickets of willow, reed grass, and other streamside growth.

Tall, spreading cottonwoods arch over the trail and the creek, but unfortunately some of these stately trees were consumed by a hiker's toilet paper fire that spread across sixty acres of the Deer Creek valley. Although charred cottonwoods stand as a silent reminder of this illegal and obviously unwise practice, willow and giant reed grass have reclaimed some of the scars of the burn.

You pass a few fair campsites among green and charred cottonwoods en route to the narrows, located alongside the small but vigorous stream. Tall Hooker evening primrose hug the banks of the creek, their large yellow blooms in season nodding in the breeze. Other campsites, offering little shade, can be located on the mesquite-clad bench east of the creek. No camping is allowed below the head of the narrows, so hikers must choose a site and then day hike through the narrows to Deer Creek Falls and the Colorado River. River parties frequently stop at Deer Creek and hike into the narrows during the May through September river running season, so don't be surprised if you are briefly invaded by a large number of people.

Where the Tapeats sandstone outcrops in Deer Creek, its walls quickly envelop the stream. The trail enters these narrows via a ledge just above the creekside. Here Deer Creek carves an increasingly deep, serpentine path through the coarse, highly resistant Tapeats sandstone.

As you proceed into the exciting narrows on the cliff-hanging ledge, the gorge becomes deeper and the creek disappears from view, though its crashing thunder reverberates up through the slot. The gorge is more than 100 feet deep, and in places barely 10 feet wide. Bulging sandstone walls require you to pass sideways at times to proceed, with the void of the gorge lying mere inches from your feet.

After 0.25 mile, you emerge from the shadowed stone hallway onto a point at 2,200 feet overlooking the Colorado River coursing through Granite Narrows 250 feet below. Views upriver are especially dramatic. Granite Narrows at, the narrowest point in the Canyon, frame the view of pine-fringed Powell Plateau, rising on the eastern skyline. The trail steadily descends west from the point, switches back once above the willow thickets bordering the vigorous springs below, and ends at the rocky beach alongside the river at the mouth of Deer Creek.

Here the Tapeats sandstone almost reaches to river level, and Deer Creek emerges in a 100-foot waterfall from the narrow confines of its slot canyon, with the appearance of a spring surging from a cave.

From Deer Creek, retrace your steps to the trailhead.

Near the head of the Deer Creek narrows.

| General description: | A part cross-country | See Maps on Pages 236 & 246 |

General description: A part cross-country route, for experienced hikers only, useful as part of the 27.1-mile Tapeats Creek to Deer Creek loop.

Distance: 4.1 miles.

Difficulty: Moderate.

Average hiking time: 3 hours.

Type of trail: Route; trail segment in good condition.

Trailhead elevation: 2,000 feet low point; 2,000 feet high point; 2,800 feet.

Elevation gain and loss: +1,250 feet; -800 feet.

Water availability: Tapeats Creek at beginning of route; the Colorado River for the first 1.3 miles; Deer Creek at the end of the route.

Optimum season: Mid-May through mid-October.

Use Area codes: AW8, Lower Tapeats, designated campsite; AM9, Surprise Valley, at-large camping; AX9, Deer Creek, at-large camping.

Management zones: Lower Tapeats, Threshold; other areas, Primitive.

Topo maps: Powell Plateau, Tapeats Amphitheater, and Fishtail Mesa USGS quads; Trails Illustrated Grand Canyon National Park (route not shown on maps).

Key points:

0.0 Lower Tapeats campsite.
0.6 Bonita Creek wash.
1.3 Beginning of trail segment at Hundred and Thirtyfive Mile Rapids.
4.1 Head of Deer Creek narrows.

Finding the trail: The route begins on the beach at Lower Tapeats campsite and ends on the east bank of Deer Creek at the head of the narrows.

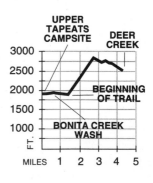

The hike: This excellent route, ranging from the trackless beaches of the Colorado River to a good trail segment high above Granite Narrows, connects the Tapeats Creek and Deer Creek trails, allowing backpackers the opportunity to trace a superb loop trip. The route involves rudimentary routefinding skills, and requires some scrambling and downclimbing. Thus, only seasoned Grand Canyon hikers should attempt it. The route is also unforgivingly hot during summer, at which time a pre-dawn start is essential.

Good camping areas on the beach at Hundred and Thirtyfive Mile rapids are exposed but inviting, yet most hikers push through to Deer Creek in one day, a trip of about three hours from Lower Tapeats campsite. The hike out via the Deer Creek Trail to Surprise Valley is less arduous than hiking out via Tapeats Creek and Thunder River, thus most hikers take the trip in the direction described below.

Tapeats Creek is the last source for fresh water until reaching Deer Creek, so hikers are advised to tank up there. From the mouth of Tapeats Creek, at 2,000 feet, follow the sandy, boulder-littered beach west downriver, passing among thickets of tamarisk and seep-willow. There is no trail here; you simply weave a way along the beach. After 0.5 mile, the beach pinches out where a black diabase outcrop projects into the river. Here cairns will guide you about 100 feet up to a rocky notch. From there you clamber down steep ledges to a fifteen-foot dropoff. Most hikers will lower their packs, then downclimb the dropoff with the aid of ample hand and foot holds.

Beyond that obstacle you cross the dry wash of Bonita Creek, then begin a long, 0.7-mile boulder-hop along the sloping beach ahead. You eventually emerge from the boulder fields onto a fine stretch of sandy beach alongside the riffle of Hundred and Thirtyfive Mile rapids. This inviting beach, strewn with large boulders, is inaccessible to river parties and affords excellent, though shadeless, camping (Use Area AM9). The dark walls of Granite Narrows enclose the river just ahead, forming a mile-long aisle that bears the distinction of being the narrowest point along the river in the Grand Canyon.

Ample cairns at the west end of the beach lead you away from the river and onto a well-worn trail. This trail, very steep and brutally hot in summer, ascends 800 feet in 0.7 mile, via a rocky draw, to top out on a 2,800-foot saddle. En route you navigate through the Redwall limestone debris of a slump that long ago filled the channel of the Colorado River. Consequently, the river carved a new channel through Granite Narrows, which is now 500 feet lower than the ancestral channel, suggesting the antiquity of the slump.

Excellent views unfold during this grind, helping to distract you from your labors. The broad river courses below, the towering walls of Great Thumb Mesa loom almost overhead to the south, and the immense bulk of Powell Plateau fills your view upcanyon. Beyond the saddle, a pleasant, view-packed traverse ensues, following ledges and slopes high above Granite Narrows. Views extend downcanyon, framed by the walls of the narrows, to the lush greenery surrounding the springs near the mouth of Deer Creek. Keep an eye out for desert bighorn sheep, as they are occasionally spotted on the rocky slopes from this high traverse.

Coarse desert shrubs scatter across the rocky trailside slopes, including the gray mounds of brittlebush and mormon tea, and the spiny masses of tall barrel cactus. After curving into several minor draws, you cross a larger dry wash beneath the Redwall tower of Cogswell Butte, where a rich growth of giant reed grass and saw grass suggest the presence of subsurface moisture.

The protracted traverse continues generally westward over the variegated slopes of Bright Angel shale, undulating as you negotiate the curves of many draws and alcoves. Finally the trail begins a steady ascent, curving north-

Excellent views of Granite Narrows unfold from high above Bonita Creek.

west to mount a 2,600-foot saddle next to the low, cliff-rimmed crown of Point 2677, 2.4 miles from the river. From the saddle, the wide valley of lower Deer Creek unfolds before you, where tall cottonwoods and willows hug the banks of the perennial stream. Redwall cliffs flank the valley on the east and a mass of boulders from a large slump define the western flanks. Deer Creek has a spacious, unconfined landscape, unlike the cliff-bound environs of Tapeats Creek. And since Deer Creek is more open, it is hotter and there is less shade.

The trail descends a moderate grade northwest from the saddle via switchbacks. Abundant barrel cacti dot the sun-scorched trailside slopes alongside other sparse desert growth. The descent passes quickly, and within minutes you proceed down a mesquite-choked draw to the head of Deer Creek's narrows. The trail continues into the narrows, but shortly it ends. Be sure to cross the creek near the head of the narrows to find the Deer Creek Trail above the west banks.

The clear, cold creek during average flows, is about 8 feet wide and ankle-to shin-deep. The ford is trouble-free, except during high flows in spring or shortly after heavy rains. Campsites can be found on both sides of the creek, though sites on the west bank are more desirable since they are shaded by cottonwoods.

To return to the North Rim via the Deer Creek Trail, a 10.3-mile trip best accomplished over two days' time, follow Hike 27 in reverse.

APPENDIX A: HIKER CHECKLIST

Hiking in the Grand Canyon requires ample planning, and one of the first steps to being well prepared is packing the right equipment. Don't overburden your pack with too much equipment and unnecessary items; bring only what you really need. Scan the checklist below before your trip into the Grand Canyon to ensure you haven't forgotten an essential item.

- [ ] Backpack
- [ ] Day pack
- [ ] Extra pack straps
- [ ] Water bottles (1 to 2 quart Nalgene bottles are best)
- [ ] Collapsible bucket (for settling silty water)
- [ ] Water filter (with brush to clean in the field)
- [ ] Pocket knife
- [ ] Hiking poles (1 or 2)
- [ ] Foam or self-inflating sleeping pad
- [ ] Sleeping bag (or sheet, or sleeping bag liner for summer)
- [ ] Tent, stakes, ground sheet and/or tarp
- [ ] Hat with brim
- [ ] Sunglasses (with UV protection)
- [ ] Sunscreen (with an SPF of 15 or greater)
- [ ] Backpack stove, fuel bottle (full)
- [ ] Signal mirror
- [ ] First-aid kit
- [ ] Medication: prescriptions, anti-inflammatory and/or pain medication
- [ ] Knee and/or ankle wraps (neoprene is best)
- [ ] First-aid tape
- [ ] Moleskin, Second Skin
- [ ] Band-aids, bandages
- [ ] Aspirin (or other pain medication)
- [ ] Lip balm
- [ ] Toothbrush, toothpaste
- [ ] Toilet paper
- [ ] Lightweight trowel
- [ ] Boots (well broken-in)
- [ ] Camp shoes or sandals
- [ ] Extra shirt
- [ ] Extra underwear
- [ ] Extra socks
- [ ] Hiking socks; wool outer, polypropylene or nylon liner
- [ ] Parka (synthetic pile works best)
- [ ] Sweater
- [ ] Pants

- [ ] Hiking shorts
- [ ] Swimsuit
- [ ] Rain gear (Gore-tex or similar fabric that is both waterproof and windproof)
- [ ] Biodegradable soap, small towel
- [ ] Cookware, cup, pot handle, pot scrubber
- [ ] Spoon and fork
- [ ] Matches in waterproof container
- [ ] Insect repellent
- [ ] Nylon tape or duct tape
- [ ] Pack cover
- [ ] Nylon stuffsacks, and 20- to 30-pound test fishing line (for hanging food)
- [ ] Topo maps
- [ ] Flashlight, with spare bulb and fresh batteries
- [ ] Resealable plastic bags (for packing out trash and used toilet paper)
- [ ] Enough food, plus a little extra
- [ ] Watch
- [ ] Compass
- [ ] Binoculars
- [ ] Thermometer
- [ ] Camera, film, lenses, filters, lens brush and paper
- [ ] Small sewing kit
- [ ] Notebook, pencils
- [ ] Field guidebooks
- [ ] Arizona fishing license
- [ ] Fishing rod, reel, line, flies, lures
- [ ] Electrolyte replacement
- [ ] Backcountry Use Permit

Add the following for winter travel:

- [ ] Gaiters
- [ ] Instep crampons
- [ ] Wool or polypropylene cap or balaclava
- [ ] Space blanket
- [ ] Layers of warm clothing
- [ ] Sleeping bag with a rating of at least 0 degrees Fahrenheit
- [ ] Waterproof/windproof clothing
- [ ] Mittens or gloves
- [ ] Thermal underwear (wool or polypropylene)

A hiker begins the long Supai traverse from the head of the Cathedral Stairs on the Hermit Trail.

APPENDIX B: ADDRESSES AND PHONE NUMBERS

For general Grand Canyon National Park information, and to request a Park map and a copy of "The Guide" (general Park and trip planning information), phone (520) 638-7888 and press 1-1.

For backcountry information, and to request a "Backcountry Trip Planner," write to:

Grand Canyon National Park
Backcountry Reservations Office
P.O. Box 129
Grand Canyon, Arizona 86023
(520) 638-7875, Monday through Friday, from 1 p.m. to 5 p.m. (Arizona observes Mountain Standard Time year-round; it does not observe Daylight Saving Time.) You can also FAX your permit request to the BRO at (520) 638-2125. Backcountry information is available via the Internet at: http://star.ucc.nau.edu:80/ ~grandcanyon/.

LODGING AND CAMPING

To make reservation for park accommodations:

Amfac Parks and Resorts, 14001 East Iliff, Suite 600, Aurora, CO 80014. (303) 297-2757

Grand Canyon Lodge at Bright Angel Point on the North Rim, (303) 297-2759

Kaibab Lodge, (520) 526-0924

Jacob Lake Lodge, (520) 643-7232

Mather Campground reservations must be booked through DESTINET at 1-800-365-2267

Trailer Village (campground with RV hookups), (520) 638-2401

North Rim Campground, 1-800-365-2267

Tele-Park, Grand Canyon and Surrounding Communities Information and Reservation Service (900) 976-7888.

Chambers of Commerce

Flagstaff, AZ (800) 842-7293.

Grand Canyon (Tusayan, AZ), (520) 638-2901

Kane County (Kanab, Utah), (801) 644-5033

Page, AZ (520) 645-2741

Williams-Grand Canyon, AZ (520) 635-4061

MAPS

To order USGS quadrangle maps:
Distribution Branch
United States Geological Survey
Box 25286, Denver Federal Center
Denver, CO 80225.

FOREST SERVICE

Kaibab National Forest
800 South 6th Street
Williams, AZ 86046.

APPENDIX C: WEATHER CHART

Average Temperature (Degrees Fahrenheit) and Precipitation

	South Rim			North Rim			Inner Gorge		
	max	min	precip	max	min	precip	max	min	precip
Jan.	41	18	1.32"	37	16	3.17"	56	36	.68"
Feb.	45	21	1.55"	39	18	3.22"	62	42	.75"
March	51	25	1.38"	44	21	2.63"	71	48	.79"
April	60	32	.93"	53	29	1.73"	82	56	.47"
May	70	39	.66"	62	34	1.17"	92	63	.36"
June	81	47	.42"	73	40	.86"	101	72	.30"
July	84	54	1.81"	77	46	1.93"	106	78	.84"
Aug.	82	53	2.25"	75	45	2.85"	103	75	1.40"
Sept	76	47	1.56"	69	39	1.99"	97	69	97"
Oct.	65	36	1.10"	59	31	1.38"	84	58	.65"
Nov.	52	27	.94"	46	24	1.48"	68	46	.43"
Dec.	43	20	1.62"	40	20	2.83"	57	37	.87"

ABOUT THE AUTHOR

Ron Adkison, an avid hiker and backpacker, began his outdoor explorations at age six. Since then he has logged more than 5,000 trail miles in ten western states. He has walked every trail in this guide to provide precise, firsthand information about the trails, as well as features of ecological and historical interest. When he's not on the trail, Ron lives on the family's mountain ranch and with the help of his wife, Lynette, and two children, Ben and Abbey, raises sheep and llamas.

Ron shares his love for the backcountry in this, his sixth guidebook.

Hiking the National Parks

The national parks have some of the very best hiking in the world, and just because it's in a national park doesn't mean it's crowded. In many parks, the roads are clogged with traffic, but the trails are nearly devoid of people.

As part of the **FALCON** GUIDES® series, Falcon plans to publish a complete set of hiking guides to every national park with a substantial trail system. If your favorite park isn't on the following list of books currently available, you can plan on it being available soon. Each book comprehensively covers the trails in the parks and includes the necessary trip planning information on access, regulations, weather, etc., to help you put together a memorable adventure.

AVAILABLE NOW:
Hiking Big Bend National Park
Hiking California's Desert Parks (includes Death Valley and Joshua Tree National parks, Mojave National Preserve, and Anza-Borrego State Park)
Exploring Canyonlands & Arches National Parks
Hiking Carlsbad Caverns & Guadalupe Mountains National Parks
Hiking the Columbia River Gorge
Hiking Glacier & Waterton Lakes National Parks
Hiking Grand Canyon National Park
Hiking Great Basin National Park
Hiking North Cascades
Hiking Olympic National Park
Hiking South Dakota's Black Hills Country (includes Wind Cave, Badlands and Mount Rushmore national parks, and Custer State Park)
Hiking Yellowstone National Park
Hiking Zion & Bryce Canyon National Parks

COMING SOON: Redwoods, Glen Canyon/Escalante, Grand Teton, and Rocky Mountain

ALSO AVAILABLE: 26 state-wide hiking guides

TO ORDER:
Check with your local bookseller or
call The Globe Pequot Press at **1–800–243–0495.**
www.falcon.com

FALCON®

get
FALCON GUIDED

FALCON®

• *To order any of these books, check with your local bookseller*
or call The Globe Pequot Press at **1-800-243-0495.**
Visit us on the world wide web at:
www.falcon.com

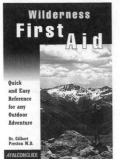

WILDERNESS FIRST AID

By Dr. Gilbert Preston M.D.

Enjoy the outdoors and face the inherent risks with confidence. By reading this easy-to-follow first-aid text, all outdoor enthusiasts can pack a little extra peace of mind on their next adventure. *Wilderness First Aid* offers expert medical advice for dealing with outdoor emergencies beyond the reach of 911. It easily fits in most backcountry first-aid kits.

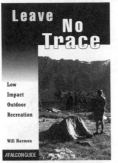

LEAVE NO TRACE

By Will Harmon

The concept of "leave no trace" seems simple, but it actually gets fairly complicated. This handy quick-reference guidebook includes all the newest information on this growing and all-important subject. This book is written to help the outdoor enthusiast make the hundreds of decisions necessary to protect the natural landscape and still have an enjoyable wilderness experience. Part of the proceeds from the sale of this book go to continue leave-no-trace education efforts. The Official Manual of American Hiking Society.

BEAR AWARE

By Bill Schneider

Hiking in bear country can be very safe if hikers follow the guidelines summarized in this small, "packable" book. Extensively reviewed by bear experts, the book contains the latest information on the intriguing science of bear-human interactions. *Bear Aware* can not only make your hike safer, but it can help you avoid the fear of bears that can take the edge off your trip.

MOUNTAIN LION ALERT

By Steve Torres

Recent mountain lion attacks have received national attention. Although infrequent, lion attacks raise concern for public safety. *Mountain Lion Alert* contains helpful advice for mountain bikers, trail runners, horse riders, pet owners, and suburban landowners on how to reduce the chances of mountain lion-human conflicts.

Also Available

• ***Wilderness Survival*** • ***Reading Weather*** • ***Backpacking Tips***
• ***Climbing Safely*** • ***Avalanche Aware***

To order check with your local bookseller or
call The Globe Pequot Press at **1–800–243–0495.**
www.falcon.com